# THE MECHANICS' INSTITUTE REVIEW
## ISSUE 10 AUTUMN 2013

The first Mechanics' Institute in London was founded in 1823 by George Birkbeck. "Mechanics" then meant skilled artisans, and the purpose of the Institute was to instruct them in the principles behind their craft. The Institute became Birkbeck College, part of London University, in 1920 but still maintains one foot in the academy and one in the outside world.

D1100585

**The Mechanics' Institute Review**
Issue 10 Autumn 2013

**The Mechanics' Institute Review** is published by MA Creative Writing, Department of English and Humanities, School of Arts, Birkbeck, University of London, Malet Street, Bloomsbury, London WC1E 7HX

ISBN 978-0-9575833-0-6

Project Director and Senior Editor: Sue Tyley

Editorial Team: Ravinder Basra, Mary Bracht, Stephanie Cooper, Pamela Gough, Ian McNab, Angela Shoosmith

The Editorial Team would like to thank Russell Celyn Jones, Sue Tyley, Julia Bell, and Anne-Marie Taylor for making this project possible.

For further copies or information, please contact Anne-Marie Taylor, Senior Administrator, MA Creative Writing, Department of English and Humanities, School of Arts, Birkbeck, University of London, Malet Street, Bloomsbury, London, WC1E 7HX. Tel: 020 3073 8372. Email: a.taylor@english.bbk.ac.uk

Website: http://www.writershub.co.uk/mir.php

Printed and bound by Berforts Limited, 17 Burgess Road, Hastings TN35 4NR

Cover design, quotations design and typesetting by Raffaele Teo

**The Mechanics' Institute Review** is typeset in Book Antiqua

# Table of Contents

# Foreword
## RUSSELL CELYN JONES

### Art for Art's Sake

Once upon a time, not so long ago, writers worked on large canvases. By large canvases I mean contemporary political landscapes that were often epic in scale. Pasternak, for instance, lived through the Russian Revolution, as did his Dr Zhivago. F. Scott Fitzgerald created a cast of unreliable heroes in an America that was on the skids. Christopher Isherwood was a private tutor in Germany during the rise of the Third Reich, the setting for his famous Berlin stories. E. M. Forster and Graham Greene witnessed first-hand the activities of the British Empire in its colonies.

Nowadays, for the British writer at least, the large canvases have become harder to fill. The Empire is no more. When empires rise and even more so when they fall, writers are usually to be seen on the ground, watching and recording the show. But empires already in ruins are for archaeologists to pick over. And that's what this country is today, a Parthenon. It's hard to date exactly when this final destruction occurred, but up until the late 1980s, with Thatcher on the rampage, you could still encounter the real, could still *walk* through a political landscape as Dickens used to do in another century, seeking material for his novels. Politics was replaced by consumerism at some stage and it felt like another Dark Age was descending.

The state-of-the-nation novel, rebooted as the trans-national novel, is now more at home in Asia – India and Pakistan – where industrial capitalism has rediscovered its Victorian roots; where poverty, migration, religious fundamentalism, etc. are key issues in everyone's lives. Meantime, if English literature has turned retrospective (the rise and rise of the historical novel) or introspective, less concerned with the ascent and fall of empire than the ascent and fall of a single marriage, that is not per se a bad thing, inasmuch as the domestic milieu is also fruitful territory. In many respects our days are good days for art; not for the wide-angle lens perhaps, but certainly for the short story and for the avant-garde. Writers have always told the story of men and women and that has not changed, even if the crucible of human relationships has been scaled down to the size of someone's apartment.

There are still upheavals in the world that impact upon us – 9/11, the Iraq and Afghanistan wars, the Financial Collapse. As subjects for fiction, they are both omnipresent *and* a little out of reach; difficult to personalise from a writer's or a reader's perspective. Even though we feel the shocks from these upheavals in our lives, we are not in the epicentre, and depending upon their vantage point, contemporary writers struggle to pin them down. At worst they download information we already know or write from too great a height, like birds of prey. Readers, of literary fiction at least, build firewalls against such pretension because pretension, and other forms of overwriting, tend to be more prevalent when a writer is expounding something he or she knows nothing about, while pretending to the contrary.

But isn't this what artistic ambition entails, writing about what you *don't* know? One of the central problems of writing fiction lies in how we go about mediating the experience and lives of others. How to bridge the gap between what you know and what you don't or can't ever know? Unless you have experienced something yourself, or know someone who has, unless you can see it, you can't usually write about it *convincingly*. And that really is all that matters. Not *should* I do it, but *can* I do it. Pasternak, Forster, Greene et al. could write big because big is what they encountered. They wrote about what they *did* know.

If fiction is to work as art it needs to be emotionally honest, and it is not emotionally honest for writers to write about things they can't understand or know. Real life is what fiction feeds upon. And life makes good art. Writers are surrounded by gifts – in terms of people they know, who expand and change from the moment they are sketched onto the page. Language is not experience but a translation of experience into another form, and that form is governed by its own terms and procedures.

It does writers a lot of good to remember the origins of storytelling. In ancient Greek drama, the action takes place offstage and is oxygenised by the reaction of the chorus to the messenger. Narrative is the aftermath of traumatic events, not the events themselves. And it engages an audience's imagination to visualise things they cannot see. Real-time action, already seen, disengages the imagination. Writers who have used ancient Greek story forms are legion. They include Melville, in *Moby Dick*; Conrad, in *Heart of Darkness*, in which Marlow recounts his adventures in Central Africa while on a ship moored on the Thames. And as for great mediated novels, the story of Jay Gatsby is told not in the first person, but by Nick Carraway. Even Jesus Christ does not tell his own account.

## Money for God's Sake

Ambition in the novel never used to be confused with financial ambition, but that's part of the story now. Writers who regard the novel as a business scheme may get rich, but will forgo the status of an artist. Do they care? Probably not, but if there is a shift in sensibility in the publishing world it has something to do with these journeymen, and with the media substituting concepts of art with concepts of celebrity.

Another new trend has been set by writers self-publishing on the Internet. When some trade publisher picks them up, it makes the news. It makes the news because it is so rare. It should be remembered, meanwhile, that there are a million virtual novels on the Web right now that will never see light of day as a printed text. The self-published writer first has to demonstrate a massive online constituency. Editors need to know in advance they can sell it before they will buy it. Any literary merit is superfluous to that decision.

What may be implicit in my remarks is that writing for money means writing genre fiction. Genre is *not* synonymous with bad writing, but it is synonymous with entertainment, and so falls outside that category of literature central to how some, but not all of us, choose to read. But hark! Among the many things I've discovered, teaching creative writing, is that one has to learn to write well before one can write entertainingly, so there really is no short cut. That said, if you are determined to try to write for money (good luck), you'll need a high-concept plot. Novels have to be big again, but in terms of size, not theme. They need to be a door-stopping five hundred pages of pulsating narrative, plot twists, audacious carryings-on. The cool sentence architect rarely has any success crafting one of those.

Such novels seem to draw as much from the Hollywood blockbuster as from any literary tradition, and is why literary writers should consider moving away entirely from its influence. There have been many films made from great novels but no great novels I know of have been made from films. People who refer to films they've been inspired by when talking about their work have simply not read enough and that will always show up in their writing as a primary and fatal weakness.

Of course, we all watch and love film, and some film-makers are great artists. The problem really is one of form. The literary novel is dependent upon language style, metaphor, imagery, psychological reality. Film is shackled to the three-act narrative structure, to real-time action, and in Hollywood at least that is becoming to look rather like social control. Plot is the opium of the people. The status quo may sometimes be the target of Hollywood films but it also underwrites the enterprise. My advice is, instead of watching high-concept films, read Alice Munro who deals with boring technical problems like exposition in a thrilling, Greek way.

It may be heartening for students to know that it is easier for the first-time novelist to publish than veterans of the mid-list, but it is not so encouraging to realise that what has always been true of Hollywood is now true of writing: you are only as good as your last opus. Writing careers now can be painfully short. So why have so many publishers lost their confidence, which is what this trend suggests? It would seem there are few curators left in the world of letters. Editors no longer act alone but need the permission of their marketing team to buy a new title. They toe the line with retailers, who really control the culture now, when it would be more admirable if they formed a resistance. Old literary publishing houses are becoming commercial publishing houses, while small independents appear to be waiting out the game on the bench. So where do good writers go to find a readership?

There are no easy, painless answers to any of these questions. I can only hazard a guess that as it becomes more and more tedious reading fiction in which proficient writers put stock characters through their usual paces, like circus animals through a burning hoop, the crop of smaller houses will become more attractive venues for the daring and inventive. And where the art goes, audiences tend to follow eventually. The subculture will then become the culture.

## MIR for Heaven's Sake

And finally to the love: the tenth-anniversary issue of *The Mechanics' Institute Review* is here. Ten years for a literary magazine is very good going indeed. What began life as a showcase for creative writing students has grown into a selective anthology, consistently and favourably reviewed in the *Guardian*, *TLS*, *Independent*, *Financial Times* and other national newspapers. It is also one of the few anthologies on the market devoted to the short story.

All the novelists mentioned in the first section of this essay were also on active duty in the service of the short story. Melville's short works are every bit as great and important as his novels. And Fitzgerald actually lived off the proceeds from writing them. Nowadays what "short stories" mean to publishers (along with "literary") is: "does not sell". But the short story is just as exacting and rewarding – to write and to read – as the novel. More importantly perhaps, it is also less corruptible as an art form. I've already intimated that the short story may be *the* form for best encapsulating the accelerated, atomised world we now live in, and it *can* sell, actually. *The Mechanics' Institute Review* has a print run of nearly one thousand and frequently sells out each year; better than many first novels fare.

*The Mechanics' Institute Review* is still primarily a road test for new and untried writers, and, for the team of post-graduate students who produce and edit it, the anthology also provides vocational skills in publishing. While many of its past contributors have seen their first novels appear in bookshops and on Amazon, several of the anthology's editors have found jobs in the book trade. Its influence is therefore broadening.

Birkbeck has developed over ten years what is now widely regarded to be a post-graduate writing programme of international standing. We have taught over three hundred students to write bolder and more interesting work than they might have done on their own, by bringing them in contact with each other, with professional writers as their tutors, and with world-class humanities academics. Universities in general and Birkbeck in particular are where the new thinking about literature is born and in such an atmosphere students are taught to read more closely and write more truthfully. *The Mechanics' Institute Review* is the end of that journey and the beginning of a new one: a real place for emerging writers to find a readership.

I have much admiration for the writers in this anthology, as I have for contributors to past issues, for pursuing their passions – their reading and writing passions first and foremost – rather than worrying about what the market is doing. They can afford to do this, *must* do this. Many may be writing their first novels, some may even have finished writing their first novels, but there are no tentative extracts on show here. These short stories offer a firm handshake with writers who are probably at this moment firing out onto the Internet and elsewhere other works large and small. I urge them to continue to do this, until such time as art for art's sake might just start to look like the best deal in town again.

# When You Go,
# You Leave a Farce
## KAVITA JINDAL

I arrive in Ujjalpur when the unbearably bright July sun is at its peak in the sky. The villagers want to know my name. That much is obvious. But they don't have to ask me. By the time I alight at my destination from the car I have hired to bring me here, the driver has already stopped a few times to ask the way to the house of my cousins. A raggle-taggle bunch of youths with nothing better to do have been following the slow-moving car at their own pace.

When the road narrows to just a *gali*, when the cows, stray dogs and bicycles-balancing-cans-of-paint all take precedence, the spanking white car can go no further, and the driver stops and points to the black-railed gate a few yards ahead. "That must be it. The house of your cousins."

The house is painted a fetching pink. I have four female relatives in this village – well, four who are of my generation – and two of them live in this house. I last saw them when I was twelve years old. One of them is my first cousin and although the other three are close to me in age the actual relationships are complicated. One is my father's cousin, but born at the same time as his daughter. Another is my father's uncle's adopted niece from his wife's side. To simplify things, I refer to them as I have always done, as "cousins", although as soon as the word "cousin" is mentioned to friends in India who don't know the family, an explanation of the blood relationship is usually pumped out of me.

When I was younger and I was taken to Ujjalpur more often by my father, we four cousins played together all day during the holidays. We played seven stones, catch, Mother may I, hopscotch. We played L-o-n-d-o-n, London! Who knew then that Daddy and I would go to live in London and hardly ever return to Delhi, let alone Ujjalpur. We played hide and seek. My favourite hiding place was in the dark quilt storeroom, where you could climb aloft a stack of ten thick folded *razai* and nap on the top till you were found.

I haven't seen my cousins in the flesh for eighteen years, but as they pour out of the pink house to exclaim over me I realise that mentally I will revert to referring to them as I have always done: Skinny Cousin, Singing Cousin, Stodgy Cousin and Simpering Cousin. Their adult selves are, utterly surprisingly, not that different from their pre-teen selves.

My suitcase and rucksack are carried inside by many willing hands while I submit to intense hugs and murmurs of condolences. We live, therefore we condole. We show we care. This is how things are done. We condole. I begin to accept the fact that I will have to repeat some parts of my father's story twenty times a day while I am on this trip. His accidental death, his last wishes. My father, who liked to be orderly in all matters, has specified in a letter attached to his will that his ashes be taken to Ujjalpur and offered to the water. To the river here, specifically. This is puzzling to me but I reason that one branch of his family still lives here and he must have had an unspoken affection for the place. Whatever the intention, I'd said aloud to Daddy after I'd read the letter twice, to be sure of his wishes, *It has been asked and it shall be done.*

There are men and children in this household, too, for me to meet and greet, and an assortment of elderly cousin-aunts has also gathered. People who knew my father are milling in the courtyard and distant relatives are dotted about in all the cool white rooms. I can see that I'm going to have to be firm about spending my short time here with my four cousins. I'd already explained my mission to them on the phone and at each juncture now I repeat my previous assurance that I don't need the entire extended clan to come with me en masse for the offering of the ashes to the water. I would like to be accompanied by just the girls I once knew. I know how this is received, but as I'm a misfit anyway, with foreign ways to boot, I can get away with it. They will say behind my back that I'm strange and I don't know how things should be done, I have been away too long, blah blah. I don't care what they say when I'm not there to hear it as long as I don't have to pour out Daddy's ashes with a crowd in tow. There was nothing in his letter about holding a memorial event or a prayer ceremony in a temple here. He would have said if that's what he wanted; he was never shy about making his views clear.

So one of my recurrent sentences today turns out to be: "I'm just following instructions." When I get a moment alone I turn my eyes up to the white ceiling and address it. *You see, Daddy, how dutifully I'm following your directions. I'm here, in the family home in Ujjalpur. I hope you're pleased.* I glow with virtue.

Skinny and Simpering live in the pink house with their families. Singing and Stodgy have stayed in the area too and both have contrived to buy homes in a new complex on the perimeter of the village. "Duplex villas" is how they refer to their terraced houses. I am taken for a tour of their fresh-yellow-painted abodes. In my mind I see a vision of the pink house (old) and the yellow houses (new) side by side, and together like this, in my mind, pink and yellow, pink and yellow, they remind me of wild lantana flowers. How abundant the massed green shrubs were on the roads that led to this village; how I loved to stare at the tiny and profuse pink and yellow florets; how I loved to smell them and pick them apart to create a dainty trail of my wanderings. Just thinking about it, the air in Ujjalpur begins to smell like winter lantana; a sharp herby tang gladdens my nostrils even in this high heat and my fingers itch to fidget with a pink and yellow inflorescence.

In the evening I'm informed by Singing's husband – ex-military, now a businessman ("property deals, this and that, you know") – that it's odd my father asked for his ashes to be immersed in Ujjalpur. Strictly speaking it's not a river that runs past this village. It's only a stream. "But," he concedes, "it *is* a tributary rivulet of the Ganges. And we're not that far from Haridwar."

"It's what he wanted," I say, for the umpteenth time. "It's equally a puzzle to me, but I am here at his request."

Singing Cousin has arranged a *pundit*, the best in the village, to help me perform the ceremony. "Must I drag the priest along?" I ask. "Can I not go to the water's edge and do the deed myself?"

Simpering Cousin's face transforms into a mask of horror. I have my answer. If you involve family for their help, then you have to let them meddle a little bit. It is only polite. I let them meddle. I decide to follow their subsequent instructions meekly.

We bathe early the next morning and each of us dresses in a white *salwar-kameez*. The pundit arrives at the gates an hour after he said he would. A Tempo van, complete with local driver, has been arranged for the six of us by Singing's husband. It is waiting at the end of the lane. We set off to the river. Ten minutes later we park on the last stretch of built road and begin to walk across a swathe of pebble and shingle to the river. Across the shingle we follow the priest but the river doesn't materialise. It is not there. It appears to have dried up overnight.

"I checked last week and the stream was normal." Singing looks stunned. "There was plenty of water."

"They are damming it further up," Skinny Cousin informs me. "To clear the silt, I believe."

"Oh yes, I do remember hearing that there would be some work upriver. The damming must have started." Simpering spreads her hands at fate. "But why today?"

Stodgy steps out into the middle of the riverbed where there is a large puddle. The remainder of the riverbed is a long damp line with a few more puddles further ahead in small basins of lower ground. "Here?" asks Stodgy, looking hopefully at me.

I look at the sky. *This is the spot, Daddy. Now what do I do?*

When she sees me hesitate, Simpering Cousin suggests that I can return when the work upriver has finished and the rivulet has been let loose again.

I want to ask her if she knows the price of an air ticket. I want to ask her if she knows that I get two weeks' holiday a year. Am I going to make a trip to Ujjalpur again in a few months? Can I tell her that I prefer to spend my holiday money on a ski trip in the winter?

How mean I'm being, how unfair to my father. He has left me with enough money for twenty ski trips, so I shouldn't begrudge this at all. I'm holding a large Tupperware jar filled with ashes and small bits of white bone that I hope belong to him, but who knows how they scoop out things in the crematorium, where it's a conveyor belt of one body after another, and a set time to burn. Even dead, you can't take too long or be stealthily quick; you just follow the timetable.

I stand on a dry riverbed of gravel wondering what to do. It strikes me that there may have been a hidden agenda in my father's request. There was no way I'd come to Ujjalpur if he hadn't specifically asked for this. Or maybe I'm over-analysing. He may just have had a huge nostalgic love for his familial village and I wasn't aware of it. He may just have wanted to rest in peace here. But although he's succeeded in sending me to Ujjalpur, and I will leave his ashes where he wished, you can bet that I will not be sending *my* ashes here. I will send mine via ski lift to a snow-clad summit, to be thrown over a precipice.

A group of five raggedy children is hovering on the riverbank. Although the riverbed is waterless they don't play on it.

The priest breaks into my silent thought. "We can perform the ceremony here anyway."

He spreads a sheet on the pebbles, at a distance from the puddle, removes his greyish Reebok trainers and sits down cross-legged. He is carrying an Adidas bag with pink piping. His white *dhoti* and his beige *kurta* are wonderfully clean and starched. Simpering Cousin dutifully sits down beside him, her feet under her hips. I remain standing. While I am considering what to do, the others have removed their shoes and sat down and the pundit has taken out his little accoutrements from the bag and, without me, they are beginning the ceremony of last rituals. The pundit chants Sanskrit *shloka* and pours a teaspoon of holy water into the cupped palms of my four cousins, which they hold for a second before letting the drops of liquid meet the dry ground.

"Your turn," says Skinny One.

I sit down and repeat the exercise.

The translucent white plastic jar is taken from my arms. The lid is unscrewed. Small heaps of ashes are duly distributed to cupped palms once again, then carried by the four cousins to the middle of the riverbed where they drop the ashes into the puddle. I find I am standing again, standing and thinking furiously, but obediently

5

I follow this exercise too. The pundit arises and walks towards where the rivulet should be, wincing at the sharp jabs of the stones into his soft bare feet. He begins to turn the plastic jar upside down to shake out the remaining ashes into the puddle. A breeze starts up and blows them towards the children. One of them, a girl with a dirt-streaked but intensely sweet face, comes running up and says, in the nicest, politest way, "Uncle-ji, when you have finished with this *dabba*, can I have it? Give it to me, Uncle-ji, not the others." She stands by his side waiting.

I shake myself out of my stupor. "Stop," I call out. "Stop."

The pundit stops shaking out ashes, holds the large container upright, and waits for me to say more.

"Shouldn't there be water?" I ask. "Isn't that the whole *point* of the ceremony?"

Singing Cousin looks at me strangely. "Is it? Is that the point?"

Simpering just says, "Well if you can't come back when the river runs . . ."

And Stodgy stands in front of the pundit, hands on hips. "Should there be water? More than this?" She points at the sad puddle.

He wavers. He looks at his watch. "Well," he begins, "we have had the ceremony and this is the requested spot –"

I cut in. "There must be water. There is no cleansing without water." Although I'm sure my father didn't believe so totally in these religious rituals, depositing him into a puddle doesn't seem right. There is going to have to be a bit more water. Something better than this. I set my lips. I am not known as Stubborn for nothing.

The four cousins are looking at me annoyed. I wrest the Tupperware container from the pundit and return to the sheet on the ground, which is now pinned down by trainers and sandals neatly placed at the four corners. I pick up the lid and slowly screw it on to the top. As I do this, I hear the pundit say, "Allotted time is up. It will cost more."

Skinny nods at him encouragingly. "No problem," she says.

"I suggest," he says ponderously, "since your sister from London wants more water, that we go to Madhuban Lake. The lake is always full and it's clean."

Skinny Cousin nods again, approvingly. The others look

doubtful. "There *is* a tradition of letting go of ashes on the lake," says Skinny.

Pundit, who is gathering up his teaspoons and salvers and little bowls of stainless steel, gives a hum of assent.

I look up at the sky again. *Ujjalpur river is not cooperating, Daddy. This puddle won't do for you. I'm sorry. We're going to have to compromise. We're going to a lake. A lake that's full and clean.*

I nod agreement at the priest.

"For the lake," he declares, "we need a small jar. Because it has to go under the water. That is the correct way to offer the ashes if you're going to the lake." He points to the Tupperware cradled to my chest. "That's not right for setting on the lake."

"There are hardly any ashes left anyway," Stodgy points out.

He rustles in the Adidas holdall and comes up with a small glass jar, which has red powder in it. Pundit considers for a moment, then he tips out some powder onto his palm, places his thumb in it and anoints us all with a red *tikka* on our forehead. He raises the glass jar but there is still some vermilion in it. He sighs and sprinkles it out onto the gravel. He holds the glass jar out towards me. I understand. Carefully, I put the lip of the plastic to the lip of the glass and, shielding the operation with my body, I pour out the ashes and the last of the bits of bone from one container into another. The glass is still tinged red with the powder clinging to it and the grey ashes inside have assumed a cheery pink cast. The priest then covers the neck of the jar with a square piece of muslin, which like a magician he has conjured from the depths of his *kurta* pocket, and ties it around the neck of the jar with yellow pure-cotton thread.

When he breaks off the thread Simpering Cousin holds out her wrist, and he separates the thick strands so that the remainder can be tied onto our wrists. We are now spiritually connected to the glass jar of pink ashes by sacred yellow cotton. Pink and yellow, I think. Pink and yellow for ashes and thread, pink and yellow for lantana flowers, pink and yellow for all my jumbled memories of Ujjalpur.

The raggedy girl comes and stands by me, her eyes on the container in my hands. I place the jar on the ground and not a beat passes before she picks it up and runs away with it. I hope it's for her mother; for grain, or lentils. The other kids chase her.

"I didn't know there was a lake here too," is my conversation offering, as our group of five women aged thirty to thirty-five, and one emollient priest, aged what? forty to forty-five? heads back to the hired Tempo.

"It's only a small lake," says Singing Cousin.

"And it's not in Ujjalpur," adds Simpering. "It's an hour's drive away."

"I've never been there," says Stodgy.

This makes the other three giggle and Stodgy looks irritated.

We arrive at Madhuban Lake. I am the first out of the van to see if there is water. I exhale in relief. There is water, plenty of it, gleaming in the noon sun. The lake is not that small; it ripples gently into the distance. I can see the shore on the other side because the lake is not very wide, but I can't see the perimeter of the lake to my right. The water stretches away in a narrow strip to the horizon, enclosed by green trees. Quite like a river, in fact. I begin to feel better.

Two boatmen approach us. We state our business. One of the boatmen elbows aside the other and stands forward. "It's me you want," he says. "That's my business. Sending off the ashes."

Simpering asks, "Why you?"

"Because I'm the one who does it. He doesn't."

He's lying, of course, but the other doesn't argue. He looks fatigued. Maybe noon is not his best time. Our self-appointed boatman bustles about, wading into the water to bring round his boat and instructing us to roll up our *salwars*. Stodgy looks faint. The rest of us take a few steps until knee-deep in the water where the boatman helps us into the boat and tells us where to sit on the two benches. Pundit on the left, Simpering on the right. Skinny on the left. "You here, *behenji*," says Boatman, settling me on the right, and "You sit here, sister," he says to Singing, seating her on the left. Stodgy is still standing at the water's edge, a distinct look of unease on her face.

"She's scared of water," murmurs Singing.

"Then she should stay on land," decides the boatman.

Stodgy hears him and is incensed. "Did you hear why we are here?" she shouts across to him. "My brother's ashes," she says dramatically. "Do you think I would not get on the boat?"

The boatman looks at Singing, looks heavenward, shrugs.

We wait. Five minutes pass. Singing is humming a muted

*bhajan* to herself, Simpering is ensuring her fair hands are covered by her *dupatta* and I am shading my eyes to take in the beautiful scenery. Why haven't I been to this serene spot on earth before? Daddy will like it here; anyone would.

Stodgy has put one foot in the water. It is on the tip of my tongue to urge her on. But I know she has many phobias and I don't want to be responsible for killing her. Fear might kill her.

I look at the boatman whose impatience has made his face red, but he stays silent. It is not his place to say anything. On a signal from Pundit, he loosens the mooring rope and the boat starts to drift out into the water. Stodgy is stunned into action. She is at the side of the boat in great splashes. The boatman and the priest haul her in. She is hyperventilating. The boatman tries to manoeuvre her to where he wants her to sit. He takes his position at the back of the boat, stows the rope, puts his hands on the oars, and addresses Stodgy: "Don't worry, auntie. If you just sit still we will all be completely safe."

"What did you say?" Stodgy glares at him as she lodges herself on the bench, causing a rocking of the vessel.

"I said not to worry, auntie. I am an experienced boatman –"

"Why are you calling me auntie?" she roars. "Do I look like an auntie to you?"

The boatman gapes at her.

"I'm the youngest of this lot," she says. "Don't call me auntie. I'm not your auntie. Understand?"

"I understand," Boatman says in a cowed voice, rowing furiously till we are centred between the two shores.

Singing, Simpering and Skinny can't control their smirks. Pundit keeps a straight face. Stodgy is still trembling with fear. I'm clutching the glass jar with the tinted ashes. The water gleams, the fronds of trees dipping in at the shoreline are the colour of old Kashmiri jade and the sun is relentless in its hot radiant beauty. I'm ready to let go of the ashes.

"What do I do?" I ask Pundit when Boatman stops rowing and lets the boat drift.

"Leave the jar on the water."

"But the ceremony . . ." interrupts Singing. "The ritual, the ceremony . . . ?"

Pundit obliges. He begins intoning a *shloka*, at least that's what

I assume he's reciting. What do I know? He looks very solemn as he slows the chant down to elongated vowels. I am waiting for him to say, "*Om Shanti Shanti*," words I *do* know. I follow the four cousins in folding my hands and looking down as if joining them all in earnest prayer. A mobile phone rings. We all look up, startled. Pundit stops intoning, delves into his starched *kurta* pocket and nonchalantly answers his phone. Into his phone he says, "Yes. No. Not now, later. Soon. I'll tell you what time. I'll try to bring it. I can't talk, I'm working. I can't talk now, I'm in the middle of work, I said." He puts away his phone and resumes the chant. There is no apology. The interruption is not mentioned either by Pundit or by the four cousins who are as saucer-eyed as I am. If Boatman thinks anything at all he is not showing it.

I place the jar on blinding sunlight in the water. It bobs away towards the far end of the lake. We all stare after it. I didn't realise the wind was rippling the water to such a degree. Our boat had felt as though it was drifting rather slowly, but I guess the boatman's oars were holding us in place. I see a bird alight on the jar. Its claws grip the cloth tied around the neck. It pecks its beak into the soft muslin.

"What will happen now?" I ask. Aren't the ashes meant to go in the water? The jar will bob out of sight before I can see what will happen to it. Will the birds pick it up and take it away? I see another one alight on it. "What do those horrible crows want?" I ask.

Pundit doesn't answer but Boatman does. "The birds want cloth for their nests. They will peck at it and their weight sitting on the jar will soon send it under. Don't worry," Boatman reassures me, "your father's ashes will go in the water."

I like Boatman better than Pundit.

I turn my head away from the others. *It's a nice day, Daddy, clear strong sunshine, sparkly water, lashings of green fronds. If you ignore the people here, everything is perfect, as Nature intended. I won't tell you to have a lovely time swirling in Madhuban Lake. I know what was important. You knew how to have a wonderful time when you wished.*

## Schrödinger's Baby
## CHARLIE FISH

There she slept, a puckered little bundle of DNA fighting to organise. She looked and smelled like a lump of dough. Her breathing rattled less than it had when she was born; I could hardly tell she was alive apart from that relentless ticking.

There was an electronic pad tucked beneath her baby mattress that sensed her breathing, translating each inhalation and exhalation into a metronomic tick. The ticks were supposed to be reassuring, but to me they sounded like a countdown.

Everything about the last year had been a countdown. Waiting to conceive, watching the bump grow, buying everything we thought we needed. At each stage I was convinced that the hidden timer would reach zero, and Elaine would get bored of our workaday lives, escape back to the wealth she'd been accustomed to. Even after the birth, the countdown seemed to continue. I stared at the baby, waiting to feel something. Tick. Tick. Tick.

She wasn't born, technically, rather pulled from Elaine's stomach like a weed. That's where Elaine was now, having her stitches tended, having her shredded dignity prodded into further submission.

I told the baby I loved her, trying to believe it.

Coffee. I went to the kitchen and prepared a really strong cup. But we were out of milk. The shop was next door to our flat; I could be out and back before the coffee cooled. Cursing, I grabbed the ticking intercom from the lounge and went out.

"Hi, Mo," I said to the Indian guy behind the counter as I entered the corner store. It wasn't always the same guy, but as far as I could gather they were all called Mo.

"Hello, Mister Franks. How is your little girl?"

I held up the ticking intercom. "Still alive."

"This is the best age, ah? You can gaze at them all day. I have seven daughters, you know. Can't stop myself."

"Really?" I said, distracted. What had I come in for? I hadn't been getting much sleep.

"They are very difficult when they grow. Our oldest – twelve years – she is chatting about eye-phones and Myspacebook and popping music. We have no idea what she is talking about."

"I always wanted a child," I said. "But I'm not sure I want an infant."

I rubbed my face. Milk – that's what I'd come in for. I grabbed the biggest bottle. Elaine called these six-pinters "the Cow". But when it came to paying, I realised I didn't have my wallet. I grumbled under my breath, set down the Cow, and scurried out.

At the door to our building I patted my pockets. Patted them again. Looked down. I was wearing my pyjamas, the powder-blue ones Elaine's mother had given me for Christmas. I put the ticking intercom on the ground and, ridiculously, patted my pockets again.

Of course the keys weren't there. I knew exactly where they were – in my jeans, next to my bedside table. On the other side of two double-locked doors. In a last-ditch display of utter fantasy, I gave myself one last full-body pat-down before the panic started to set in. A prickle at the back of my neck; a tinge of whiteness in my vision. I contained it and willed myself to think. My first instinct was to walk away, pretend the baby didn't exist, and live the rest of my life under a bridge.

Elaine's mother had a spare key. She lived just a few bus stops away. I could call her and be there in ten minutes. But – no. I couldn't call her: my mobile was also in the pocket of my jeans.

Back to the shop.

"Hello again, Mister Franks. You forgot something?"

"Mo, have you got a phone I could use?"

"Not for customers, sorry."

"Please, it's an emergency."

"*Ji*? Problem with your little one?"

"No, it's, uh . . . it's . . . Can I use your phone please?"

Mo must have seen something in my face. He handed over his mobile. But I had no idea what number to dial. I called Elaine instead, the only number I could remember.

"Hello? Who's this?"

I felt a blush of warmth, an abdominal tug.

"Elaine, it's me. How're you doing?"

"Still waiting. You know how it is with hospitals. Waiting, waiting, waiting. How's the baby?"

"I'm just calling . . ." Why was I calling? What was I doing? Elaine had entrusted me with the baby and I was about to admit that I was the worst father in the world?

"What number is this?" she asked.

"The baby's fine. She's asleep."

"I miss her." Her voice became shaky. "Sorry, still feeling a bit fragile."

"I just . . . What's your mother's number? I wanted to call her to . . . thank her for those pyjamas. I'm wearing them now."

I made a frantic scribbling gesture towards Mo, who took a few seconds to realise I was asking for a pen. I scrawled the number onto the back of my hand, filled the air with sweet platitudes, and hung up.

"That did not sound like an emergency," said Mo.

"Shut up, Mo."

I dialled Elaine's mother's number.

"Hello?"

"Mrs Leclerc, it's –"

"Daniel! What a surprise. How lovely to hear from you. How's my gorgeous granddaughter? She is simply the most ravishingly beautiful baby I have ever set eyes on. She gets it from me, darling."

"She's fine."

"She's fine, he says. Men are always so articulate on such matters. My husband –"

"Mrs Leclerc, I wonder if you can help me."

"Ah! Seeking some parental advice? Well, you've come to exactly the right place. You only need to look at how wonderfully well-mannered Elaine is to see –"

"Do you have our spare set of keys?"

"Yes, dear. You endowed us with responsibility for them and we've taken that responsibility seriously. They're in the jewellery box at the back of the cutlery drawer."

"Could you please bring them over? Or can I come and get them?"

"I'm in Brighton, dear. The Conservative conference. It would take me an hour at least to get home, and Sebastian's away on business, in Monaco. Is it an emergency?"

I gritted my teeth.

"Darling?" she prompted.

"No. Sorry to bother you."

I hung up.

Mo glanced at the baby's ticking intercom, which I'd left on the countertop, and then looked sideways at me, grinning. "You're in a bit of a pickle, aren't you?"

I could feel the panic spreading in my veins like a poison. I wanted to shout, lash out. Instead, I closed my eyes, took a deep breath. My hands shook with the effort of containment.

"Mo, have you got the number of an emergency locksmith?"

Mo shrugged.

"I'll call directory enquiries." I held up the phone. "If you don't mind?"

Mo made a concessionary gesture. His lips clenched as if suppressing a smirk.

I got numbers for two locksmiths, and called the nearer one. "Hello," I said when a man with meticulous received pronunciation answered. "I've locked my keys in my flat and I need someone to come and let me in. It's urgent."

"Certainly," said the man. "We charge £250 for changing locks, and a £50 call-out fee."

"Fine, fine." I told him my address.

"We can be there in ten minutes. Do you have a form of identification?"

"No. My wallet's in the flat."

"A driver's licence? A utility bill?"

"I'm in my pyjamas."

Mo leaned over, cupping a hand to his mouth. "Very nice

pyjamas they are too!" I elbowed him out of the way.

"I'm afraid we can't change the locks unless you can provide valid identification showing your address."

I tried not to let my irritation show. Unsuccessfully. "I can provide ID as soon as you let me into my flat."

"I'm sorry, sir," came the snitty reply. "I'm afraid we can't help you." He hung up.

I let out a primal roar. Mo looked concerned that I might cast his phone into the liquor aisle. I swallowed my rage and stabbed in the number of the second locksmith.

"Hello, Securelock Limited."

"Hi. I'm locked out of my flat."

"Right. I can sort that out for you, no problem."

"It's an emergency. And I don't have any identification."

"What's the address?"

I told him.

"I'm on another call at the moment, sir, so I can be with you in . . . say . . . forty-five minutes."

I checked my watch. My face must have been a picture – Mo actually looked sorry for me. "Can't you come any faster?"

"Forty-five minutes."

I sighed tensely, hung up, and handed over the phone, blinking back a tear. "Thanks, Mo."

"My name is actually Sukhvinder."

I picked up the plastic intercom from the countertop. It wasn't ticking any more. I shook it. Held it to my ear, straining to listen. Popped the back open and rolled the batteries around. Nothing.

"Batteries, batteries!" I barked.

Mo fumbled, spilling several packs of batteries onto the countertop as he reached up for them. I grabbed one, ripped it open. Levered out the old batteries and shoved in the new ones. Nothing.

I checked and double-checked. The batteries were in correctly, the intercom was switched on, the volume was turned up, yet there was no sound. I looked up at Mo. His eyebrows formed an inverted V. He covered his mouth with his hand.

I ran out of the shop and banged on our front door. I rattled the handle, uselessly, then stepped back and ran at it like a battering ram. Mo came out of the shop to watch as I banged at the door again and again like a wasp against a window. It wasn't going to budge.

I stopped. Tried to think rationally. Failed. "Mo, help!"

Mo shrugged. "Do not to go crazy. Probably she scooched off the sensor or it has malfunctioned."

"I don't know if I've got an alive baby or a dead baby until I can open this bloody door!"

I looked up at the windows. Our flat is on the first floor. An old Victorian metal drainpipe led up past the nursery window. I clamped myself to it and tried to shimmy my way up.

Turns out that kind of thing is only possible in cartoons. The drainpipe was rusty and flaky, and in my effort to gain purchase I managed to pull it off the wall. A stinking slosh of stagnant water landed on my face. I spluttered and retched as the pipe arced gracefully down, twisted to one side, and landed heavily on my neighbour's Subaru Impreza, popping out the passenger-side window.

I stared at the car, my shoulders jerking with dry sobs that were almost laughter. It was parked near the porch; now that the drainpipe lay across the front of the house it might be possible to climb from the top of the car up onto the roof of the porch.

I jumped onto the car, denting the hood, then reached up to the broken pipe. Hanging, hand over hand, I worked my way up. I tried to haul myself onto the porch roof, but the drainpipe bowed. "Mo!" I shouted. "Give me a leg up!"

Mo glanced nervously at the door of his shop, then slunk over and held up his hands. I stepped on them, then onto his turban, and heaved myself onto the porch roof.

Leaning precariously over the edge, using a stretch of broken drainpipe for support, I stared into the nursery window. I could see her, just, but there was no way of telling whether she was moving. Never before had I appreciated what it meant to have a lump in your throat, but now I felt like I'd swallowed a lemon.

Directly over the porch was the lounge window. I braced myself and kicked. It resonated loudly, but didn't break. I wound myself up for a firmer kick, and nearly slipped off the roof with shock when a siren sounded not ten metres behind me.

I crouched on all fours to keep my balance. Cautiously, I

turned my head to see a policeman stepping out of his vehicle. From the corner of my eye I saw Mo slip quietly back into the store.

"Hold it," shouted the cop.

"This is my house! I need to get my baby!" At least that's what I intended to say. It came out a little garbled.

"Down. Right now," ordered the policeman. "We'll discuss it at the station." He yelled more orders and threats, but I could only hear the rush of blood in my ears. I turned back to the window and gave it a powerful kick.

My foot went through the glass. The sound was surprising, a staccato of hollow ringing. Even more surprising was that when I retrieved my leg, a large triangle of glass came with it, embedded in my calf.

I staggered, reaching out for something to hold on to, but my leg gave way beneath me. As I fell, I saw every mistake I'd ever made, and I had just enough time to register that none of them had been as bad as this one.

THWACK. The pavement tasted salty metallic. I blacked out.

I woke with a start. Horizontal. Tried to get to my feet, but my leg was braced and my head felt like someone had stuffed it full of nails. I squinted my eyes to try and focus. I was in hospital. Without the baby.

A pressure built up on my chest, and kept building, like a marching band trampling my ribcage. It grew into a full-on military tattoo. I was officially the worst father – no, the worst person – in the world. If I was on a life-support machine, it should be switched off now.

"Please try to relax." The voice belonged to a robust-looking female doctor. "You're in King's College Hospital Emergency Department being treated for shock, head trauma, a broken leg and a partially severed Achilles tendon. You'll be all right, but you need to settle down."

I tried to say something, but my voice sounded like it was coming from somewhere else and I lost my train of speech.

"Calm down or you'll do yourself more damage. Stop moving about and tell me your name."

I looked up at the doctor with pleading wet eyes.

"What is your name?" She enunciated every syllable.

I concentrated, struggling to cut through the morphine mist. "Dan. Yel. Franks."

"Daniel Franks?"

I nodded. "My . . . baby . . ."

"Can we contact someone for you?"

"My baby my baby my baby!"

The doctor's face tightened with concern. "I'll be right back, OK Daniel?"

"No!" I bawled, but she'd already left. I needed to concentrate. I needed to speak to someone. I had to get to a phone. I searched my bedside for an emergency pull-cord, thinking that this couldn't possibly get any worse. Then it got worse.

A familiar figure loomed above me, leaning on a crutch. My heart swelled and fluttered. It was Elaine, wearing a hospital gown. I gawked at her helplessly. She looked crestfallen.

"Oh, Danny," she said. "I was just about to have my check-up and I got a call saying you were here. Oh, honey . . ."

I wanted to gouge my eyes out with a spoon. "I'm . . . sorry, Elaine – so sorry . . . The baby –" The word caught in my throat and came out as a kind of hiccough.

"You must have been terrified. Sukhvinder told me all about it."

Sukhvinder?

Then I saw him. Mo – Sukhvinder – standing behind Elaine. In his arms, a tiny miracle. My precious doughy baby. He winked at me. "I called your wife on my mobilephone and told her about the *bewakoof* burglar who broke your window and attacked you while you were responsibly babysitting."

Elaine leaned over and stroked my hair. "I don't know how you had the presence of mind to drag yourself downstairs and ask Sukhvinder for help. Or should I say: Mo." She flashed me a wry smile and kissed me on the forehead. I sank back into the crisp hospital sheets; felt like I was floating.

Gingerly, Mo bent down and placed the baby on my chest. He lingered a moment to whisper in my ear. "The locksmith arrived. I took the baby and called your wife from my last-dialled numbers." He straightened up, then ducked down again to whisper one last thing. "You owe me three hundred fifty for the locksmith. And four pound ninety-nine for batteries."

But I barely heard him. I stared at the baby wriggling on my chest. She glowed with life. The thought that I might have lost her – that I might ever lose her – filled me with butterfly panic. She was small and perfect, yet so precarious. I caressed her yielding fontanelle, weeping with joy and apprehension.

"The world always seems brighter when you've just made something that wasn't there before."

– Neil Gaiman

# The Cull
## LUCY HUME

### Spring

Jim rose at five. He had slept in fits, waking at two-hourly intervals through the night. He pulled on jeans and a jumper and laced his boots over his pink bed socks. The nights were still cool and the fire in the wood-burner had died, so his breath was visible as he dressed. There had been no rain, though; that was good. Downstairs he unhooked his whistle from the coat rack. Poppy leapt off the sofa and trotted after him out of the house.

The sun was beginning to rise and the sky was lightening. A tapering column of cloud hung above the trees at the end of the field. The Ministry had given twenty-four hours' notice: the disease had been found in the Kemps' cattle over in Halesden. Yesterday the valuer had been round. Today the vets and slaughtermen were due.

Jim stuck his whistle in his mouth and Poppy ran off to the edge of the field, crouching close to the hedge. He called her back to heel; there was no work for her today. He wanted only to walk the circuit of his three fields, to check on his flock, to make sure none of the ewes was lambing and in trouble.

The sheep ran together in clumps, alarmed by the presence of Poppy, then broke up and grazed grass already worn down by the movement ban. Some of them had lambed, their young gathered at their feet or head-butting to get at a teat. Others were slow with pregnancy.

Jim spotted Kylie lying down, her week-old twins nestled against her haunch, curled up like dogs. He named his ewes only occasionally, wary of sentimentality. It was usually the ones marked out by some odd feature – a lumpy head or black specks of pigmentation that gave their noses a freckled appearance. He named them after singers: Debbie, Siouxsie, Bonnie, Celine.

"Name one for me," May had said to him, about this time two years ago. She'd been standing at the kitchen sink in tracksuit bottoms and the same pink socks he was wearing now.

"What, love," he had said, "call her May, you mean?"

"Call her Kylie," she said.

Jim had found the perfect lamb in that year's newborns, the smallest of triplets with a slender head and dark-ringed eyes. Kylie. She had been lucky with her twins, which were born easily, forelegs first and no complications. Jim had lost more ewes than usual so far this year, the Ministry having decreed no movement even within farms, so he couldn't bring them into the barn to lamb. Little Robbie Ilari from down the lane had been helping him out, bottle-feeding the sock lambs. Jim had been struck again by the maturity of his skinny eleven-year-old neighbour. Though his mother would probably point him towards a career in law or accountancy, he had the right temperament for farming – calm and capable, with just enough worry in him.

It took Jim less time than he had anticipated to complete his round of the fields. Back in the house he made tea, his hand shaking as he poured water from the kettle into his mug. After a single bite of buttered toast he took his plate over to the bin and tipped the two slices into it. Outside in the yard Poppy began to bark, her chain rattling against the kennel where Jim had left her tethered. He noticed the sound of the engine only when it fell silent. A car door slammed shut, followed by another.

There were two of them. They looked the right ages to be father and son, though there was no similarity between them. The younger one had white-blond hair and long limbs, his shirtsleeves not quite reaching his wrists. His tanned skin was patchy with flush at the jaw. The older man was small, with black hair to his collar, receding severely to the crown. He introduced himself as Grant.

"And this is Barney," he said. "He's in his final year of studies."

Barney leaned across the bonnet of the Land Rover to shake hands. His palms were clammy, but he looked Jim in the eye and gave a little nod.

"This will take a while," Grant said. "If you've got something better to do, you might want to go off and do it."

"You're all right," Jim said. "I'll stay."

"They'll use what's called a captive bolt gun," Grant said. "So after impact the bolt is retracted and used again."

"Fine," Jim said.

"It's safer than your so-called free bullet gun because there's no danger of the bullet ricocheting off and shooting the wrong thing."

"Good," Jim said.

Grant opened the back door of the Land Rover and pulled a small shoulder bag off the seat. He unzipped it on the bonnet, took out a syringe and passed it to Barney. He turned away to speak, but Jim turned too so he could listen in with his good ear.

"Only inject them once the mother has been killed," Grant said in an undertone. Barney nodded. Grant turned back to Jim and looked at his watch. "The others should be here soon," he said.

"Yes," Jim said. He was feeling dizzy, and he had to hold on to the wing mirror to steady himself. He was in the business of death, and would be paid. It was no different from lambs going to market as they did every year.

Gordon Richardson's battered blue Peugeot struggled noisily up the steep incline in front of the farmhouse. Gordon had only just avoided the cull: his sheep farm was three miles to the north of the Kemps'. He eased himself out of the driver's seat, a massive man, twice as broad as Jim and half a foot taller. It seemed every second tooth was missing, but the ones he had were white against his brown skin. He slapped Jim on the back, leaving his hand resting on his shoulder. He had brought his two sons with him, Danny and Stu, and Gav, the young farm worker who had come round yesterday to help build the pyre. Gav was barely sixteen, with ears that stuck out from his shaved head so the sunlight glowed through them.

A silver van arrived soon after Gordon, and the two slaughtermen climbed down, dressed in white hooded overalls like spacemen. Their movements were slow and reluctant as they opened the back doors and unpacked their equipment. Many of them were working sixteen-hour days and seven-day weeks, so Jim had heard. He was glad he had enough food in the house for everyone to sit down to lunch after the work was finished, even if it was only sausage rolls and cold cuts. May would have had something in the oven, a casserole or pie. Since her death Jim's appetite for all that had disappeared.

"Off you go, lads," Gordon said. "We'll be along." He assumed charge of any situation, whether captaining the tug-of-war team at the village fête or chairing the quarterly parish council meetings. Stu and Danny led the way down to the field. When they reached the gate, Gav performed a jaunty vault over it.

Jim waited for Gordon to start talking, to go off on a rant about the government, the Ministry or the pig farmer in Northumberland whose fault it all was. But he remained silent, keeping his hold on Jim's shoulder. After a while Jim's awkwardness about being so close to the other man began to ease, and, if not for the smell of wax on Gordon's jacket, he might have forgotten about the heavy arm around him.

The first shot sounded like a slap. Jim cried out and started forward, but there was no strength in his legs and his knees gave way. Gordon kept hold of him and hauled him upright. The other ewes had burst into a panic of bleating that almost drowned out the second shot. Another one followed, and another. The two men stood with their arms around each other and listened until the last of the animals had fallen silent and the first tendril of smoke drifted over the hedge towards them.

## Summer

Marco lit the touchpaper with a match. Flames licked the coals and a watery panel of heat hovered above the barbecue. Emma sipped her white wine, which had lost its chill after only a few minutes in the midday heat. Marco took the glass, drank from it himself and returned it to her with a lingering look. His fingers had left dirty charcoal marks near the rim.

He levered the cap off a bottle of beer, nodding in time to the tock, tock of Siena's racquet as she played swingball by herself. Emma loved the countryside's summer sounds – a distant lawnmower, the call of a cuckoo, a sudden flapping of wings in the hedgerow. But this year there was a strange absence of background noise without the sheep bleating on Jim Daly's farm.

Once the coals had cooled to a smoulder Marco slid the kebabs onto the grill. The smell of meat cooking alerted Emma to her hunger. Marco had marinated the lamb overnight in one of his mysterious "mama" recipes and assembled the kebabs this morning on skewers with wedges of green pepper. Emma wondered how long this campaign would last. Marco had never had a problem with contrition; it was sticking around he struggled with.

This time he had shown up at the front door without warning or cash to pay the driver of the minicab from Gatwick. Emma had been forced to upend the change jar for pound coins.

While the children slept upstairs Marco had ground pepper onto the scrambled eggs Emma had made and detailed the demise of his latest business venture. The economy was stagnant even in Rome and luxury holiday apartments on the Amalfi coast were in short demand.

"What about Ana?" Emma had said when Marco finished talking.

"She threw me out," Marco said. "She just wanted my money."

Emma had met Ana the previous summer, the last time the children saw their father. Emma had escorted Robbie and Siena over on the easyJet flight, and Ana had driven Marco to da Vinci airport to meet them. She was bosomy and unkempt, with a mole at the tip of her greasy nose, wearing an oversized T-shirt with a leopard's face on the front. She had not seemed the money-grabbing type.

"She realised I still loved you," Marco had added hastily, reaching for Emma's hand across the table.

Emma was not jealous of Ana. She was grateful to her, even, for the temporary respite from their marriage, that endless string of concessions made on the grounds of intimacy. Marco's return had brought with it the daily dusting of bristles in the sink, curled toothpaste rind around the cap and a rapid depletion of toilet paper. After two weeks living with him again Emma was already feeling the tug, the need to pull away from careless make-up and sheets that needed washing, and to escape to her ideal – the uncrowded landscape, the precision of solitude that had first prompted the move here.

Marco needed other people, though, at his most vivid when surrounded by his noisy cohort of sisters and their overweight husbands. If Emma ever saw him walking alone – through the arrivals doors at the airport, or along a station platform – he looked lost and childlike. He seemed to regard the space here as a void needing to be filled with ceremony and clutter – these new cooking utensils, the brightly coloured plastic plates and wine glasses.

The swingball string wrapped itself around the pole and unwound again; Siena ran forward to hit the ball but missed, falling to her knees on the grass. She got up, skipped over, tapped her father playfully on the bottom with the red plastic racquet and ran away. A flinch of irritation passed over Marco's face, but he handed Emma the barbecue tongs and chased Siena, laughing, round the garden.

Emma used the tongs to turn the kebabs. They had burned on the side nearest the flame and in places the meat tore where it had stuck to the grill. Marco got hold of Siena and lifted her up over his shoulder as if she were a much lighter child. The soles of her bare feet were dirty and her hair hung down, almost touching the grass. Marco spun her around and she squealed with delight.

But where was Robbie? With no work for him on Jim Daly's farm since the outbreak, he had taken to sprawling in front of the television or the Nintendo, ominously aping the adolescent he would too soon become. Emma placed the lid on the barbecue and went into the house to look for him. She found the door to the downstairs bathroom closed, and knocked. There was no reply, so she opened the door. Robbie was sitting on the floor beside the toilet, his head resting in his arms on the mahogany seat. When he looked up his face was flat with pallor.

"What's wrong?" Emma said, hurt that he hadn't alerted her, that he should prefer to suffer alone than make a nuisance of himself.

"Feel sick," Robbie said.

Emma crouched down next to him and felt his forehead, which was cool.

"It's probably a bit of heatstroke," she said. "Come on, sweetheart, let's get you up."

She helped Robbie stand and led him over to the basin where she ran the cold tap. She took the bar of almond soap and rubbed it into a lather in her own hands, then washed Robbie's shaking hands with hers, smoothing the soap along his fingers. She rinsed them under the water.

"How does that feel?" Emma said.

"Better," he said.

"What is it?" she said.

Robbie closed his eyes and said nothing.

"It's strange having Daddy back, isn't it?" she said.

He opened one eye. "No," he said. "It's good. Siena likes it."

"Do you like it?" Emma said, finding she wanted the answer to be "No".

"Yeah," Robbie said.

They went back outside. Marco was taking the meat off the barbecue and Siena was making a show of laying the table with blue napkins. They never had napkins.

"Food is ready!" Marco said. He picked up Emma's hand, brought it to his mouth and gently bit her knuckles.

They sat down and Emma helped everybody to food. She was pleased when Robbie managed to eat most of his chicken breast and a forkful of potato salad, though he left his kebab untouched.

"What's wrong with it?" Marco said, gesturing with his knife.

"I can't eat it," Robbie said.

"Why not?"

"Mum knows."

"It's fine, Marco," Emma said, unsure of what she was supposed to know.

Marco rolled his eyes, took the kebab from Robbie's plate and slid a chunk of meat off with his teeth. Emma tried to smile at Robbie, but he was watching his father eat, his eyes inscrutable behind his dark fringe.

## Autumn

"Have mercy on us," Robbie said, as the rest of the congregation intoned "Grant us peace". His voice sounded louder for the words being wrong and his mother, standing beside him, turned her head. Siena was kneeling at the altar, her head bent over her little gold bell, looking like a stupid, fat angel in her white robe. An acorn struck the windowpane like a flung pebble.

After the service, Father Barry stood inside the church door.

"Enjoy the half-term holiday, Robert," he said. A purple throat sweet glistened on his tongue.

"Thank you, Father," Robbie said, dropping into an accidental curtsey. He pressed his fingers into the sponge in the basin next to the door and made a sign of the cross. He could feel the cool spot of water on his forehead as he stepped outside. His parents were talking beside the car, his father holding the tip of his mother's finger. She was wearing a new dress with seashells on it.

"Can I walk home?" Robbie said.

His father turned, frowning, as if Robbie were a stranger.

"All right," his mother said, "but take your sister with you." Then she said something Robbie couldn't hear, and his father laughed. They climbed into the car, pulled the doors shut and drove off. Seeing his mum lift her hand at the window, Robbie waved back, before he realised she was only pulling on her seat belt.

Last night they had gone out for dinner at the pub, leaving Robbie and Siena with Carey, their babysitter. Robbie had stayed awake until they got home, reading by the light of his bedside lamp and snapping it off as soon as the headlights shone through his curtains.

The nightmares came less often now. It was rare that he woke gasping with no breath in him, his pyjama top damp with sweat. His mother put this down to his father's return, but Robbie knew it was just the spread of time slowly relieving the dread that had breathed down his neck since the bonfires of spring.

Siena ran up to him, still pulling on her coat. Baby hairs stood up on the top of her head.

"Mum and Dad have gone without you," Robbie said. "They knew you'd only nag them for sweets at the paper shop."

Siena rearranged her hurt into a pout. "Ha-*ha*," she said. "Ha-*ha*."

"Come on," Robbie said, and set off on the path through the leaning gravestones.

When they reached the kissing gate at the top of the footpath Siena climbed onto it, threw a leg over and clung on as it swung to, her jumper riding up and exposing her stomach. She vaulted off and stumbled, laughing. Robbie ignored her. Weekends meant forced companionship, but at school they were strangers to each other, him blank-facing her in the corridors, running away with his friends when he saw her standing alone in the playground at break-time eating her Frusli bar. Her solitude made him itch with annoyance. He couldn't understand why she didn't do something to make friends, approach a huddle of girls talking, or join in with the big games of red rover in the school car park.

On the far side of the valley Mr Daly's fields were silver with dew. Since the cull in April they had remained empty, but back then they had been full of new lambs, giving fragile bleats and leaping just for happiness. Robbie had been up there helping Mr Daly feed the sock lambs, spooning three tablespoons of powdered milk into hot tap water to make up the bottles of chalky liquid. When they fed, the lambs shook their tails madly and pulled on the rubber teat so it was all Robbie could do to hold himself steady.

When Mr Daly sheared a sheep it was like he was hypnotising it. With other farmers, sheep fought as if they were about to have their throats cut, but between Mr Daly's thighs they were calm, almost dozy. The shears drove through the fleece like a plough pushing snow, exposing soft white skin underneath. They looked ridiculous shorn, like goats, and they seemed to know it, their cropped tails pressed against their backsides as they ran out of the pen into the field. Sheepish, Mr Daly said. He let Robbie bundle up the fleeces for him and pack them into plastic sacks, and the lanolin in the wool left Robbie's hands smelling like petrol.

They reached the wood. The light in here was poor, the air sweet with the scent of damp earth. As he walked, Robbie kept his eyes on the ground, looking out for the chestnuts that had just begun to fall from the trees. Whenever he found one he trod on it with the heel of his trainer to split the casing, picked it up carefully and eased the prickly shell away from the shiny brown nut inside. He stored his collection in the pouch of his hoodie.

Copying him, Siena tried to pick one up but cried out and dropped it again, examining her fingers for prickles.

"Here you go," Robbie said, and gave her one of his chestnuts. She inspected it suspiciously before slipping it into her coat pocket.

Last year his mother had roasted the chestnuts in the oven and the three of them had sat around the kitchen table, burning their fingers trying to get the skins off. Robbie had a feeling his father would hijack this somehow, wanting to do something complicated and Italian.

In the close shade of the beech trees, Robbie could just make out a large object up ahead. As he drew nearer, he saw it was Mr Daly's old blue Toyota truck, parked a little way from the path. It had been weeks since he'd last seen it careering along the lanes. Poppy usually sat in the back, her tongue hanging out, blown back along her cheek. She couldn't be in the truck now, though; Robbie could hear her yelping and rattling her chain against her kennel in front of the farmhouse.

Closer, the truck looked like it was smoking. It was surrounded by a grey fog that smelt like traffic fumes. There was a long, green tube attached to the exhaust pipe running along the side to the driver's window. Maybe Mr Daly had broken down, and the tube was one of those jump leads used to kick-start car batteries.

Holding his breath against the stink, Robbie approached the driver's door. The tube had been fed through the top of the window, the gap covered over with silver tape. He made a cap with his hands and peered through the window. Mr Daly's seat was tilted back and his body was turned slightly to one side. His hands, resting in his lap, were swollen and pink. His mouth hung open. Just as Robbie raised his hand to tap on the glass, he saw the eyes, wide open and staring.

Robbie drew back. Siena was at his shoulder. He pushed her away roughly with his arm.

"Ow!" she said, and rubbed her elbow.

"Come on," Robbie said. He grabbed her sleeve and pulled her away from the truck. "Race you home," he said, and ran. Despite her size, Siena could never resist a race. Robbie sprinted to the end of the track and out into the sunlit farmyard where Poppy was straining at her chain so it looked like her neck would break, barking furiously.

*He was wearing his seat belt. Why would he wear his seat belt?*

Robbie kept running, past Mrs Arthur's bungalow and the Maschlers' big white house on the corner, up the lane to home. Chestnuts were falling from the sides of his pouch and rolling down the road back towards Siena, but he didn't stop to retrieve them. He slowed down to let Siena catch him before sprinting again at the end, beating her to the front door.

In the kitchen their parents were having breakfast. The cereal boxes were lined up in height order at the centre of the table. Siena plonked herself down in a chair, breathing heavily and fanning herself with her hand.

Robbie's father held a piece of burnt toast in one hand and was bent over the newspaper. He was using a biro to underline sentences in the article he was reading. In places, he had drawn a circled star in the margin. His mother was eating muesli and listening to a programme on the radio. Her mouth was occupied with chewing, but every time the audience on the radio laughed, her eyes creased.

It occurred to Robbie that this was what a normal family looked like on a Sunday morning. He was the only one who knew what he had seen, which meant that for as long as he didn't tell anyone, it wouldn't be true. He pictured his mother flying up from the table, his father dropping the pen. He saw them all in the wood, his father opening the door of the truck, the foul-smelling smoke billowing free.

Still regaining his breath, Robbie fetched two extra bowls from the cupboard and poured Cheerios into each. He felt strangely disconnected from his actions, as if someone else were performing them. He poured milk onto his cereal only; Siena preferred to eat hers dry. He stuck a spoon into her bowl and slid it across the table to her. His mother finally looked up at him, surprised, and gave him a nod of approval.

He sat down, and though his throat was constricted and his stomach felt full of sand, he forced a spoonful of sweet cereal into his mouth and swallowed.

"Let the world burn through you. Throw the prism light, white hot, on paper."

– Ray Bradbury

# Wendy
## GAYLENE GOULD

Wendy's dolls are cardboard and flatter than a fish. Dolly One has bright-red cheeks and blue eyes and a grin like she's mid giggle. Dolly Two is a brunette with peachy skin and two thick plaits. Dolly Two is prettier but Dolly One has a tufty yellow fringe that makes me melt when I stroke it. Their colourful dresses are painted on, cleaner than anything I've seen since I arrived at Ryders. Soon I discover their fresh innocent faces are a perfect cover for their vicious tongues.

**"Now, Wendy, don't just sit there, looking stupid."**

*"Yeah, why don't you get yourself some friends?"*

"I have friends."

**"So, where are they then?"**

"They're waiting for me at home."

*"Now. There you go again, you daft ha'p'orth. You don't have a home."*

"Yes I do."

**"What you doing here then?"**

"I'm here on me holidays."

*"Ha ha! What d'you call this place then? Butlins for retards?"*

I'm stiff all over from trying not to move. My body's wrapped around my Survival Box and my arms and legs ache from where it's dug into me. (It's not really a box. It's an old McVitie's biscuit

33

tin which lost its biscuit smell a long time ago. Marma used to keep odds and ends in it. Some of the more useful odds are still inside it.) I'm still dressed in the clothes I arrived in a few hours ago, even though I'm under the covers. The mattress is lumpy and the bedspread smells musty.

From the outside, Ryders looked like a place where grandfather clocks strike thirteen. It's the high wall that runs along the front and side of the house that makes it stand out from the others, that and its red roof turrets. It seemed grander than the other ones on the street, which are red-bricked and flat-fronted with tiny walls and concrete gardens. Ryders' garden sprawls out all the way to the corner – so the waving treetops told me. The street is long and straight and stretches way into the distance. You could never reach the end of it, no matter how far or fast you ran.

"That's a park right across there. And if you stand on tiptoe in the back bedroom you can almost see the footie ground. Ain't you the lucky one?"

Julie, the social worker, had her hand on the large wooden gate. She turned back to see if I was following.

"Well? You wanna see your new home or don't you?"

I tried to be Dorothy putting my first ruby-red shoe on the Yellow Brick Road, like the time I skipped around the living room to Marma's claps as the film played in the background. But this path was all smashed black stones and wild weeds.

Now, they've put me in a room they say is mine. But this room will never smell of Saturday Soup and I'll never hear Marma talking back to the telly, or Miss Baptiste's hymns coming up the path. So I find myself turning towards a sigh. It sounds so lonely.

Sitting on the floor, with her back against the other bed, is a small girl. Her legs are crossed and her head bowed. She's balancing two cardboard dolls on her knees. As I turn she looks up at me. Her flat blank look switches to a scrunched smile.

She flings herself forward, pushing their three bright faces into my stunned one. I scrabble backwards towards the wall, clutching my Survival Box. One of her front teeth is chipped and her cheekbones are dusted with freckles like they've sprinkled from her round brown eyes. Her hair, the colour of gravy, coats the bedspread in thin straggly strands.

"Hallo. I been waiting for you to wake up. I'm Wendy what's your name? I'm nine. How old are you? This is Dolly One and Dolly Two. You can play with them if you like but Dolly One's arm is falling off so you have to be careful with it. She broke it in a fight she had with Dolly Two so you have to keep watch over them. They fight all the time, see? *Take that.* **Ouch. You bitch.** *How dare you speak to me like that? Take that.* **Ouch. I'm gonna get you. I'm gonna strangle you in your sleep.**"

Dolly Two is laying into Dolly One but not doing much to wipe the smile off her cardboard face. Wendy pulls them apart.

"I bandaged Dolly One's arm with Sellotape but it's still a bit loose. Look."

Dolly One waves at me with her artificial joint. Then Wendy leans in some more so her nose is an inch from mine and I can smell her stale sugar breath. She drops her voice to a whisper.

"I got a house out back. It's no one else's but mine and the dollies'. We've got our very own kitchen and living room and bedroom and everything. It's got fitted carpets throughout. You can't tell no one about it though cos it's a secret and only we can live there. But I'll let you come too because you're my friend so you can have a key. Want to see it?"

She stands up. Her grey socks fall to her ankles. She pulls them up and they immediately concertina down again. She holds her hand out to me. I slowly let go of the Survival Box and reach out from under the bedcovers. I take her hand. It's warm and clammy like real flesh.

I didn't tell Marma about the Box. She might've thought I wasn't God-fearing enough. I didn't tell her that I was preparing for Just In Case. Just In Case I hadn't read my Bible thoroughly or helped out in the kitchen or learned my sums properly. Just In Case Judgement Day came and I was left behind. And I was right to have the Box because Just In Case happened. Marma made it to Paradise and I didn't. And if Marma is in Paradise, there is only one other place this can be.

I wait until Wendy thunders away down the landing before climbing out of bed. There's not much choice. There's the wardrobe, but I'll be sharing that with Wendy. There's the chest of drawers, but people always look in drawers for secrets. So I stoop down and, throwing a last look over my shoulder, slip the Survival Box into the lonely place under the bed.

Wendy's house is a tree. Not just any tree. It's like the one that stood at the bottom of our garden. The same broad trunk and those leaves like pretty hands. The ground underneath is littered with the helicopter seeds.

It's tucked away in a corner of the back garden by the high wall that circles the whole house. Above the wall, the gas-tower spaceships are so out of this world that they make me dizzy.

To get here, you come out the back door by the kitchen and cross the grass that's trampled bald by hundreds of careless feet. The garden stretches the length of the house and continues round to the car park on the side. It's lined with bushes, not flowers like Marma's garden. This one's given up.

The shady area, underneath the branches, makes up the kitchen, living room and hall. Wendy tells me off when I somehow sit half in the kitchen and half in the living room. Her broom's a broken branch and she sweeps the imaginary wall-to-wall carpets. She stands at the sink and washes up a lot. She pulls roasts out of the pretend oven. She moans when the babies cry and shakes them up and down to settle them. She sits on the sofa and gossips about the no-good neighbours. She stands by the window and cusses her rubbish husband, Big Jim. This game is called mums and dads.

"So I told Big Jim not to come round when I pick up me Social cos he only wants to get his hands on me Family Allowance. Why should he when he ain't gave a penny towards them kids?"

I look down at the kids, thrown to one side but still smiling despite Big Jim and his lack of pennies.

"Want a drag?"

She holds two fingers out towards me like a pistol. I look from her face to her fingers and back to her face again. Her eyes narrow into suspicious slits. I touch my fingers to hers nervously. She narrows her eyes even more. I sit there, fingers awkward. Slowly, I lift them to my lips and blow out cautiously. She relaxes and so do I.

"What about your Ted? Have you seen him since he ran off with that bit from the pub?"

My fag hand freezes in mid-air. I have a *Ted*? He has a *bit*?

"No," she continues, "I bet you haven't. The little bugger. I told my Jim to make himself useful and knock Ted's block off next time he sees him. But they're as bad as each other. Men. They're all a waste of space if you ask me. Better off without 'em."

She stands suddenly and stretches, rubbing her pushed-out belly.

"Let's go to bed."

Crouching low, she waddles over to a shaded part of the tree where the bottom branches have been twisted to the ground. I follow her through a hole in the broken branches into a dark, cool cave. We can't see out and no one can see in.

We lie side by side in our bedroom. The leaf shadows dance across her face. She's got blue ice-pole traces tucked in the corners of her mouth.

"My mum's a *bomb-buster*."

I lie dead still and watch her mouth move.

"She is. She busts bombs, she does, down at Greenum Common. They camp out there, they do, and at night they dress up like James Bond – all in black, they are. They got these *massive* scissors and those wire things that shoot on top of a roof and pull you up at a hundred miles an hour and they do secret missions to dis-harm the bombs. Sometimes the bombs go off and kill people, like *millions* of people, but my mum ain't been killed. She's the best bomb-buster in the business."

She pulls her knees up to her chest and drags her socks up. I watch them slip down again.

"And one day she's gonna come and bust me out of here so we can be the first mother and daughter bomb-busting team."

I play quietly with the buttons on my shirt. She thumps over onto her side so her face is inches from mine and I can smell her blue breath.

"She is 'n' all!" she hisses.

I freeze my fingers and don't let my breath out until she sits up and says, "Come on, it'll be teatime soon."

Wendy talks – a lot – so she doesn't notice I don't. She ain't noticed I'm coloured either and never wants to touch my hair. She doesn't even want to see inside my Survival Box. So I follow. Even though she's nine and I'm eleven I don't mind her taking the lead. By the time I've climbed over the branches to take my place beside her in the dapply light, I've promised to follow her anywhere.

I'm shadowing Wendy round the breakfast room my first morning at Ryders. Micky Bull's steely eyes follow me with an "'ark at 'er" look. Micky Bull's dad, a plumber, fixes Dave from Showaddywaddy's waterworks so, to prove the point, Micky wears kick-flared tartan trousers with six-inch turn-ups. He tries to brush his hair so his sidies hang low in front of his ears but he's only twelve so he has no sidies. Instead he spits on his hands and sticks bits of his hair to the side of his face.

Wendy doesn't notice him looking at me, though. She's too busy prattling away for the both of us. I'm busy trying to shrink to nothing.

"So Weetabix for me and Sugar Puffs for Jess. Jess likes her Sugar Puffs, don't you, Jess?"

I don't like Sugar Puffs. Sugar-coated puffs of nothing. What I like is Marma's crunchy dumplings that you can feel the weight of in your mouth, but I don't say owt. I watch Micky Bull out the corner of my eye. He's sitting across the other side of the room, leaning over to his mates without taking his eyes off a me.

"Now hold your bowl out, Jess silly. There's the Sugar Puffs. 'E y'are, I'll gi' you some more cos you like 'em lots, don't ya? Now here comes the milk . . ."

Micky stands, bends his knees John Wayne-style, and saunters towards me, his turn-ups flapping round his ankles. He's hooked his fingers in his belt loops, which sit on his ribcage. His mates, blurry in the background, nudge each other like birds fussing on a telephone wire. The air tightens in my chest.

"Now, where do you wanna sit, Jess? How 'bout by the window, so we can see our tree?"

My Sugar Puffs are rocking from side to side in my bowl. He stands above me now, too close.

"Who's the jungle bunny, Wen?"

Wendy blinks slowly, like she's waking from a dream, before rolling her eyes.

"None of your beeswax, Micky Bull."

He leans forward and pushes his face into mine. His teeth are green and his mouth smells mouldy.

"Don't you speak the Queen's English, Bunny?"

He pushes out each word with a loud puff of stale unwashed air. My stomach does a long slow turn. I hear a chorus of laughter come from behind him.

He scratches under his arms, rocking from one foot to another to the sound of a laughing chimpanzee. The room grows louder and chairs drag to get a better look.

"You better not put that bowl back with the others, cos we don't want to be eating out the same bowl as a *monkey*."

Then his long curved finger hooks under the rim of my bowl and flips it up and over. The first few splashes of milk tickle my shoes and soak through the front of my flowered skirt before the slam and mushy thump of the Sugar Puffs bowl hits my feet. The edge has caught the tips of my toes and they throb, empty, like they've come clean away. The room breaks apart in peals of laughter. The soggy empty puffs of nothing ease out around my feet.

"Oi, clown. Siddown."

And he's there in the doorway. Fists as wide as shovels sit on his large hips. The stripes on his egg-stained sweatshirt are stretched wider round the belly. His stomach is too heavy for the waistband it rests on. His eyes are surprisingly young, a sandy colour that matches his thin, spiky hair. Sleep's printed in long deep grooves on the side of his stubbly cheeks. Chris. It's the first time I've seen him. He wasn't on duty when I arrived yesterday. "House Father" they call him. But I don't have a father. Not any more. Not like him.

Chris is smiling at Micky and Micky is smiling mischievously back, like they're conspirators. He jerks his thumb suddenly and Micky immediately obeys, performing a stylish stroll back to his seat. The others applaud. Chris folds his arms and looks me up and down, those golden eyes soaking me up like blotting paper. I know I should move but I can't. Something about the way he's looking fixes me to the spot. Outside, the leaves are rattling on the tree. I wish my shaking would loosen me away like that.

He takes his time to shamble across to me. When he reaches

me, he kneels down and studies the bowl, holding his chin like he's fixing to shift a boulder. He shakes his head and gently lifts the bowl up and away. My feet are heaped in piles of soggy Sugar Puffs. He cups his big shovel hands and slowly begins to paw them along my feet, scooping away the mess and dumping it back in the bowl. Sometimes he opens his hands and, for a few seconds, rests them on the top of my feet. They are big enough to take my whole foot in his palm. Their heavy heat seeps through the patterned holes in my socks. When the mess is cleared, he covers my feet with both hands and circles his thumb and middle finger around my ankles. Then he starts to squeeze slowly, until his joints bore painfully into my bones. Suddenly, he lets go and he's smiling up at me but there's no warmth in it.

"Go on with you. And don't go trailing Sugar Puffs round the house."

After he leaves, I stand shivering. My feet have turned into blocks of ice and they're beginning to freeze my entire body, jamming my throat and frosting my eyes. I'm scared because I'm in this hell and I'm freezing over. My jaw begins to flutter. Then Wendy jolts me with her elbow.

"Come on, silly. Let's get you another bowl."

I free-fall, that first summer at Ryders Children's Home. I try to skulk along the corridor but the twins still barrel into me as they aim kicks at each other's groin. I learn what happens when you get in the way of the older girls as they swing by wrapped in their cloud of Charlie perfume. The vicious cracked voices, the hysterical tantrums and the constant wailing jangle me. Micky Bull tortures me. And Chris's strange smile haunts me at night. When I wake my feet are blue with cold.

No one seems bothered about my silence which is the only good thing. Julie, my social worker, drops by every now and then, and I hear her chatting to the House Parents using words like "adjustment" and "taking time". I stand on the side like Dobbin from *Rentaghost*.

Wendy and me spend a lot of time lying side by side under the cool of the leaves. It's the only place I don't have that falling feeling, maybe because these are Marma's leaves too.

Then one summer's afternoon, Chris is here, standing with his two big feet in the middle of our living room.

"What's up, girls? What you playing?"

I've seen him watching us before, from the back step. I'd smell the fag smoke first. I'd stop bathing the babies or peeling the potatoes and he'd be there, silently watching. Wendy was always too busy to notice and I never said anything. And now he's here.

Wendy stops cooking and I stop plaiting Dolly One's hair. We stare at him like he's a Martian just hopped over from the gasworks.

"You cooking there, Wen? Smells nice."

He smiles slowly, in that chilly way, and blows smoke all over our just-cleaned house. My stomach tightens.

"We're . . . just . . . playing," says Wendy. Shyly, she tucks her chin into her neck so her hair falls in front her face.

"Can I join youse?" and just like that he sits down – plonk – right on top our telly. Wendy, shocked, drops the pot and pulls him up by his arm.

"No! Not there!"

She's not sure what to do with him, so she quickly points to a spot next to our kitchen table.

"Sit there."

He does and she puts one hand over her mouth to hide her giggles. With the other hand, she stirs the pot, slower now.

"If you're playing" – her hand makes a wide empty circle – "you got to be Big Jim."

"Oh aye," he says, winking at me. I'm holding on to Dolly One tightly round her neck. "I'll be Big Jim, then. You cooking my tea?"

Wendy nods. I move an inch away. I wonder where Dolly Two is. I wish I had both with me.

Suddenly he smashes his fists on his knees and barks, "So where's my dinner, woman? I'm hungry."

I gasp. I can't help it. What with Wendy already being mad cos Big Jim stayed out all night, she's really going to let him have it. I swivel my head from him to her. But she don't say nowt. Instead she begins serving him big dollops of nothing.

"Here it is, Jimmy," she says quickly. "Roast potatoes . . ."

Dollop.

"Beef . . ."

Dollop.

"Yorkshire pud . . ."

Dollop.

"And peas."

Dollop.

"Just like you like 'em."

I want to ask how all that comes out of one pot and how does she know how he likes 'em? But by the way she's looking at him I know this ain't the time. They swap a smile which makes me look away. Big Jim rolls up his imaginary sleeves, picks up his imaginary knife and fork, and slowly begins tucking into his imaginary dinner. He takes a few slow mouthfuls. Wendy holds the pot, watching his mouth work. He's thoughtful for a minute.

"Aye. Delicious, Wendy love. You're not just a pretty face, are you?"

He smiles up at her and Wendy smiles back, broader than I've ever seen, and dollops more on his plate.

Now it's all "I better get the dinner on. Big Jim's coming" this and "Put the babies to bed. He's on his way" that. I don't know how to be around this new Wendy. Since he's been coming, it ain't about Wendy and me no more. It's about Wendy and him. I'm just the neighbour. So I keep my back to him cos I can't stand to watch him eat.

This time when he shows up, something different happens. This time, after he finishes eating, he stretches noisily and says, "Ooh, that's lovely, but I'm dead tired now after all that hard work. I think I'll go and have a lie down."

He stands and, crouching over, makes his way past the broken branches to the place where our towels lie side by side. Big Jim glances at me with an odd look then says to Wendy, "You gonna come up wi' me, then? Show me the way?"

I look at my knees. I don't want to see what's on Wendy's face and I don't want to see what's on his.

"'Course." Her bright voice is hiding something. "You go on. I'll finish washing up and then come."

After Big Jim has climbed through the hole in the branches, I put down the dollies and go over to help Wendy wash up. Her face is blank and closed. She's facing the pretend window, looking out onto our pretend street. I pick up a tea towel and start to rub the faces of the pretend plates dry. Something new and real is about to happen and I don't like it. I lean over to her so I can whisper it.

"We could play a new game? Hide 'n' seek? He could count to a hundred and we could hide, somewhere he'd never find us."

Wendy's washing up like she wants to break the dishes. She nudges me hard with her elbow.

"No." Her mouth is a firm, flat line. She looks old, older than me, like I'm the one too young for this. "You finish cleaning. I'm going up."

She turns without a smile and climbs over the branch. I watch her go. I realise I'm holding the plate in my two hands so I turn and dip the plate into the soapy bowl. I scrub its face round and round. I turn on the tap. I let the stream of water rinse off the suds. Wendy never does the last part. She leaves the suds on.

The first time I hear it, I think it's a jumbie come to eat us in our sleep. Marma told me all about the spirits that would trouble you at night.

I clutch the covers more tightly. Wendy's snoring already, so don't hear the sound of breathing outside the door. It's wet and heavy. It stops and I think it's gone away but then it starts again, slower than before. A laser beam of light suddenly cuts across the edge of my bed. I duck quickly under the covers, clenching my lips to stop my heart from spilling out of my mouth. The light disappears. It's inside with us. Its dark footsteps are moving closer. It's standing between our two beds. I can hear the mucus in its fag-stained breath, then the sound of fat, flabby skin falling to the ground.

Wendy's bed creaks. I crack a tiny hole in the folds of the blanket. It's sitting on Wendy's bed and it's naked. Wendy makes a small cry but then she's muffled. The bed shakes.

"Shhhhhh."

It's leaning over her. It's getting under the covers. It's wearing socks.

"Hey. It's only me. Big Jim." The voice is soothing. "Been a long day and I'm dead tired. It's OK. Budge up."

The struggling stops. Then his voice comes.

"Oi, Jess."

My breath stops too.

"Jessie."

I push the blankets back a little.

"Go get yourself some biscuits. There's some nice Bourbons downstairs."

I climb out quickly into the cold. My racing heart is making my fingers fumble so I can't pull on my slippers. Even though I'm not allowed into the kitchen on my own and after six p.m., I'm desperate to leave the monster behind. In the end I slip out barefoot. Before I shut the door, I peep back into the darkness. There's only one large lump in her bed. He might've eaten her. I want to check she's still alive but instead I close the door quietly behind me.

When I wake the next morning, Wendy's already gone. She never goes down to breakfast without me. I dress, fear making my fingers jittery. I don't even brush my teeth, not that anyone would notice. I run downstairs to the breakfast room but she's not there. Micky and his mates are the only ones left.

"Here comes blackie."

His voice is like sandpaper. But today's a different day to yesterday. Yesterday a jumbie hadn't eaten my friend. I make a beeline towards him.

"Where is she? Where is she, I said?"

It's the first time I'd heard me sound dark like that. It's the first time Micky Bull has too. I watch his stupid face go slack. He looks me in my eyes like he's trying to catch me out. I don't know what he sees but whatever it is makes him look away. He jerks his head towards the back door and I'm pulling on the doorknob before he finishes.

"Cat gi' you back your tongue, did it?"

I slam the door behind me.

She's sitting with her back leant against the tree trunk. Her legs are stretched in front of her and crossed at the ankles. As I move closer, I realise what's odd. The dolls are scattered about the ground and they're not talking back. I shiver a little because summer's coming to an end and the sun is starting to die.

I lean gently on the tree trunk next to her. From this angle, she looks littler than usual, like she might snap if you touch her. I want to stroke the top of her head but I don't. Spilled out on her lap is a pile of penny sweets, red liquorice laces, fruit chews, coke bottles and pineapple bombs. She's chewing noisily.

"Look at all me sweets."

She don't look up and I don't say owt. She's whirling a liquorice lace around her finger.

"He says I don't have to share 'em with no one."

The liquorice lace winds and unwinds.

"And anyway, he don't want you cos you're a nig-nog and he ain't partial to them."

Something tightens in me, stealing my breath. I try to focus on the top of her head and not the tight feeling inside. Her hands suddenly fall limp in her lap. Hot tears are tingling the backs of my eyes. Maybe he did eat her after all, cos all her insides have been scooped out. I kneel slowly beside her because if I stomp or make a loud noise, cracks will appear and she'll break apart. All that will be left will be bits of Wendy, and piles of sweets.

"Oh yeah," she says, her voice already dead, "and he told me to tell you, you can't say nowt. To anyone. For ever and ever."

I take her hand. It's hot like warm putty between mine. She stares straight ahead like she can see right through the brick wall.

I let go of her hand and pick up one of the red laces that are lying lost on her lap. I drape it under my nose and then push up my top lip to make a cradle for the drooping red moustache. I give her a nudge. I wait till she's looking then cross my eyes. Little bubbles of laughter start in her chest. She picks up some Jelly Tots and sticks them to her cheeks. I stick a few more on her forehead and she sticks some on mine.

That night, after he's gone and I'm back under the covers clutching my Survival Box, I slip off the lid like usual. This time, my hand swims past the Bible and the scissors, the postcard and the emergency tin of corned beef, and finds the small packet of Jelly Tots. I have to move very slowly so the packet only makes one crinkle at a time. I know Wendy said I couldn't have any, but it's not really stealing, is it, if I have to keep the secret? Cos it's her he wants. Not me. He's not partial to me. I just have to keep the secret and this is where my secrets are kept. I put a strawberry Jelly Tot in my mouth and chew silently.

## Shouting at Cars
## ADAM MAREK

Every Christmas Eve, we took a hamper to the troll beneath the East Bridge. Me, my little brother Alex, my dad, and my step-mum – Magda. The hamper always got a lot of attention on the tram on the way over. People couldn't help but stare at it, this big wicker box on my dad's lap, tied up with red ribbons. It was so heavy that by the end of the three-minute walk from the tram stop to the bridge, Dad was sweating and changing his grip all the time. At the top of the steps down to the tow path along the river, Dad would call back over his shoulder, "Go carefully," even though he was the only one in any real danger, not being able to see the steps at all while carrying that big present.

Since my dad's building had gone up on Peak Street, a newly created wind tunnel sucked up all the discarded newspapers from this district and heaped them here, on the steep bank. Rain had turned the papers into papier mâché, which coated the stone steps an inch thick. Magda's heels punctured holes in it, and each of my footsteps caused these holes to fill up with an inky reservoir.

No one ever came down this part of the tow path – because of the troll – so it was the only place you could walk along the river without having to worry about stepping in dog poop. But it did still stink, of the troll's hurled garbage, which accumulated and rotted on the opposite bank faster than the gulls and crows could carry it away.

By now, we were all quiet and anxious, Dad in front with the hamper, Magda holding Alex's hand, me behind. Far above us, slow-moving cars argued with their horns.

Dad stopped a fair way back from the dark arch of the bridge and called out, "Merry Christmas!"

There followed a few moments of stillness while we waited. I'd always get an awful sensation right about now, like I'd swallowed a croquet ball and it was stuck in my throat. The sensation came no matter how hard I tried to resist it. This was Magda and Dad's fault, them having built up such a sense of dread at home in the weeks leading up to this moment, whispering, bickering, scowling at each other and shutting doors that didn't need shutting. At the centre of this anxiety, there was the hamper, always prepared early and sitting on the breakfast bar, waiting for us to deliver it.

When the troll came out into the light, we all jumped. I could never learn how not to jump, his size always a shock, no matter how many times I'd seen him. He shuffled on his knees, the grey boulder of his nose and the tussocks of his eyebrows emerging first from the gloom. He pulled a face when he saw us, projecting his chin forwards and curling over his purple lower lip. This time, the troll was wearing something like a poncho, made from the blue tarpaulin they use to dress scaffolding.

"We've brought you a gift," Dad called up, lifting the hamper a little and nodding at it, then taking a few steps towards the troll and setting it on the ground. The pretty hamper was a strange sight there in the mulch. The troll glanced at it for a second, then made a huffing noise that caused his nostrils to widen. Resting his bristly cheek against his shoulder, he gazed instead at the river, where the water was black, carrying rafts of ice on which lazy gulls were passengers.

"How are you?" Dad said.

The troll did not look well. His enormous eyes were bloodshot. The underside of his nose was crusted with snot. He sniffed and dabbed there with what looked like a bedsheet. The troll coughed into his curled fist, and the sound startled two pigeons from beneath the bridge. My little brother squealed, and the troll looked round at Magda sheltering him inside her long wool coat.

The troll looked at her for the longest time without blinking, and when he finally did, the flick of his leathery lids gathered tears that clung to his lower lashes, not quite heavy enough to fall.

Magda paled to have that big gaze on her.

She signalled to Dad by clearing her throat. He looked back at her, at the state she was in.

"Well," he said, turning back to the troll, "we hope you like it." Dad pointed at the hamper unnecessarily, holding his fedora on top of his head as the icy wind gusted. "The kids picked out most of the things. There are biscuits, jams, crackers, cheese, chocolate. Some honey too I think." Dad retreated two steps and put his hand on Magda's back. "Well, merry Christmas again," he said, then signalled to the rest of us with a subtle hand gesture we were all familiar with.

"Merry Christmas," we said, a little out of time with each other.

When the troll moved in to take the hamper, he moved quickly, each squelchy footstep squirting filth-water up between his toes. How small that hamper looked in his hand, compared to how big it had looked these last weeks in our kitchen, next to the little decorated shoeboxes for the children in Africa. The troll sniffed once, rolled his eyes up high as if trying to think what should be said, then swivelled quickly on the balls of his feet, still crouched, and scrambled back into the darkness beneath the bridge.

All the way home, I rubbed my frozen fingers together and breathed on them, worrying about whether the troll would be able to open the marmalade, the smallest of the jam jars, in this miserable weather.

That was the last hamper we would ever deliver.

The policewoman arrived almost a year later, on the day before my thirteenth birthday. She gave three quick knocks on the door and Magda opened it and my brother and I hid behind her, looking at the policewoman holding her hat in her hands, and at the early snowfall, heaped in terrific drifts against our neighbours' houses. I wish Dad had been there to help us receive the news.

I stayed in my room all afternoon while Magda called Dad, and Dad went to identify the body. I don't know why they needed him to do it. There's no one else with a body like that.

I went back to the bridge one last time that winter. No one else but me knew about the troll's birds, and if I didn't release them they would have rotted in their cages.

That morning, I put on my school uniform and headed out at 7.30 as usual, but when I got to the station, I hailed a taxi. The driver dropped me at the bridge, giving me a look of concern in the rear-view mirror as I paid him.

"You know not to cross the bridge on foot, right?" he said.

I nodded, not wanting to tell him that the troll was dead. While people continued to live in fear of him, he was still alive, in a way.

Under the bridge, by the light of my torch, I could see that everything was just how he had left it: the nest of blankets and coats, the tasselled standing lamp which could not be plugged in, the photo albums of which he was so fond, and all around, hundreds of jars filled to the top with coins people had thrown down as they scampered over the bridge.

Hung from hooks on the mossy wall were the two bamboo bird cages. The troll had liked nothing better than to creep out into the park in the middle of the night when everyone else was asleep and string up his nets – each one an inescapable maze of thousands of knots he'd tied himself under the bridge by candlelight. He'd string them up between the trees and then wait for the finches to wake up and go blundering into them.

Sometimes I would be there to marvel at the way he untangled their tiny bodies from the nets and dropped them into his cloth bag without putting a feather out of place.

Today, the troll's finches were silent and I was worried for them. Ten days had passed since the policewoman came to the house – maybe I had waited too long – but then my torchlight glinted off their hard black eyes and I was relieved.

I unhooked the cages from the wall, then covered them with a single layer of newspaper so the finches' eyes could adjust slowly to the light outside. I sat in the crunchy snow on the edge of the tow path, my feet dangling over the river, which was frozen white all over. The finches began to move about in anticipation, flapping their wings to bring them back to life.

What made me most angry was how everyone else in the house seemed so much more relaxed after the troll died. So light and warm and happy, once they were freed from their obligation. Dad even started coming home from work on time and Magda began cooking elaborate dinners.

I'm ashamed to say it, but it was a relief for me too, not having to deliver the hamper on Christmas Eve with the whole family. Them being there cast the whole experience in a terrible light. This is not how it looked to me whenever I went there alone. The troll was different when they weren't there. *I* was different when they weren't there. You wouldn't believe it if you only visited in winter, but in summer it was so pretty on the tow path. There were goslings on the river. Little white flowers forced their way through every crack, and the sun baked the papier mâché so dry it was soft and warm to sit on.

Late on summer nights, when I cycled for an hour to get there, the streets were almost empty and they were ours. We shouted at cars going by, folded bottle tops in half – he with his thumb and forefinger, me by stamping on them. We threw rocks in the river, threw in bricks, threw pebbles at seagulls roosting on top of lamp posts. We caught crayfish with bacon tied to lengths of string and then threw them up onto the bridge for cars to run over. We filled shopping trollies with clothes left outside charity shops, set them alight and sent them tumbling down the steps of the Central Library. We hung festoons of videotape pulled from cassettes over telephone wires. We spray-painted arrows pointing nowhere on paving stones, scooped up dog poop on pieces of card and posted it through the letterbox of the Museum of Natural History. We lit candles on park benches and left them unattended. We shot rats with catapults, shot rats in their hundreds. We made dolls from wax candles of people we hated and threw them from the roof of Peppard's Toy Store. We ripped letters from shop signs to spell out our names on that same rooftop – because he did have a name, of course – so that they could be read by helicopter pilots. I rode on his shoulders as he charged, hollering, around the empty market square. We lifted manhole covers out of the road and raced them down the slope of Chalk Hill till they smashed into the marble face of Coley's Department Store. We hid from police cars. We listened to music on my Walkman, one earbud each, him having to hold it in place in his giant hairy earhole. We drank beer and I was sick in the river. We counted all the stars. I read his favourite cookery book to him. We said goodbye at sun-up and I understood nothing of the next day's lessons and growled at my friends when they remarked on the state of my hair or said I needed to brush my teeth.

Eventually, I let the finches go. Most of them burst out right away, green and gold and red, struggling to keep a straight line in the wind tunnel. I kicked the cage to drive out the reluctant few.

One last time, I crowed at the traffic. I crowed till my throat was sore and my tongue felt like someone else's in my mouth. I crowed till a silver coin came flying over the edge of the bridge, flashing in the sunlight as it turned, and plunged into the snow in front of me. I picked it up and it was warm from living inside someone's pocket. I put that coin, the first I'd ever earned, in my own pocket and walked back up to street level, taller than when I arrived.

Everything I know that's worth knowing I learned from the troll. How to charm crayfish from the river. How to call coins down from the sky. How to belong to no one.

# Roxburgh
## GEMMA THOMAS

It was hard to be a bluesman on the Tube. First, Roxburgh had to audition at the Transport for London offices to a man called Stu who made sure all the musicians were of a certain standard and weren't going to sing songs with swear words or offensive lyrics. Stu looked about eighteen and told Roxburgh the most successful busker at the moment was the man with the little harp who played Celine Dion. Roxburgh wanted to choose a big interchange station, but apparently there was a hierarchy in these matters and, until you'd been busking for a while, you got assigned the smaller stations. He got Westminster, which he thought wouldn't be so bad as surely all the politicians would have money.

When he arrived at the station for his first session, he found his busking spot was in an underpass near the toilets. It had been raining so the floor was flooded and the whole place stank of piss. Still, as he said to Murray in the Crown later, Charles Kennedy gave him a few quid.

"Champagne Charlie is a very fine man indeed," said Murray, raising his whisky glass. "Not that I have much faith in his politics, but the man knows how to enjoy himself, which is what you want in a politician. All that dour-faced do-gooding from the other lot and where's it got us? Bring back Ken Clarke, I say. Or Alan Clark, God rest his soul. But not Charles Clarke, oh no. And then there's Petula Clark. Petula Clark would make a lovely politician, don't you think, old chap?" Murray oscillated on his bar stool and started to sing *Downtown*.

Roxburgh checked his watch. It was four thirty in the afternoon.

When Roxburgh woke up the following day, his mouth tasted like a small animal had died inside it. His head felt as if it were locked in a vice and nausea roiled in his stomach. He opened his eyes unwillingly, the lids gummy with sleep. The bedroom came slowly into focus, the pink floral wallpaper and matching curtains, the white veneer dressing table with oval mirror. Roxburgh shifted position slightly and the constriction behind his eyes became javelins of pain. He moaned softly to himself.

By mid-afternoon, Roxburgh had gravitated to the kitchen. Murray had already put the kettle on and was laying out some biscuits. After six months of living together, this was becoming something of a routine.

"Pearl's texted to say she's coming over later," Roxburgh announced.

"Oh dear. Another dose of tea and antipathy."

Roxburgh slammed his mug down, slopping coffee on the kitchen table. He glared at Murray, who jumped up, got a cloth and wiped up the spill.

"My dear fellow, please forgive me. Take no notice of silly old Murray. You know I think she's quite a girl, and utterly ravishing to boot."

Mollified, Roxburgh nodded. "She gets her looks from her mother, thankfully."

"I can't imagine you as a married man."

"I was a disaster. I did try, you know. I loved Josephine. But being a roadie and being a husband don't mix. If it's Tuesday it must be Tokyo."

"And you must have had thousands of groupies."

Roxburgh snorted. "I'm no Mick Jagger. Not thousands. But when you're on tour with the Stones, well, girlfriends were not hard to come by. It's just relationships I'm terrible at."

"Well, no more roadie-ing for you, not with your bad back.

Isn't that what the doctor said? You might find life in one place can be rather fun. Look at me. A footloose and fancy-free bachelor, not a care in the world." Murray wrung the cloth out over the sink. "I'm just popping to Tesco, old chap. Do you need anything?"

After a stint at Westminster station debuting his version of *Wild Horses*, Roxburgh returned home having made a profit of £3.54, two euros and a button. The house was empty. He stood in the kitchen, not knowing what he was going to do with the rest of his day. With the rest of his life. What did people do? How did people fill the hours, the days? How did they not go mad from boredom and claustrophobia?

Six months ago he'd been standing by the side of the stage in Madison Square Garden watching twenty thousand screaming fans and known that he was part of that magic. He wasn't in the band, but he was a Rolling Stone. What was he now? A piss-poor busker, a shitty father, a drunk. He paced round the kitchen. His eye was caught by the newspaper on the table. There was Mick Jagger, with yet another beautiful girlfriend young enough to be his daughter. He stared at the photo, stared until the image went out of focus and all he could see was a collection of black-and-white dots. He grabbed his keys, shoved them in his pocket, and slammed the front door on his way out.

Pearl's text had said she'd be round at seven. At seven fifteen Roxburgh returned home to find his daughter sitting on the edge of the sofa as Murray stood above her, leaning on the bookcase.

Roxburgh walked over and his lips found the air just above Pearl's ear as she stiffened slightly and turned her head.

"I'm sorry, love, I got caught up. Unavoidably detained. I hope Murray's been looking after you."

Roxburgh cursed himself for the last whisky chaser in the pub, for being late for his daughter, and for not saving her from a very drunk Murray.

"Would you like a cup of tea? Why don't we sit in the kitchen, leave Murray to watch some telly?"

He gestured Pearl through the door, switched the television on and steered Murray to the armchair. At the sight of *Emmerdale*,

Murray sighed happily and immediately fell asleep.

Roxburgh closed the kitchen door quietly behind him.

"Cup of tea?"

"Thanks."

"Milk but no sugar, cos you're sweet enough."

Pearl rolled her eyes. Roxburgh filled the kettle and got out some mugs.

"You stink of booze."

"So you don't like my new aftershave?"

"For God's sake, Dad."

"It was just a wee dram."

"It's always just a wee dram."

Roxburgh put the mugs down on the table and sat opposite his daughter.

"I'm sorry, love."

"And you're always sorry."

Roxburgh started to speak, and then shrugged, apologetically. "How's your mum?"

"Fine. Always at church. If she's not praying she's sending Bibles to Africa. She tries to get me to go to church with her. But I'd feel like such a hypocrite. We're not close, you know. She has her life, and I have mine."

Roxburgh hadn't seen Josephine for almost twenty years. He struggled to reconcile his memory of the swaying-hipped, Afro-haired beauty he'd met at a gig with the picture of religious piety that Pearl described. He knew she'd been born again not long after they divorced, but in his head she was still a young, sexy music fan.

"And how's work?"

"They're transferring me to the Covent Garden salon. Daniel says my styling's really good. And he never compliments anyone. I'll start to maybe get some magazine work, get some high-profile clients."

"Sweetheart, I'm so proud of you. This Daniel bloke knows talent when he sees it. Bloody brilliant."

Roxburgh sniffed loudly, and rubbed at his eyes with the backs of his hands. He didn't deserve to have such a beautiful and talented daughter, when he'd been such a terrible father. Although he'd sent money, he knew he'd forgotten birthdays over the years. And now he was back in London, he was too busy drowning his sorrows at the pub to make it home in time to see her. He blinked, and saw the crumpled newspaper on the table. Next to Mick Jagger was the employment section.

"I'm getting a job," he said, surprising himself.

"You're what?"

"I'm getting a job," he repeated, with more certainty. "B&Q, they're looking for people for their superstores. More mature candidates welcome, it says here. That's me."

"Dad, you've only ever been a roadie. You don't have the right experience."

"I need to do something. And I need the money. I go busking, but I've made less than a tenner this week. I want to make you proud, love, be a proper dad."

Pearl raised her eyebrows. "Proper dads work down B&Q, do they?"

"Proper dads have jobs." As he said it, Roxburgh felt certain this was the right decision. He made an anxious mental note to ask Murray, once he'd sobered up, how to go about writing a CV.

"Hi, my name is Euan."

Roxburgh looked at himself in the changing-room mirror. When he came for his interview he'd seen the staff in their orange dungarees, so he knew what to expect. He knew he would look like an idiot in the uniform, so it was no surprise to see that he'd been right. He hadn't spotted that all the staff had name badges. When his had arrived in the post he'd called up and asked if it could be changed.

"But Euan is your first name," the HR woman said. "It's on your CV."

Roxburgh had explained that he hated the name Euan. No one ever called him Euan apart from his mother, and she'd been dead for eleven years. His name was Roxburgh, and he'd be far more comfortable with that on his badge.

"I'm sorry," said the HR woman. "I can't be using people's nicknames on these badges, now can I? It could lead to all sorts of trouble. Euan's your name and Euan's on your badge."

Roxburgh spoke to his reflection again. "Hi, I'm Euan. How can I help you?" He sighed. "Hi, I'm Euan and I'm fifty-three years old. I live in the spare room in the house of one of my drinking pals, I go busking for coppers and fag butts on the Tube at weekends, and this is my first proper job. My daughter thinks I'm a loser, and she's right."

A tall, skinny lad with over-gelled hair stepped out from behind the row of staff lockers. "Nothing like a bit of self-motivation in the morning, is there?" He stuck out his hand. "Asif. This your first day, Euan?"

"Oh God, I didn't think anyone else was in here. It is my first day, yes. I'm Roxburgh."

"Roxburgh? Is that name for real? Cool. They made a mistake with your name badge. You need to tell them."

Roxburgh started to explain but Asif was already walking towards the doors to the shop floor. "Come on, man, I'll show you around."

By the third week, Roxburgh was getting used to his new job. He wouldn't have said he enjoyed it, but he found an unexpected satisfaction in the routine. On Friday afternoon the store was quiet, and he and Asif were restocking shelves ready for the weekend.

"I mean, it's not as if I want to be doing this the rest of my life. There's no way I'm still gonna be here when I'm like, thirty. No offence, mate."

"None taken."

"I just wish my parents would get off my case. My older sister, Nisha, she's a pharmacist now and my younger sister, Parveen, she's at university and my parents are like, 'Asif, when you gonna get a career? When you gonna get some qualifications? When can we start looking for a wife for you?' Man, I wish they'd just listen to themselves sometimes, they're like a broken record, you know. I told them once I wanted to be a DJ, and my mum she started to cry and my dad he was shouting. So now I just don't talk about it. My mate Ramesh's got a lock-up and we store our records and decks there, and we practise there, you know. We're serious about this. I'm gonna be the next Bobby Friction. Anyway, so we're playing a gig next Saturday night down Harrow Road. You wanna come, Rox?"

"Thanks for the invitation, Asif, but I'm . . . you know . . . I'm not . . . I don't know if you'd want people like me there."

Asif narrowed his eyes. He put down the can of paint he'd been holding.

"People like you? What do you mean, mate? White people?"

"No, God no. Old people."

Asif grinned and stuck out his hand. He'd been teaching Roxburgh the complex choreography of a modern handshake, and Roxburgh had been a good student. Their hands slid over and under, and Asif clicked his fingers with a flourish.

"Shit, man, you ain't old. You're my boy, one of my crew. I'll give you a flyer. Come down and check us out. Even Mick Jagger can't make nectar for your ears the way DJ Asif can."

"Excuse me," a soft voice interrupted them.

Roxburgh turned, opened his mouth, but found that he'd forgotten how to speak.

"I'm looking for garden lights," the voice continued, as Roxburgh concentrated on a point in the middle distance, just behind the woman's ear. He'd caught a glimpse of the curves, the golden waves of hair and the big blue eyes, and didn't want to get himself into trouble for staring.

There was a silence, until Asif said, "Aisle ten. My colleague Mr Roxburgh would be delighted to show you. He is very knowledgeable."

Roxburgh nodded enthusiastically at the point in the middle distance and took off towards aisle ten. He realised the woman was dropping behind, so he slowed his pace and focused on remembering his product training.

"I'm looking for some lights to illuminate my patio. It's getting warmer now, and I like to host barbecue parties. What do you recommend" – she looked at his chest – "Euan?"

Roxburgh winced. "Roxburgh," he said, thankful that the power of speech had returned. "They made a mistake with my badge. Well, not a mistake. I mean, Euan is my first name, but nobody calls me that. Roxburgh's what everyone calls me. I hate Euan. Always have. Only my dear old ma called me Euan, and she's dead. These are good lights for a patio." Roxburgh pointed at a box on the shelf in front of the woman, and wondered to himself if he'd ever sounded so pathetic.

"I'm sorry to hear about your mother. Roxburgh's a beautiful name. So unusual. I'm Linda, Linda Cotton." She held out her hand.

Roxburgh shook it gently, not wanting to crush her delicate fingers.

It turned out that Linda was having a lot of work done in her house. She came back to the store every afternoon, after finishing work as a secretary at a doctor's surgery. She'd recently become a grandmother, although at fifty she still felt like a schoolgirl. She'd been divorced for five years, she liked to go to Greece on holiday, she was a Sagittarius and she loved the Rolling Stones. All of this Roxburgh found out as he helped her to find shelf brackets, and door handles, and washers for her taps. She said he'd had the most exciting life of anyone she'd ever met. Roxburgh had even been able to forget that he was wearing orange dungarees as she said it.

Asif had taken to giving him pep talks in the changing room in the morning. "Thing is, man, women love a sense of humour. You gotta tell her some jokes. And show her your sensitive side, you know, be caring. They love that shit. But don't be too soft. A woman like Linda Cotton looks like she's after a real man."

"I don't know. Maybe she's just after stuff for her house."

"Are you insane? I've seen the way she looks at you. She is into you. She's after some of that Roxburgh magic. Believe me, man, she don't get like that when she asks me where the radiator keys are."

Roxburgh looked down at the orange dungarees. "I'm not exactly a catch, am I? Ex-roadie, no place of my own, finder of lost door handles. She's way out of my league."

"Rox, you've seen the world. You've got a history. And I'm not gay or anything, but you're a good-looking dude. You're cool, and women go mad for that. Trust me. Oh, and here's some of my flyers. You'd better come, man. Tomorrow night. Don't forget."

After spending most of Saturday mooching round the guitar shops on Denmark Street, Roxburgh was about to head home. He remembered Pearl saying her salon was in Covent Garden, and on a whim he decided to surprise her. He would tell her how his job was going, about Asif. Maybe even about Linda Cotton. He found his way to the middle of Seven Dials and paused. He wasn't sure exactly where Pearl's work was. Daniel someone-or-other.

He asked a smart-looking woman, who smiled indulgently and pointed him in the direction of Mercer Street.

Roxburgh stood outside the salon, looking in through the window. The staff were young, beautiful, and looked deeply serious. The customers were checking their phones, then checking their reflections, and then checking who else they could see. They were a mixture of ages, but they all looked rich.

He saw Pearl, and watched her for a moment. She was lifting the long hair off a woman's neck, indicating a shorter length with her hands. She looked absorbed, focused. The woman nodded and smiled, and Pearl smiled down at her reflection in the mirror. She was the most beautiful girl in there, and she looked so professional. Roxburgh felt as if he would burst with pride.

He knocked on the glass. A couple of heads turned, so he pointed at Pearl and knocked again. Most of the salon was looking at him now. He pointed at Pearl again. A young man tapped Pearl on the arm, and gestured towards the window. Pearl turned, saw Roxburgh, and her beautiful smile curdled. She looked around wildly, and Roxburgh waved again, worried that he'd startled her. Pearl bent towards her customer and said something, and then walked outside into the street. She was shaking.

"How dare you. How dare you come and embarrass me at work like this."

"I'm sorry, love, I just thought –"

"No, Dad, you didn't think. I'm in the middle of seeing a very important client, and in front of all my colleagues you turn up looking like some pathetic ageing rocker and humiliate me. What do you want?"

Roxburgh felt his eyes prick, and he swallowed hard.

"I wanted to see you." He shoved his hands in his pockets despondently, and felt the flyer for Asif's gig. "I . . . er . . . I wanted to give you this. That's right, that's what I wanted to do. A lad at work's a DJ. He's playing a wee gig. For youngsters. I thought you might be interested." Roxburgh handed Pearl the flyer.

She shoved it in her apron pocket without looking at it. "You're pathetic, Dad." She turned on her heel and went back inside.

Moving away from the salon so as not to embarrass her further, Roxburgh lit a cigarette with shaking hands. He'd wanted

Pearl to be proud. Instead he'd humiliated her, and himself. He took a long, miserable drag. He wanted to disappear. He knew he wouldn't even be missed.

Murray had put *You're So Vain* on the jukebox for the third or fourth time. Roxburgh had lost count. He'd lost count of the number of drinks he'd had, of how many hours he'd been in the Crown.

"You prob'ly think this song is aboutchoo, don'tchoo, don'tchoo?" Murray had one eye closed, making him look like a mad pirate, as he swayed and gestured in Roxburgh's direction with his cigarette.

There was a buzzing noise and Roxburgh's pocket started to vibrate.

"It's for you-hoo," Murray sang, working the words into the tune of the song.

Roxburgh snorted. "The only text messages I ever get are from the phone company telling me I'm at the end of my credit. Or from Pearl, but she's not speaking to me. So it'll be the phone company."

"But you topped up yesterday, old chap. I remember you doing it when we were watching *EastEnders*."

Roxburgh pulled his phone out of his pocket, still unwilling to check the message, to get his hopes up.

"Aren't you going to see who it's from?"

"Only to shut you up."

It was from Asif. "Dont 4get gig 2nite. Station Rd Harrow. Arches under trainline. C u l8r."

Roxburgh groaned. It was nice of Asif to invite him. He was a good kid. But Asif was only being polite. There was no way he'd actually go. His phone buzzed again.

"Rox, ur on the guestlist. U gotta come. A ;-)"

"Someone's popular."

"It's Asif, my friend from work. He's a DJ, and it's his gig tonight . . ."

Roxburgh hadn't finished his sentence, but Murray was draining his glass.

"Good-oh. Are we leaving now?"

Roxburgh didn't know whether to be touched or annoyed at Murray's assumption that he'd be coming too.

"No, Murray. We're thirty years older than everyone going. We'll look ridiculous."

"Speak for yourself, old chap. We'll show these youngsters a thing or two about partying. We invented it!"

Murray flounced out of the door. Roxburgh sighed, and followed his friend out into the night.

The music was so loud, Roxburgh could feel it reverberating inside his chest. He clutched his overpriced bottle of European lager, and watched hundreds of lithe young people sliding and shimmying round each other. He remembered Pearl's words, and looked down at himself. In his tight black jeans and crumpled Dylan T-shirt, he was a dinosaur. Murray, standing next to him, had perfectly ironed slacks and a linen shirt. What were they thinking?

At the back of the club, Roxburgh could see Asif up on a stage. He was completely in control, headphones on, head cocked to one side as he put the records on the decks.

"Your friend's ever so good." Murray was shouting into his ear. Roxburgh could feel his stubble against his face. "I imagine you're a musical guru for him."

"I don't know anything about this sort of music."

"Don't put yourself down. You're always putting yourself down. You're an incredible man."

Murray swayed, pushed by the crowds perhaps, and as Roxburgh turned towards him their faces were centimetres apart. He looked into Murray's eyes, and saw himself reflected.

"Murray, I . . ."

Murray pulled himself upright and looked away, out into the dancing crowd. "Take no notice of silly old Murray."

Roxburgh put his arms around his friend, and gave him a big, awkward hug. He held Murray for a moment, and then released him as quickly as he'd embraced him. The two men stood side by side in silence, gulping back their drinks.

Roxburgh looked over at a knot of people in the middle of the dance floor. He noticed a tall woman with her back to him, in a tight vest top and baggy army trousers. She was an incredible dancer, her body moving in perfect time with the beat. She turned, and Roxburgh recognised his daughter.

She raised her eyebrows, and snaked her way across the dance floor towards him.

"Dad, what are you doing here? And what's he doing here?" Pearl gestured towards Murray, looking rather like Noel Coward, moving spasmodically on the dance floor and smiling beatifically. Some of Pearl's friends were smiling back, and starting to dance alongside him.

"Asif, the DJ, he's my mate."

"You told me that when you gave me the flyer. I didn't think you were actually going to come. It's not exactly your scene, is it?"

The crowd suddenly started whooping and cheering as Asif finished his set. He waved triumphantly, handed the headphones to another young man, and jumped down from the stage. He made his way round the dance floor, people coming up to him to shake his hand, pat him on the back or kiss him. He looks like a rock star, thought Roxburgh, and felt very proud.

When Asif saw Roxburgh, he grinned and offered his hand. The handshake was seamless.

"Rox, my man, you made it."

"I wouldn't have missed this for the world."

Asif looked at Pearl, and didn't stop looking.

"Dad, you going to introduce us?"

"Oh . . . yes. Asif, this is my daughter, Pearl. Pearl, this is Asif."

Pearl kissed Asif on the cheek. "You were amazing. Great set."

Asif smiled back at her. After a long pause, he turned to Roxburgh. "What did you think? How did I do? I mean, you know, professionally speaking, how was I? Was I OK?"

Roxburgh patted him on the shoulder. "You were great, really great. You've got real talent."

Asif nodded solemnly, absorbing the commendation. "Thanks, man. That means a lot."

Pearl looked at Roxburgh, and linked her arm through his. "Dad knows loads about the music business."

"Your dad's a legend. Total legend. He's really inspired me, you know."

Roxburgh shifted in his seat as the night bus lurched around a corner. Murray was across the aisle, sprawled over a double seat and snoring contentedly. They'd left Pearl and Asif outside the club, swapping numbers. He wiped the condensation off the bus window with his sleeve. He could see an aeroplane blinking across the sky, above the sleeping city. Garden chairs, curtain rings, a stepladder and some window locks. Roxburgh ran through Linda Cotton's latest order in his head, and realised he knew it off by heart. He wondered whether Asif was right. She did come in every day, and she did only ever speak to him. Roxburgh looked up. The plane had disappeared into the clouds, which were turning pink with the coming sun.

"The idea is to write it so that people hear it and it slides through the brain and goes straight to the heart."

– Maya Angelou

# Valediction
## AMANDA CRANE

**Level zero. 0700 hours. Wilton Aerodrome**

"This is Bravo Echo Lima Fifty-One, requesting clearance for the runway. Over."

"Receiving you, Bravo Echo Lima Fifty-One. Good morning, Jim. You have a twelve-knot westerly down here. It'll be silky smooth at two thousand. What is your destination? Over."

My destination?

Cumulus over the North Sea? Perhaps. Cloudspotting. One big fat cauliflower and a clear ocean. My name is Jimmy James. I am a pilot. Ex-RAF. Ex-commercial-airline workhorse. Ex-aerobatics champion. Ex-aerobatics instructor. Ex-husband. Yes, I am that too. Widower, to be precise. My destination today is backwards. I plan to fly backwards to the beginning, to better understand the end.

I can see the windsock, plump and kicking with the twelve-knot westerly. We're waiting under a mackerel sky, ready to fly, destination east. We're going back in time with a tailwind, girl. It's going to be a beautiful day. This little Piper Cub is ticking over – fuel full, compass set, instruments checked, canopy down. I nod to Bill's lad to spin the propeller. Hear the sound change, Bel? We're ready. Headphones on; radio on.

"My destination is north-north-east, Bill. Over."

"You have clearance, Bravo Echo Lima Fifty-One. Have a good flight, Jim. See you later. Proceed to taxi. Over."

"Thank you, Wilton. Thank you, Bill. Over."

I flew solo in the Rockies in 1943. I didn't know you then. I was a cocky little shit – you'd have hated me. We were twenty. You were running away from becoming a farmer's wife like your mother; I was in Canada, running away from Bryngoed, from becoming my dad, or his dad or his dad before him. We volunteered the same year. "I liked the WAAF uniform, I liked the pilots, but most of all I liked the chance to get on," you said. Well, it was not so very different for me. My sister Dell flattered me: the RAF was my colour, she said, a good match for a blue-eyed blond, as I was then. Our lives were parallel; you and me, rolling on different runways, thousands of miles apart.

After I landed, before the customary shindig in the mess, I wrote home – cramming all the gen and swagger onto tissue-blue airmail, jamming every moment right to the edges of the paper. Getting my wings – you have no idea, Bel, what it meant. I found bundles of these letters in Dad's old leather case in the loft when I was sorting out your stuff – your clothes and paintings. Spent hours up there. Didn't notice the day escaping; forgot to eat again.

I've packed the letters up now – sent the lot to Duxford. You'd have loved them. I wish I'd found the hoard sooner. Dad had kept them all. Dell passed his collection to me after he died and I just stuffed it away, forgot about it. Duxford will do something with the airmails. Archives, for a pukka snapshot of an era, full of the new language I was learning. New accent, too – although you always said you could still hear the Welsh. I sent them my uniform. It's amazing it's survived – rough old bit of shoddy twill it was. I thought it was Savile Row at the time. Gold-thread wings, gongs, flamboyant facial hair – it was all a blueprint, fooling young men into believing the lie of invincibility. The army hated us. The officers, that is. Jealous, they were – we stole their thunder on the dance floor and didn't know our place. Snobbish bastards.

I dropped Dai – took on my mess-room nickname. We all had them: Chalky White, Nobby Clark. I became Jimmy James. All part of the process. Going solo felt like being born into my real life. The twists and corners of a two-year passage to wings had squashed and bruised my ridiculous ego, squeezed the breath nearly out of me. As I climbed – two hundred, three hundred, four hundred feet – the waiting vacuum was lifted and my future got sucked in.

Dad managed to turn it into a negative somehow, though. Wrote that it was good I'd got my wings but it was a shame my mam missed it and that I'd never see service. The war for the skies was over; it was all down to the army now, he said.

We're moving, Bel. Like riding a sitting trot, you always said. Every dip and crack in the concrete connects in a craft this size. You really feel the earth under you. Taxi-ing a jet was the difference between piloting a dinghy and an oil tanker. Too big, too cut off to feel where you are. Hell, it paid the rent though, didn't it? And much more besides – we lived well on it. We had plenty.

Stick back, right pedal, left wing down, keep her rolling. Nose straight. Little more right rudder, that's it, Jim. It comes back every time. I could do it in my sleep. How long have I got? Grounding is only a few more millimetres of mercury away on the blood-pressure scale, according to the quack at the last medical. What does he know, Bel? He was the same bloke who said you were the picture of health.

We're up. Feel the crosswind? Won't last. Wait, it'll be silky smooth up there at two thousand feet.

## 500 feet. 0710 hours. Hennington village

Home just ahead, Bel. Morning shadows on the ground, a weak sun struggling to burn off the chill. We're on the way up, this little craft groaning like an old horse in harness, but willing enough. We'll be over home in a few minutes. I'll give you a last wave.

No, it didn't start with the solo. It started at Willie Flowers' Flying Circus. Nineteen thirty-three it was. A novelty even for England, let alone Wales, I can tell you. There were hundreds of people there. All set out on one of Prosser's top fields. It was flat, you see, made flat by the ore pits, from years before – a perfect runway. Bit of a crosswind up there but they were mad buggers, didn't care much about mud landings or crosswinds. God knows what the sheep made of it but we were all mesmerized. They'd a man walking on the wing two to three hundred feet up, parachutists dropping into the crowd, aerobatics – loop-the-loop, belly-rolling, you name it. Later, they were offering twenty minutes in the air for two and sixpence. Dad and my mate Eddie Penny bet me a threepenny bit I wouldn't get in. They didn't need to but I didn't let on. I was gagging for a go. Auntie Eadie was there. It was she who gave me the money for the ride, as always, helping out her brother-in-law, giving his kids her best love to make up for the lack of her sister.

"Go on, Dai, have a go. You'll catch Merthyr from up there, you'll see," she said.

"The only thing Dai'll catch is a cold. That'll learn him." Dad coughed a laugh like a sneer.

I queued and went up. Shaking, I was. Excitement or fear, I don't know. It was a chance to do something to confound Dad. He expected me to chicken out – the claustrophobia, you see. Eadie Pearl was right: I could just see Merthyr, like a grey shroud, and the villages, long seams of houses cut into the red hillsides. As we cleared the heads of the valleys, we saw the pit, the farms, cream dots of sheep and people. It was like playing at the world on a giant board game. It reminded me of the school trip to the model railway in Cardiff, the thrill of discovering some epic secret. I could even see the steam over the viaduct at Bryngoed, the train like a wet snake, cutting through the valley floor. I could see everything, hear nothing but a roaring of the wind, the buzz of the Avro Anson engine. Faithful Annie, they called her. She bucked and dipped, her wooden seat like riding one of Joe Evans's donkeys at Derby day. My teeth were rattling together, cheeks stinging and quivering with the slap of cold air. None of that mattered, least of all the lack of space. The sky was pure, bright and crisp with the smell of freedom.

We weren't up for long. It was all over so quickly. No time to ask questions and I couldn't see or speak to the pilot behind me – I wanted to ask so many questions. Twenty minutes was enough to know nothing else would ever do. I wanted to be Willie Flowers. I wanted to take my Avro Anson all around the country, flying tricks into the light and wowing the crowds. I told Dad to have a go but he gave me a look. "What the hell would I want to do that for?" he said.

Eadie asked me on the quiet, "How d'you manage up there, Dai? The little space you squeezed into. Didn't seem to bother you, did it?"

"It did a bit, at first, but when we got up high I could see everything, Auntie Eadie. I could see everything around me for miles and then I wasn't scared any more."

"You're a funny one, Dai," she said, but she was pleased with me. Eadie understood what Dad pretended didn't exist. He wouldn't connect my claustrophobia with the trench tales he'd employ to stun me to sleep at night. I believe he took a perverse delight in describing to his only son rank images of filth and flesh, of unrelenting horror, of confinement – images that lived long into my adolescent dreams.

I made myself a promise that day. No bugger was ever getting me down a mine, or a trench, nor any stinking hole in the ground. Never. If I was going to fight, ever, I'd fight up there or nowhere. Six years on as Chamberlain finished his speech I blurted it out, made brave by the memory of the feeling from the sky. I squared up to my father that day and told him straight and clear. Him the war hero, the decorated soldier. He spat when I told him, as though the taste of my words was bitter, like a rotten nut.

We're right over Hennington now. I can see the mist leaking from the river, the village barely awake. There's the odd car, not much else happening yet. I can see our church, the graveyard, huge dark yews, stately old headstones all angled like teeth, their morning shadows long thin crosses in the struggling sun. I can just make out our corner – can see the rows of shiny squares crammed in the western edge; new marble catches the light from up here.

"Find me a village, a village school, where I can teach and paint and wave to you as you fly over. I'll know it's you when you tip the wings. That's all I want," you said.

Did it measure up, Bel? Were you happy? We had almost everything we wanted.

Down there the fields are dying beautifully: beans, grey brown, dull, tangled; wheat stubble burning black and gold, the smoke filtering to starboard. I can smell it over the fuel: a clean fire, the sour smell of cooking sap and summer wood mixing with the sweet smoke of smouldering leaves and cut logs. The trees are turning, last greens dark, old, ready for the morbid breath of night frost, the sift and breakdown of winter. The cycle moves on, Bel, turns like a turbine. I can see it from here better than anywhere – combed brown plough, knocked up with next season's seedlings, sunk in furrows, linked and stippled over the land, waiting for the stink of muck to kick-start spring.

And here's our house.

"It's my favourite view of our home," you said, whenever I took you flying. "We can put ourselves in context up here. It's one of the reasons kids climb trees, why people climb towers, rocks, mountains even. Anything to reference scale, anything to get high, to get the long view."

If you can peep past the fear, it fascinates most people – to see how small we are. That's what I said to you the first time I took you up.

Looks a bit overgrown, Bel. Our garden.

Let's circle once and wave for old times' sake. Left rudder down, throttle hard over, thirty degrees bank – that's it. Now straighten and wave, one last wave, right, left, straighten. That'll do. I can still see you now, a dot in the garden looking up, waving back.

That's low enough, Jim, you used to say. No aerobatics, please. It spoils the view and ruins my lunch. I remember, Bel. No aerobatics. Not yet.

## 1000 feet. 0745 hours. Cambridge

"Bravo Echo Lima Fifty-One, Bravo Echo Lima Fifty-One, this is Cambridge Airspace here. Requesting immediate climb to two thousand feet. This is Cambridge Airspace. Raise your altitude immediately. Over."

"Cambridge this is Bravo Echo Lima Fifty-One. Climbing to two thousand feet. Over."

There's the city on the horizon, a big grey smudge. The city where I first saw you a week after I'd moved in with Chalky White from Canada. His dad was a good bloke, Bel. Bank manager. Gave me a job eventually.

"I escaped the chicken shit and grain silos. Got a job out of it," you said. RAF West Holding was your free finishing school. It did a good job on you, Bel – took a fresh farm girl from Cambridgeshire and converted her into an efficient secretary, neat as a pin in WAAF tailoring. I've still got the photos, the black-and-white heads and shoulders of a generation. When you took me back to your parents' farm, the urbane young city woman I'd met on a hot day by the Cam, I could see you'd grown out of place in your own home. The big sister, surrogate mother to seven brothers and sisters – no wonder you never wanted our own. Your dad wasn't sure of me, ex-RAF, burdened with a full-on wartime swagger, no job yet to speak of. All he could hear was the new boys-in-blue accent stitched to my tongue. If I could have stuck my wings onto mufti I would have done. Fake. I was a fake and he knew it. You could hear the south Wales accent, buried in layers underneath, breaking to the surface at times, exposed like treasure. Still can.

"Did you kill any Germans, Mr James?" Your brothers dared to ask what most adult males wanted to hear, coyly hushing the kids, yet greedy to hear the detail all the same.

"Not exactly," I told them. I missed active service by a hair, but I'd collected a cache of stories for small boys. Second-hand and colourful, embellished with as much gore as I felt I could get away with.

It struck me how much I wanted to tell war tales. Just like my dad did. And I began to understand his need to tell me about his war. But I wasn't ready to forgive him. It stung to have to admit that my war had been a clean one. What, all that training and no murder to show for it? No retributive burning Fokkers spiralling into the Channel? No, my war was different.

"You didn't do badly out of it, then, did you, either of you?" your father said. He called me lucky and he was right. War gave me a career for life. I joined a nation on the move and together we took off towards plenty. It didn't happen overnight, though. You in a tedious office, me in the bank, when all you wanted to do was teach and all I wanted to do was fly.

"It's work, Jim. It pays the rent and keeps me in lipstick and you in petrol. How else will you afford to keep your licence going at the flying club? Something else will come up. Be patient, Jim." I did as you said, worked and waited and flew at weekends. Waited for the jet age to start recruiting.

"What do clouds feel like?" you asked me at the start of it. I gave you a lecture, about cloud formations, how they affected the handling of the aircraft, the effect on aerobatics – my dream – how clouds challenged and altered the journey, the landing, the vision. I can picture you listening to me in the garden of the Jolly Farmer, on a July evening in 1951, one of the first weekends of our first summer; the New Look dress you wore, spring green with white polka dots, belted tight to flatter your post-war waist. We filled out in the years of plenty, didn't we, Bel? You had a cardigan over your shoulders, the colour of Welsh earth, rust red. You listened patiently, smiled shiny cherry lips, brown eyes crinkling at the edges, the teacher-in-waiting, always a good listener. You looped a dark-brown permanent curl behind your ear, touched my arm. Your touch excited me.

"That's all very interesting, Jim, but I meant what does it actually feel like? To touch."

"I don't know. I've never touched one." Clouds were technical data, clues for an aerial puzzle; my log book had no place for abstract concept. I hesitated to answer you. Touching clouds sounded like a pilot's euphemism for death, like twisting the twig or hitting the deck.

"Well, why don't we do it?" you said.

"You want to fly with me?" I asked.

"Of course I do, if you'll take me."

You looked up to the sky, the skin on your throat bare of powder, soft downy brown, slightly freckled like a ripe apricot.

"I want to touch a cloud," you said.

So I took you up in a little Piper Cub, bright yellow. You said it looked like a canary. I liked that. Eadie had one in our front room. Pipers have been my planes ever since.

We did it in the air. Me in the front seat, my feet on the rudder, stick back and climbing, you on my lap. No words; too much engine noise to speak. I could see and feel your laughter through me, you watching the wings. As if anyone could see us five hundred feet up. There were no clouds above Cambridge, no cauliflower clouds, the sort you wanted to touch – fat, white and fluffy. Only low stratus – thin and layered like mist, the sort the sun shines through, the kind that doesn't even shut out moonlight. We flew due east, to Suffolk, to the sea.

"Where're we heading now, Jim?"

We're going to the sea, Bel.

\*

"What's that whining noise?"

"It's only the wind. There'll be turbulence. Hang on – this'll be fun. Ride the turbulence, Bel, pretend we're at the fair."

The sound of your laughter that day has faded to a whisper.

Are you ready, Bel? Are you ready?

This is the one.

When we found it, the cumulus was high, four thousand feet. We lost momentum as we climbed, the controls sluggish, the Piper screaming into the incline. Inside the cloud, in the rushing grey mist of it, we levelled, pulled back the canopy; the noise, even with headphones on, beat our eardrums. You held your arm out, towards the wing, your hair wild, whipping around your headphones, the sleeve of your jumper moulded to your arm. On the ground, much later, you said the cloud felt rough. "It didn't feel how I imagined it at all. No, ice cold and rasping, like a cat's tongue. Surprising – a rough surprise. I don't know what I expected really. Something beautiful, I suppose. Softness."

Our climb stalled the engine. We were hanging, suspended, only the sound of the wind around us, watching the propeller blades slow to the speed of a ceiling fan, the Piper riding the air like surf. I had performed tricks like this before – I knew I could handle it – but your fear unsettled me. It took a few moments to recover the stall and we corkscrewed to two thousand feet.

It was the first time I made you cry. And you told me off, didn't you, Bel?

"I was terrified when we stalled. Never do that to me again, Jim."

I never did.

You had no time to tell me what you wanted because it was going to be me first – I was the one rattling with pills every morning. Ironic. No, this is all for me, Bel.

### 4000 feet. 0800 hours. North Sea

Not far now. My course is level to the horizon and I can see what I came for – right ahead, a little high. Look, can you see it? Let's go. Are you ready, my love? We're climbing a slow steady scramble to the heart of this bugger. Here we are. This one's a beauty, topped like an anvil, a cartoon cumulus, a cauliflower cloud. Are you ready?

I lift the steel urn from between my legs, unscrew the top and let the wind take you. Your dust is sucked out and swirls backwards, a curl of silver grey, like a silk scarf, little pieces of you spinning like winged seeds. I wipe my eyes, a mess of tears from the blast of the air. Some ash blows in my face. I'm not crying. I've done enough crying these past few months. The ash turns my tears charcoal. As I wipe my face my hands are streaked with you.

My altitude is dropping. I'm pirouetting down, the engine in silent stall, the propeller blades solid; a fearful, thrilling image. Peaceful. Only the lonely whine of the wind. I can see the sea.

Two thousand feet.

Willie Flowers looped the loop with me in 1933. I have walked the wing untold times in my life since then. I queued for an hour to talk to Willie Flowers after the show. When we got to the head of the line he shook my hand and smiled at me. His fingers and teeth were yellow, his hand felt damp and sticky and quivered slightly as he squeezed mine. He was only a little man, no taller than my dad.

Six hundred feet.

I watch the altimeter move like a stopwatch.

Four hundred feet.

I pull the nose up, level to the horizon. I can see the waves breaking on the surface of the sea. I'm not sure where to go now, but it doesn't matter. I'm a pilot, navigation is part of going solo. I understand nothing else. Fly on.

# 1,619
## LENYA SAMANIS

It's immediate and involuntary: in spite of everything else that happened, Eleni's the first thing I see when I think back to that trip we took to Nicosia, on the last leg of our search for the painting. "It has to be there," my father said. "This time, it has to be there."

We set off, flush with confidence, pretending not to notice the pinch in Maria's smile as she stood among the sun-strangled flowerbeds and watched us leave. Minutes later we were on the motorway out of Limassol and my stepmother was left behind, along with most of the ill feeling. For me, the looking was incidental, the painting – a vast canvas of a man on a train – no more than a detail from my small store of childhood memories. For my father, though, it was something else entirely. We'd chased its trail all over the island, and this level of persistence was unlike him. It wasn't until we started out for the capital that I realised: it was a self-portrait in disguise. He was wanting to find one of those bright fragments of self that get lost as the years wear on – the hopeful, beautiful parts which give that sense of strength and sturdiness. The search for the painting wasn't about the two of us spending time together at all: it was his own, private attempt at retrieval.

Nicosia meant leaving the blue line where the sea meets the spirit level of the horizon to head into the stony heart of the country and its butchered, divided capital. It meant time alone in the Land Rover with my father – no small thing in view of the preceding weeks. The argument still felt fresh and the blow to our fledgling relationship close to fatal. We'd simmered and skulked for days and the silences had soured with all the unspoken recrimination still thickening at the bottom of things, and yet we both agreed to pick up the thread of the painting.

We were still in June and the air was heavy with moisture. Looking back, it's difficult to separate out the individual parts: sticky-skinned scenes and snapshot conversations blur, changing colour and tone with each overlap. Eleni stands out, though, stark and stirring. I can still see her standing at the edge of the road in black, a photograph in one hand and her free arm wrapped around her middle, as though she were holding herself together. I can see her hunch-rolled shoulders; the invisible weight on her neck. Eleni was the reason I heard about the 1,619. She was the catalyst for that conversation. Without her presence on the periphery, how would I ever have known? Who would have brought it up?

We were humming along in the Land Rover when she first appeared as a smudge on the verge up ahead. The radio crackled and cut out, the signal repeatedly lost in the space between the mountains. A car of nuns pulled onto the hard shoulder in front of us. I caught a glimpse of her face, and then we were gone, the same old bone-dry landscape grinding on beyond the window. Dried out by the heat and the African air, we stopped at a place by the side of the motorway – the kind of place where travel-logged bodies sit at cheaply varnished tables to eat their *souvlakia*. When we emerged into the bright sunshine with our sandwiches, there she was again: an old lady with a photo in one hand, pestering tourists where the cars were parked. "Who d'you think she is?" I asked. My father shrugged, and when I looked back for the old woman, she'd disappeared. Back in the elevated seats of the Land Rover, I picked the *lounza* from my sandwich and spun it out of the open window while my father filled the tank with water. My thoughts were already back on the discord between us – a brittle-tempered, thorny-backed beast that was hard to placate – but their focus was fugitive.

We hadn't been on the road a minute before we saw her again and, for some reason, my father pulled over.

Looking at Eleni's face in too much detail was like staring too long at the sun: there was a crazy kind of intensity there that stayed with you after you'd looked away. She thrust the photo at me from the back seat at the first opportunity. A young man stared out of it, his features softened in well-worn sepia. Her fingers smoothed at his face in a constant, compulsive motion. It seemed quite probable that they'd been wearing out his features for years. "What's with the photo?" I muttered to my father. He stared out through the windscreen, a pinch to his mouth that suggested he was annoyed about something, and my question mumble-bumbled around the front of the car pointlessly before becoming background.

The motorway unfurled interminably onwards. Just as I'd given up any hope of a response, he spoke. He told me about the 1,619 Greek Cypriots, missing since the 1974 invasion. The number came flying out of the picture: It was unlike him to be so precise. 1,619. People get lost in times of war, even in times of peace, but 1,619? The number was so naked and definite. 1,619 mourned and searched for. 1,619 marked individuals, missing for three decades. "So they're dead?"

My father gave another of his shrugs. "Who knows? Probably. Officially, they're still missing," he said. "Officially, they're still married, still own houses . . ." His hand described a spiral over the steering wheel.

I glanced in the wing mirror and saw her there, half obscured by a circle of vivid orange where the sun had superimposed itself over everything else. The lines on her face led nowhere. Eleni: all white-knuckled clutching, holding on to the hope of something long since lost.

If it wasn't for Eleni, appearing on the road like she did, her story might never have come up. Perhaps I'd have read of the 1,619 paper ghosts later, researching on my own under a dark-grey English sky. If it had happened like that, things would've been different. Filtered through the cold, fine gauze of intellect, the story would barely have touched me, but I was dealt the narrative out there, on the dust-layered road, with all the heated illogic and atmosphere needed for such a story to thrive. Shades, it whispered. People gone and not gone – frozen in time. These 1,619 postcard people blended with the ghost town of Varosha in my mind. Both belonged to the hollow and the chill.

Her eyes, in the wing mirror, were in constant motion, flitting to and fro without proper pause. Her mouth, too, never stopped. I asked my father what she was saying.

"Just stories," he said. "She's in the past." He offered me one of his fluid shrugs.

"Translate for me," I said.

He pressed his lips into a line.

"Just for a few minutes."

"It's nothing important."

"Please."

He sighed, glanced in his rear-view mirror and caught a hand-hold in the flow of her narrative. "That was the year he found the sparrow," he began, "out in the fields. This tiny thing, it fitted perfectly into his hands. And he was small, still so small, I remember, stepping slowly through the long grass, this boy of mine, who was never still, no, not for ten seconds. He was coming carefully, like the land mines were already there, coming back to the house, his arms held out, coming so slowly, but almost breathless. His cheeks, his cheeks were pink and his eyes were bright. 'Mama,' he said. 'Save him.' He begged and he cried, such a gentle heart, such a good boy, but there was too much blood, so much blood for such a small thing. His father put it out of its misery, and he cried, like all children cry, but he lost it after that, that easy childish joy. My Christaki. He –"

The Land Rover swerved violently onto the hard shoulder as a BMW careered past, veering from right to left, four laughing young men leering out of the windows and screaming on the horn. My father shouted and cursed until the sleek black slick of car was out of sight. Eleni's monologue had risen in volume. There was a fresh urgency to it, but my father was done translating.

There's a point on the road to Nicosia where something breathtaking appears in the distance, but it's easy to miss through the soft focus of the heat haze. I saw it for the first time when my father stopped there that day, as we chased our third lead to the capital. He pulled the car onto the side of the motorway and got out without a word, slamming the door behind him. In the back, Eleni shrank into the seat, her mouth busy but silent. I watched my father walk away. The smears on the window obscured his face when he glanced back, but I knew he was expecting me to follow. The dust claimed my shoes the moment I stepped out. Cars sped past, fast and hard and too close, as I picked my way to where he stood waiting. When I drew up beside him, he put an arm around me, not out of affection or in the spirit of reconciliation, but to pull me into his perspective. He pointed with his free hand into the distance. "You see that?" he asked.

I squinted.

"The mountains," he said. "You see what they've done to the mountains?"

His grip on my shoulder was uncomfortable. Sweat collected in my eyelashes and ran into my eyes, making them smart. I blinked it away; squinted again. There it was, impossible to miss: a white crescent and star on a scarlet background, branding the landscape, flagrant in spite of the dust in the air and the blur of the heat. It made the mountains look small.

"You see it?"

I nodded. I saw it.

He snorted. "Now, tell me why they did this. What reason could they have to put their flag so big on our mountain? It's pointed at us. It's for us, this flag." His arm fell away.

I didn't know what to say. I felt again that welling up of a distress that wasn't mine. In an instant, I recalled film footage I'd seen of the morning of the invasion: parachutes floating down onto the island like dandelion seeds waltzing on a warm and wafting breeze. Underneath that airborne enemy waltz, people were panicking, lending the footage a surreal quality. I felt the Greek displacement and erosion as though it was a personal loss. More potently, standing there beside the motorway that day, I felt my father's bitterness, and the resistance that was in him, as if it was chemical, inherited. The capacity for hatred was in easy reach. There was still a part of me that watched all this happen with a detached and suspicious eye, but I was tired of being pulled in two directions at once. The impulse was there to belong to something wholeheartedly for once, and I was dangerously open. I looked around for my father. He was leaning against the bonnet, blowing smoke rings, and smiling. That was the thing about my father's smile: there was room for me in it. I didn't have to shrink to fit. I walked towards him, amid the smell of tobacco and exhaust fumes, with the sun in my eyes, on my back, and the sound of my father coughing. And then the sound of a car door slamming shut, puncturing the moment. Eleni shuffled past us, dangerously close to the cars as they tore along the motorway. Her gaze was set straight ahead, the one hand still worrying the photo, the other opening and closing into a fist at her side. A soft humph of laughter eased out of my father, causing his chest to rise and fall. He threw me the car keys, and set off after her, hands in pockets. "Start her up," he called over his shoulder.

The flag on the mountains disappeared from view as we slipped back onto the A2. We were almost there. Eleni had been getting quieter, to the point where I couldn't hear her at all above the background muddle of the radio and the roar of the African winds at the windows. We lost her altogether alongside the great, hulking walls of Nicosia's Old City. Spotting the densely packed crowd there, her muttering resumed. My father pulled up at a red light and she was out, gravitating towards the crowd. He raised his shoulders, resigned. I glanced at the back seat and saw that it had grown holy with all the devotions: sunlight streamed through the front windscreen in beams full of glittering dust motes to caramelise the spot where Eleni had been sitting. And there, under that golden spotlight, on the faded and ripped fabric of the car seat, was the photograph. I turned back to the window to call her, but she'd vanished.

We found Paniotti close to the border, in the section of the city where time loops in on itself and squares into confusion. Where the Green Line bisects the city, in the middle of buildings and crossings, through the most exposed and central arteries of its heart, there is a band of streets mostly made up of still-empty, derelict premises. It's where the city borders the buffer zone. Army lads on sentry duty guard the line. Here and there, shops have been put back into use; here and there you can see washing hanging out to dry on a balcony up above the shop fronts: splashes of colour, spots of life, but they're surrounded by the accoutrements of a savage history. It's said that rats and roaches thrive here, in this small, half-deserted labyrinth. Graffiti brands walls; windows are opaque with dirt, and broken. To walk here is like stepping into a magical and brutal moment. It has one foot in the past; it's a place to bring on the shivers.

It was where we found the bar, half hiding behind a shop selling lace and mass-produced Roman statues to the tourists. A tenacious ivy had spread to every corner of the building's façade, blocking any windows it may have once had so that the door was the only visible feature. Inside was a gloomy, cool space that smelt of leather and oranges. Brass horseshoes gleamed on dark beams of wood. A vaguely African carving of a naked woman with a drum sent dramatic shadows across the room. What looked like a primitive farm tool was hung high on one wall alongside a large poster for Polanski's *Chinatown*. My father, apparently unfazed by the incongruous décor, spoke to the barman who, with an ear-to-ear smile, put down his cigarette to lean across the counter and shake my father's hand. We were offered seats, and furnished with drinks. The barman went to shout around a door.

"D'you know him?" I asked.

My father tutted. "No," he said, popping a few peanuts into his mouth.

"Ah," said a sonorous voice.

Behind us stood a man with crinkled-to-twinkling eyes and a full and riotous beard. Paniotti was delighted to meet the painter of The Train, as he called it.

"Ah, *The Train*! It was up there a long time." He gestured to an empty section of wall by the entrance. "A very good painting." He shook his head and pursed his lips until they disappeared entirely into his beard. "I liked it very much. Your father is very talented," he said to me, in his clean, crisp English. Paniotti was easily the most polite Cypriot I had ever come across.

My father held up a hand, and they raised a glass to one another.

"Yes," Paniotti continued, "I liked it very much. This is why I'm sorry to say I no longer have it. A man came and offered me more than I could refuse." He held out his palms. "Times are hard."

My father was smiling his "I should've known better" smile and looked his age. "Do you know where it is?" he asked.

"It was bought by a man from Kyrenia. He owns a taverna in the old port. Your painting, my friend, is on the Other Side."

And that was that.

Paniotti seemed sad to see us go. "I'm sorry about your painting," he called out as we left. "If you go to the old port, I'm sure you'll find it. It wasn't so long ago."

My father ended the conversation with a good-natured nod, but once we were back in the car with the doors closed, his shoulders seemed to sag. The painting was beyond the line; that piece of him, that repository of self, was in the possession of the enemy. "What's lost is lost," he muttered, as we drove away.

We headed back onto the motorway in silence. In the closed-off space of the car, we settled into our seats, and into silence. I surrendered to the rhythms of the road under the tyres. It loosened my mind, as the momentum of irresponsible travelling will, and I drifted. And through the smog in my head, I realised that the bitterness which had surfaced before we'd started out on this trip had already been shunted into the background by as simple a thing as our being stuck together in that car, biologically tied. None of it seemed to matter as much any more. Then I saw a road sign and I realised we weren't going home: we were heading to Paralimni and beyond, to the beginnings of the Dead Zone. He was following the trail to the very edge. Outside, the landscape looked two-dimensional and flatly unreal and the heat was leaking out of the sunlight.

Eventually, he brought the Land Rover to a stop with its nose pressing up against a fence. In the distance, the coastline blurred against the turquoise sea. We watched the light die over the north of the island, and smoked the joint that he'd been saving in his shirt pocket for the drive home. It was slow-grinding, seductive stuff. It instigated a network of illuminated cerebral connections webbing ever outwards. My body sank into its memory-foam embrace. And for a while there, up against the edge of the Dead Zone, that image of the ladies' man he'd been, the man of few words and smouldering looks, the artist, and the misanthrope, came together in a temporary focus with the father and the storyteller. All the borrowed memories and pictures, all the scraps of detail and the different versions managed to coexist for a brief moment, converging to make a singular, solid, real thing. My father: the adventurer, the cheat, the philosopher, the liar, the free spirit, the war-torn wreck. He appeared there before me, suddenly, razor sharp and slightly surreal.

"It's all about the journey, *mana mou*," he said. "That's all there is."

Famagusta lay spread out in the distance, too much of a stretch for my sun-tired eyes.

"So we came for this, in the end," he said. "So what? We came."

A faint breeze ruffled some long, scraggy grass sprouting from the edge of the gravelled parking space, and the sea could be heard – a faraway sound, like breathing. A dangerously nostalgic, golden light tinted the world. We sat for a while, looking out at it. I was picturing the streets of the ghost town, Varosha, when he spoke. "Shall I tell you something that'll freak you out?" he said. "At least, I think it'll freak you out. It freaks me out. Do you want to hear?"

"Go on," I said.

"But it goes no further."

"Fine," I told him.

"I haven't kissed her in sixteen years," he said. Sixteen years was as long as he and Maria had been married. His profile was on its way to being a silhouette. "Sixteen years. Can you believe that?" He took a brief lungful of smoke. "You know, I married her to get the house," he began.

"I know," I said.

He nodded to himself. "You know." Another story I'd already heard. "And now here we are." A wry smile twisted on his mouth.

I lit two cigarettes and handed him one. It made him cough. He snorted his distaste at my brand of choice, then, grinning mercurially, turned the key in the ignition. "OK," he said. "Fuck this place. Let's get back on the road."

The drive back to Limassol seemed long, even nestled into the warm and fragrant comfort of the grass we'd smoked; even curled up with the bewitching story of the missing Cypriots wrapped around me. I pondered these twilight figures, reliant on old photos and other people's memories to stay alive, as we shuttled westward. Encased in that electrical hum that you find on an aeroplane or a coach when the passengers are all asleep, my father navigated the lonely road with an instinctive, almost disinterested grip. Oncoming headlights from the other side of the motorway flashed sporadically across his face. Then, in a moment of darkness, he said her name: "Eleni." He smiled. "Imagine it," he said. "Thirty years! All that waiting. This is waiting, now! This is faith!"

"It's hardly an advertisement for either," I told him.

"It doesn't matter," he said, shifting in his seat. "You know why? Because before anything else," he said, "it's a story. We have all the bricks. Eleni! What a character! A woman for telling, or painting." He pinched his fingers together in the air and the dark lines of shadow on his brow deepened. Oratory behaviours: my father, the dramatist, knew how an illustrative face could sweeten speeches. "A woman searching for a missing son so long, she goes missing herself." He nodded. "It has a nice shape," he said. "People would enjoy this story." The Land Rover grumbled over a few cat's eyes and my father swung it back into the lane. The highway was desolate, the hills black as pitch. "So," he said into the dark, "we were on the way to Nicosia, and we found this old lady walking along the side of the motorway. And she had some trouble walking, you know, so we offered her a lift."

"Don't forget the nuns," I said.

"What?"

"Those nuns."

He shot me another sideways glance.

"They gave her a lift first."

"You think anyone wants to hear about that? There's something you need to understand about people – most of them can't concentrate for too long. You have to remember this. It's important not to expect too much from them."

I was out of smokes so I lit one from Maria's pack, which was rattling around in the glove compartment. It tasted of musty attics and old sun-cracked sandals.

"So," he said, "we gave her a lift to Nicosia."

For my father, it was an ironic anecdote that supplanted the story of the failed search for the painting. He liked the idea of her disappearance; he used it to rewrite our day. For me, her vanishing only became meaningful when I realised she'd left the photograph behind. Somewhere along the way, something must have happened to change things, I pointed out. He wasn't interested. We couldn't agree on the focus. We went over and over it, and seemed to get nowhere. By the time we were hitting that point in the road where Limassol appears, spread out and sparkling, I was fairly certain our encounter with Eleni wouldn't survive the translation into the mythologies that were being polished and perfected and passed through my father's house. The thought of it vanishing lent those minutes in the car, where the end was finally in sight, a sense of gravity. I wondered if it wasn't a trick of timing, like the image of Limassol and the feeling of relief that the sight inspires in the heart. A trick of timing, because no car journey on Cyprus is terribly long, and Limassol was only familiar, never held in the heart. Just because a place is home doesn't mean you have to love it. Sometimes it's just a place to kick off your shoes. Sometimes, when you've lost your real home, all you want is a place to kick off your shoes. But Eleni resisted all attempts at closure. She was the untied end, the unresolved narrative; impossible to shake.

And those 1,619 missing Greeks and their loved ones, they started turning up at night in my dreams. In those dreams, I was in a car driving down a dusty, half-familiar road, and they were lining the verges – the grief-stricken, photo-wielding relatives of the 1,619. Mothers clutching pictures of sons, daughters, husbands, holding them out, certain that somebody, somewhere, must know. The photo-flat faces loomed at me and, beyond them, the eyes of the bereft brimmed and begged. In the dream, I'd realise it was they who were moving, not me, and that their ranks were endless, and I would wake, sweat-soaked, disoriented and short of breath. It's what remained. Eleni: wandering between the eras, her back bent from the weight of her years. Eleni and her empty-handed vanishing. Eleni: the reason I started to carry in my purse a sepia-toned photo of a young Cypriot man I didn't know, just in case.

"When we are young, the words are scattered all around us. As they are assembled by experience, so also are we, sentence by sentence, until the story takes shape."

– Louise Erdrich

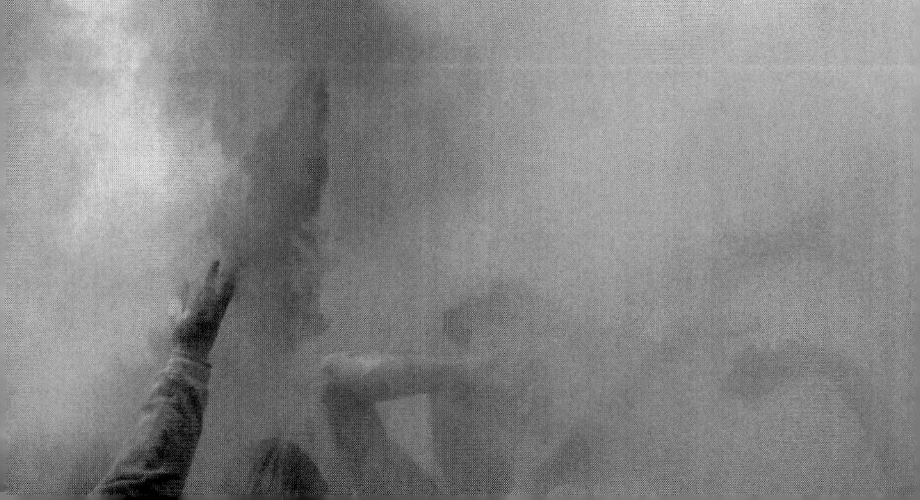

# The Upstairs Room
## AMY BIRD

There are only so many conversations you can have about naming children who aren't yet conceived, and so after a wet three-hour drive back from Suffolk, we arrive in equally rainy London with talk of tea and collapsing on the sofa before the business of the evening begins. That's what it takes to propel us inside. As Mark opens up all five doors of the car we bought, in hope, for my thirty-fifth, I climb out of the driver's side and heave our two sleeping bags to the front door, throw them down, and look up at the porch of number 36 next door.

A woman is standing there. White hair, white skin, translucent mac, clutching a shrivelled, almost empty plastic bag in front of her. She's not looking at us, at the unloading-of-the-car ritual, but instead staring into the middle distance. We've met the paternal grandmother – this must be the other one, Katie's mum

I could ignore her. But she is old, it's getting late, there is rain, and next door's windows are dark. Sociable face goes on.

"Are you OK there?" I ask.

"Oh, hello. Yes, she said she's back at eight – I'm a bit early."

Back from what? I wonder. Katie doesn't work. I look at my watch. It's twenty to eight now.

"Oh, well, not long to wait. The porch will keep you dry!" I say, as I fish out our front-door key and insert it in the lock, willing it to turn more quickly. I'm in, and the burglar alarm counts down my seconds. I try to kick off my shoes so as not to soil the carpet, but there isn't time for all that, it's bleeping away, so I teeter on my tiptoes to press the fob against the alarm console, hoping the mud from the rain won't leave any trace that Mark will notice. Then the alarm's off, the time pressure's gone, and I'm home.

I hear Mark go through the same routine as me outside.

"Are you OK there?" he asks.

"Yes, I was telling your . . . I'm a bit early. She'll be back at eight." There's a pause.

"Well, that's twenty minutes!" Mark exclaims.

Oh Mark, idiot, I think, don't invite her in.

"Do you want to come in?"

I groan to myself. That cushion of time before evening creation rites must begin, lest we become too tired, will be gone. Still, it's only twenty minutes. We can wait that long – just – says my internal egg timer. I head to the kitchen and put the kettle on. I hear Mark chivvy the old lady in.

"Come on, come round through the gate – or you can just squeeze through the gap in the hedge there if you want. No? Closed up, has it? All right, come round the old-fashioned way, then."

I poke my head back into the hall as Mark breezes in ahead of the old woman, does a half shrug, half head-duck at me, and leads the stranger into our home.

"Sorry, we're just back from holiday, everything's a bit crazy." He throws his hands up in the air to indicate the craziness. The old woman stays mute. Mark and I usher her through into the living room, following the trail of mud her shoes leave behind her. Mark grimaces, but doesn't demand she take off her shoes, Debrett's etiquette trumping carpet conservation. Good job – I doubt she's got the flexibility to bend down.

"Would you like a cup of tea?" he offers her.

"Oh, that's very kind. But only if you're having one," she says, meekly.

I would love some tea, too, but private tea, on my sofa, without having to wait on this dodderer.

"Right! Coming up!" promises Mark.

We back out of the room.

"Holly, darling, would you mind making . . . ?" Mark asks me.

"The kettle's almost boiled."

"Oh, great. Well done! I'll finish unloading the car."

I mooch back to the kitchen. The water is ready. But milk. Tea needs milk, doesn't it? Or maybe not. I dart into the living room.

"Hi, sorry, my husband should have asked – milk? Sugar? Sorry, I'm Holly, by the way."

"I'm Gloria."

I shake her hand and tell her I'm pleased to meet her. Her fingers feel webbed with loose skin. She tries to maintain the grasp but I end it.

"So, has she taken the boys out late, then?" I ask.

Gloria looks at me blankly.

"Sorry?" she asks.

"The boys, Rory and Aled, has she taken them out past their bedtime?" I repeat.

"I've just come about the room. She's got a room to let, upstairs," says Gloria.

"Oh, OK. Sorry, did you say milk and sugar?"

"Just milk. Please."

Times must be bad, taking a lodger. Katie did say that it was tough on finances with the kids, but still. Right, milk. Can I provide milk? I open the fridge and peer inside. I spy some, right at the back, almost beyond reach. Stretching to retrieve it, I inspect the label to check it's still in date. It claims to be. I grasp the green plastic lid and wrench. Too hard – the ridges nip my skin – but not hard enough. It's one of those bastard bottles that won't open. I run my ring finger over the central areola of the lid, its middle pimple raised where the suction mould has been removed, looking for a way in. I go and find Mark, in case he can help. He is getting the last cases out of the car, slamming the back doors shut, leaving it empty inside.

I pause at the gate to give right of way to a mother and pushchair, following them down the street with my eyes. Pink for a girl. Mark interrupts my gaze and I remember the milk.

"Could you . . . ?"

Mark tuts affectionately. He manoeuvres the bags so that he has a free hand. "It's all in the wrist," he jokes. He takes hold of the bottle in one hand, presses it against his chest and twists the lid. And twists again. His grasp on the bottle slips and he has to snatch it back into his grip to stop it falling. "Out of practice," he breathes, red-faced. He hands the milk back to me, unopened. "Never mind, she'll have to have tea without milk."

I stare at him. "We can't just give up."

Mark shifts his hold of the bags. "Come on, I'm tired. Let's go in. It's dry there."

I stay where I am. "We have to keep trying," I protest.

Mark trudges to the house, baggage weighing him down. He turns and looks back at me as he gets to the front door.

"Go and see if they've got milk at 40, then." He nods at the house that doesn't spawn old women on its porch.

I stand in the road looking at 40. The exterior is not as fresh as ours. Another coat of paint would hide the decay. They have failed to remove the moss left by the summer's lack of sun. The gate is firmly closed. Behind it, for those inside, there will be baths and bed. It's past the time for worrying them about milk and I doubt there will be any spare – there'll be just the right amount for those within. Protocol aside, I could go and ring the bell and proffer the milk bottle, peer in and see the fluffy terry-robed occupants round the legs of mother Sandy. I could feel the familiar longing.

Instead, I turn back towards 38, bedraggled by the rain, and walk up our path. All swept and clean, no sign of moss growing.

"They were out," I say, as I come in.

Mark is unzipping sleeping bags from their coverings and laying them out in the hall.

I stick my head into the living room. The old woman is still sitting there, without purpose, just clasping that old Tesco's bag on her knee.

"Just having some problems getting milk," I say.

She turns to me. I can see the little creases round her mouth shift in preparation for speech. "Take your time," she says.

I stride back into the kitchen and pull out the corkscrew. If Mark won't help me, I'll have to do this without him. I ram the stainless-steel screw-thread into the top of the milk bottle. It leaves only a dent. I try again, tightening my grasp on the handle. Still nothing. Tears begin to form in my eyes. Again I aim, catching my index finger as well as the lid. Jesus! I suck my finger to ease the pain, then examine it. The skin is broken. It might even bleed, I think. Always blood, when it's not wanted. But I've been rewarded with a small break in the green. Not enough for milk, but a start. I blink away the tears, and push the screw deeper into the hole, to pierce the inner membrane. White spurts out. Success! Hopefully that will be enough. I re-boil the kettle, fill the pot, and squeeze out as much milk as I can.

I bring the milky tea into the sitting room and look for a place to set it down. The old woman is resting a magazine I don't recognise on the coffee table, the plastic Tesco bag on her lap now looking even more deflated.

"Here we are, Gloria," I say. "A nice cup of tea."

She turns to me with a smile, relieved, I can see, to finally have the tea. I hand her the cup. She closes the magazine and puts it down on the table. The cover shows a silver-haired lady smiling and laughing as a little boy plays on a scooter in the foreground. "Be their favourite grandparent!" offers the cover-story tag line. It reminds me of the conversations with my mother. The weight of expectation, unachieved, the answer to her favourite question always negative. I should just post her the used tests each month, save her the bother of asking if she should start knitting.

"Your milk's off," says the old woman.

"What?" I ask, startled.

"The milk in the tea. It's off," Gloria repeats.

"But it can't be – it's before the use-by date!" I protest.

She holds out the cup to show me. I notice little flecks of congealed milk.

Through the walls from number 40, I hear bathtime squeals of laughter. From outside, I hear a police car's urgent cry. In here, the clock on the mantelpiece ticks loudly.

I take the tea cup from the old woman without a word.

"I don't mind," she says, as I leave the room. "I'm used to off milk. I just thought you'd like to know."

As I carry the cup back to the kitchen, the tea slops onto my hands, until they are covered in the sour liquid. I slam the cup into the sink. Mark hears the noise and comes in.

"What's wrong?" he asks.

"I told you we should have stopped for milk on the way home!" I tell him.

"What's wrong with the milk?" he asks.

"It's sour!"

I pick up the plastic milk bottle and hurl it into the bin.

"You should empty it first. It will just stink the place out, souring away in there," Mark reprimands me.

"Fine, fine, I'll empty it," I say, rummaging around in the bin, pulling out the milk, and storming over to the sink.

Mark peers over my shoulder. "It can't be sour, it's in date," he observes.

"Oh, for God's sake!" I mutter. I turn round to him. "Look, it's off, OK? Her Highness in the front room said so."

He shrugs. "So give her tea without milk." He walks out of the kitchen.

I contemplate throwing the milk bottle at his back, but I need him later. I squeeze the rest of the milk down the sink, drop by drop, and rinse it away. I press the switch on the kettle and inhale deeply. The kettle hisses. It is almost dry. I shouldn't let it reach boiling point. I flick the switch off again, just in time.

I get a fresh, boy-coloured cup out of the cupboard, and add a tea bag and the water. I carry the milkless tea into the living room just as Gloria is saying to Mark, "I don't know her, I'm just here about the upstairs room."

"Oh, OK," says Mark. "Well, better get on."

We leave the room.

"I thought she was one of the grandmothers," Mark whispers.

"I know, I know." I put on a smile, to share in his misunderstanding. "But apparently they've got a spare upstairs room at 36."

"I know they have," says Mark.

I stop smiling.

"You've been upstairs at Chris and Katie's, then?"

Mark stares at me. "Not this again."

"Lots of space, is there, upstairs? For 'lodgers'?" I hiss.

"Jesus! *One* slip, years ago, and you still –"

There is a rattle of a tea cup from the front room. Perhaps we have stopped whispering.

We stick our heads into the front room. Gloria is reading her granny mag again, milkless tea perched on her lap.

"How are you doing, Gloria?" I ask.

"Fine, don't mind me," Gloria reassures us, her voice quavering with age.

We withdrew our heads from the room again.

"Very accommodating, these lodgers. Maybe we should get one for our spare room, too," Mark suggests.

I glare at him. "We need that room," I remind him.

Mark shrugs.

"What was that?" I ask.

"Oh, I don't know. I'm tired."

"Perhaps you should stop paying visits to Katie, then."

"Just go upstairs," Mark says, running his hands through what's left of his hair. "I'll look after her."

I go upstairs. I stand on the landing, in limbo. Downstairs, age seeps out from the living room. Up here, on my own, all is too quiet.

I look at my watch. It's dead on eight. Evening. I hope Mark remembers we don't want to leave it too late.

"So, she'll be back soon!" I hear Mark say, downstairs.

"Yes, she says work usually finishes pretty promptly," says Gloria.

I go back downstairs and pick up my handbag from the living-room floor, muttering something about having to do shopping online.

Mark follows me out of the room.

"Katie doesn't work," he says.

"I know," I reply.

I return upstairs, taking my handbag to safety. It weighs heavy with my work BlackBerry. I put it down on the landing, then, thinking better of it – what if our unwelcome guest claims she needs the bathroom in order to avail herself of other facilities? – take it through to the third upstairs room, the room we paid an extra thirty thousand for when we moved here, three years ago. I stop at the doorframe. I have no reason to go in there now. I take out my BlackBerry and wonder if I should turn it on. It will invade the last of my holiday, make me forget there is life to be had outside work. Imagine not checking it for a whole year, on maternity leave. Incredible.

I don't have the pleasure of that excuse, though. I turn it on and sit down on the landing, nestling against the doorjamb of the non-spare room. Messages with increasingly pressing timeframes flood in as I cradle the device in my hands. Red exclamation marks, items flagged by the sender for action, subject lines declaring the contents to be urgent. My colleagues should learn that unless an activity carries an innate time limit for completion, a genuine deadline is rare. They should know that under false time pressure, all my responses will just be fraught, superficial, avoiding the real issue. I toss the BlackBerry into the empty room. It lands underneath the stork hanging-mobile we got from John Lewis in a moment of window-shopping weakness. The BlackBerry flashes its red light in the darkness, demanding attention. I don't want to go to it. But the flashing red jars with the calm green we chose for the room. We did the rest of the house blue, but not this bit. We wouldn't want to have to redecorate. If we got a pink. I crawl to the centre of the carpet to retrieve my electronic charge. The room could do with airing, I think. It's stale and the dust has found a home here. The wallpaper borders form a dark line round the edges of the space. I switch off the BlackBerry and, back outside on the landing, return it to my handbag.

Downstairs, time is ticking on.

"Do you think perhaps you should give her a call?" I hear Mark ask. "It's gone eight now."

"Oh, I don't think I have her number, actually. Let me look . . ." comes Gloria's response.

"I've got Katie's mobile number on my phone," I call down. "Or maybe you already have it, darling?" I can't resist the jibe.

"No, darling, why would I have it? Gloria, my wife's got Katie's mobile number. Shall we . . . ?"

"Katie?" asks Gloria. "Sylvia."

"No, it's Katie who lives next door," says Mark.

"It's Sylvia I'm here to see," insists Gloria.

"I can phone Katie if it helps," I call out. It's evening. We need to get our house back. I hover round the door of our bedroom and flick on the switch. There is the bed, the usual blue covers laid neatly across it before we went away, to welcome us back in. It would be too easy just to crawl under them and sleep, made barren by tiredness. I flick the switch off again. I have seen enough of that room.

Mark comes upstairs to get my phone. We hold a whispered summit.

"I was starting to think something wasn't right, you know," he confides. "The lights are off next door, there are no noises through the wall, no signs of life."

"I know, and who has space for a lodger?"

"No one," Mark answers, looking at me full square. He takes my phone and dials Katie, going downstairs. I hear the chain being taken off the front door.

"Hi, Katie," he says. "It's Mark. At 38. Yeah, hi. We've got a lady here, Gloria, says you've a room going? Oh! Well, no spare room there, then. Congratulations!" There is a forced jubilation in Mark's voice. I stick my head over the banisters.

"Pass on congratulations to Chris. If that's appropriate," I say. Mark rolls his eyes at me.

"Well done to you both. Just popping them out!" Mark says into the phone, before ringing off.

I press my head against the banisters. Well done them. Mark passes my phone up through the railings and takes hold of my hand, caressing it.

"I love you," he whispers.

"Chris is certainly virile," I say at the same time. Mark flinches slightly and takes away his hand. "I'm sorry, I –" I begin.

"And Katie's clearly fertile," he retorts, cutting me off.

Mark goes back downstairs, his shoulders high. I love you too, I say silently to his retreating back. I go into the bathroom. I don't look in the mirror; I know what age looks like. As I lock the door, I shout downstairs, "She could try number 40 – Sandy might know a Sylvia."

"Oh dear, oh dear. I must have made a mistake," I hear Gloria say. "But I was sure it was Sylvia at 36."

Below, Gloria sounds worried, but I see no reason to surrender hope, just yet, this month. I leave the bathroom again. I stand on the landing, looking down.

"You don't understand what it's like, when you're young," Gloria is telling Mark, her back to me. "So confusing!" Gloria fusses with her plastic bag, trying to stuff the magazine back into it, ripping a hole.

I drum my nails on the banisters. Mark darts a look up the stairs to me. "We're young!" I mouth, waggling my eyebrows. I see

Mark's body relax. He smiles up at me, ignoring Gloria's request for a replacement bag.

"Get her out," I mouth, jerking my head in the direction of the door.

"You should try *Loot*," Mark tells Gloria. "They have details of rooms to let."

Mark opens the front door, and fresh, damp air rushes into the house. The sound of rain has eased. "Or actually, the local papers sometimes have ads." Mark bends down to pick up a copy, which he'd already placed in our recycling pile. "Have a look in there, see if you can find anything."

"But Sylvia should have a room spare, you see –" Gloria begins, trying to wrap the broken Tesco bag round the paper.

Mark puts his arm around Gloria's shoulder and ushers the old woman out. She stands outside looking in, discarded newspaper and useless bag held to her chest. In here, it is just me and Mark. For now.

With a "Sorry, you can try Sandy next door, but . . ." Mark shuts the old lady out.

He turns to me. We exchange glances as he stands at the bottom of the stairs. We begin to laugh.

"Lord knows how long she would have gone on waiting if you hadn't come along!" I cackle.

"Yes, and who is this mysterious Sylvia? If she even exists!" He starts to walk up the stairs towards me. "Our Gloria was probably just gagging for a cuppa!"

Curving my finger, I summon Mark to me. "Up here, young man!" I order. Lowering my hand again, I run my fingers along the place where I tried to pierce the milk. I'm pleased to see no blood has come through after all.

"And where is this room that needs filling with some random lodger, do you suppose?" Mark asks as he mounts the stairs.

"Who knows?" I reply. "Not here."

I walk to the entrance of the upstairs room and flick on the light switch. Now illuminated, playful sheep frolic on the wallpaper borders. Mark follows and folds his arms around me, kissing my neck lightly. Our toes hug the threshold.

# For Ever
## REBEKAH LIN

(and so to dark)
e. e. cummings

A sharp blare of light, a magnificent crash and then the curtain of darkness fell as it always does at the end of any show. I remember little else of what came next except that when it went cloudy grey inside my head, you were the only truth I knew and that was all I wanted with me on the other side.

This is how it happened:

It was April 11, a cold Wednesday with mad skies that coloured over in a strange palette of pink, orange and dark blue. I went to work dressed to the nines – a crisp brown shirt with new clover-shaped lapel pins, grey brogues and a mousey-grey sweater that was once, before a laundering mishap, the colour of cottage cheese. I was rather happy and I felt somewhat cool and snazzy enough for my mid-week tipple with you later in the evening. Work went by quickly and I dragged my preppy, lazy bottom to Masala, your favourite Indian restaurant, for dinner.

We were purple from our fourth serving of basmati rice and spicy chicken curry; our cheeks blushed paprika red as we let our heat-stung lips linger in the cool beer. We decided, in the moment, to take a drive down the M4. As we accelerated aimlessly past one exit after another, you realised it was two a.m and we'd both be fucked if we didn't get home soon. Work started at nine and we weren't morning people. Making a U-ee (heard a friend slang that terribly before) was impossible, but two slip roads and a few spins of the roundabout later, we were on our way back, the beer finally finding its bloated presence in our tummies.

We must have been driving at about sixty miles an hour in the dead of the night. My dashboard clocked minus four but it really felt like twenty below. The heater wasn't working – I was wearing your jacket as well as my own but still I felt the chill. I touched my frozen fingers to your face and you recoiled slightly before placing your warmer hand over mine.

We'll be home soon enough. Do you want me to take over now? you asked, your lips crinkled like grapes on a sun-dry spin.

I shook my head and glanced at the number of miles our GPS reported across its flickering screen, with us, hovering, the solitary blue dot. The figures seemed to have stuck, like in *Groundhog Day*. I stared through the windscreen, hoping that if I concentrated hard on the dark shadows muddling outside in the maybe-turquoise fields – possibly the occasional herd of goats drunk with sleep – my eyes would return to slightly fewer miles to go.

No, pull over love. You're tired and I'm feeling all right – let me.

And so I did. I'm a yes person (unfailing and true) and even if that wasn't so, I could never say no to you. Twenty minutes passed and I saw that your eyes were a sleepy red and your hands were fixed awkwardly on the steering wheel; your knuckles bristled white in the cold morning.

I could distract you, I offered as one hand strayed to your lap. You grunted and waved my hand away bashfully, but your gesture was weak so I kept at it, tugging greedily at your fly, and soon the corners of your small mouth produced an embarrassed but extraordinary smile. Kiss me, you said, and as you clasped your hand gently over mine, you turned slightly to offer me lips. I leaned over quickly and that was when it happened. Lights; the opening orchestra; swift blows to both chest and face; and so to dark.

I remember the first time you got high.

You were a brisk kind of happy – talking quickly, chewing hard, your walk a dizzy dance of sorts before you climbed clumsy into my car. There was a vulnerability about you that I've always admired, a quiet part of you that I love completely and you know

I've always been attracted to you – not in a sexed-up, I-want-to-bed-you-now way but in a we're-two-of-a-kind, happy-souls way that drew me to you like plush mangoes on a hot summer afternoon.

Your eyelids were fluttering and I could recognise joy behind the spectra of grey-green that were your irises. You'd never been there before, and, clearly, you were enjoying it. You repeated yourself many times over and your stray comments about the dancing lights soon became the punctuation in our loosely held conversations. Most of the time you were slurring, mumbling indistinctly then bursting into short spurts of giggles. Your speech took on a lisp I never knew you had (I bet you didn't know it, either) and I kept on driving, my hands held steady in the usual, driving-manual-type ten-to-two position, eyes on the road.

How much did you have, love?

Just half a tablet, I promise, just half.

I tried hard to concentrate on the driving but I was worried about you. I looked over quickly and saw you slouched over with your knees on the dashboard, feet tucked in close to your behind. You had one hand on my thigh to remind me that you were still there, and the other running amok as you struggled with your cigarette case jammed tight in the front pocket of your skinnies. We hit a red soon after and I reached over and unpacked it easily. You grinned at me, your eyes narrowing into barely-there slits that made your face look small and white as a sheet. It took all of you to light up but once you did, I watched as your face relaxed into a sleepy smile. As you exhaled softly, you turned to me and said, I feel OK, love. I feel so happy. I'm going to miss him but I know he's in a better place.

Something wet formed pools of silver in my eyes and I remember raising a sleeve to my face, feigning a sneeze to avoid looking at you full on. It had been four months since your brother died and you were quiet, distant and limited – a far cry from your usual sprightly, sarcastic, wisecracking self. For once, I had Ecstasy to thank for this *in extasio* (yes?!!) *veritas* moment. You looked over but I was quick to wave you off dismissively with the poor excuse of a bad cold as the reason for my tears.

I drove you home speedily and as you slept, your face pale

with fatigue, a noiseless pulse flickering your eyelids, I knew then that I would love you for ever.

I was unconscious for six weeks.

You slept like a baby, said my mother in her best effort to cheer me up.

I woke to a room full of people. It was almost secretive, the way I came to. My parents had near given up and I didn't respond well to any of their attempts at rousing me. Something about my cerebral cortex being messed up. There was a pastor somewhere to my left and I could hear the drone of his voice bore my motionless self to tears as the sounds of crying and mumbled prayers became desperate love languages that filled pocket corners of the room. No one dared to speak too loudly. There was a clicking of heels as people entered one by one, in pairs, in groups; muted greetings. Others shuffled in meekly, embarrassingly conscious that six forty-five was never going to be the new six thirty.

I was awake but an impregnable force of sorts, perhaps glue, glue to prevent infection of any kind, forced my eyes shut. I reasoned with myself inwardly, circumventing all possibilities that I might . . . that I might just be blind. I refused that immediately, allowing myself to identify colour within the dark concaves of my sockets, envisioning that decorated Christmas tree I saw at Harrods the year before. And then the most surprising thing happened – I saw you hurtling through the air as we crashed head first into the oncoming lorry. My eyes shot open with such strength that the small envelope of light allowed into the room felt hostile and hot against my contracting pupils. As I surveyed the room, I could feel the crust of sleep that had formed rough edges on my lids.

I wanted to speak but my lips were stuck at their corners, crisp and ignored. My arms were resting by my side and I could feel cotton beneath my fingers. Something terrible had happened and I knew, from the air of marked silence and interrupted prayers, that my immovable self, lying here, proved normality was absent and that I would fail in any attempts to find it. I lay there, still as a capped bottle of Evian, my ears confounded by the hammering absence of noise that made obvious the obese, overfed elephant decked in boughs of holly, standing there in the room, ignored. The mounting inaction drove me crazy. No one realised I was awake. Everyone was busy or deep in prayer. Fuck prayer, open your eyes damn it – open your eyes.

I saw Mother, Father and my siblings collectively bowed towards each other as they spoke in tongues and prayed unintelligibly. I saw Ian, Joey, Lisa, Marie and my best mates in the other corner, staring blankly at the praying crowd, uncomfortably aware of their helpless, religionless selves. There were members of the clergy standing just behind the pastor, crying inaudibly even though they never knew me. Even Jack and Kate, my childhood friends, were there, their hands stuffed awkwardly into their pockets as they closed their eyes in an attempt to pray. My frustration, however, was eclipsed by the crashing disappointment that, too, fell unnoticed when I realised you were not there.

Father put the pieces of what happened together for me. A lorry driven by a sleepy, cocaine-fuelled double-shifter had crossed the central reservation and crashed head first into us. Even though you made a quick, violent swerve, the lorry still collided directly with the left side of the car, explaining my now useless pair of limbs. The car had overturned and crumpled itself some thirty metres away into a grizzly heap of mangled parts like a sandwich messily ripped in half, and I had been dragged out unconscious as the unhurt lorry driver, now frightened awake, dialled an ambulance for damage control.

I nearly bled myself dry and needed packs of refrigerated blood from the hospital bank to pull me back to safety. I was in intensive care for the first three weeks but was transferred to a normal ward once my blood pressure stabilised. Plenty of prayer and the power of God, said my mother. I believed her just a little.

There were about a hundred people who made up excuses for you. Everyone told me just how sorry you were, how guilty you felt that I had lost the use of my legs and how tormented you were, knowing that you had escaped unscathed save for a deep, unsightly scar just above your forearm. You didn't hurtle through the air as I saw in my dream and you did not come to see me. I called you tirelessly, my finger blistered on the speed-dial button of my phone, anxious for the ringing to stop, nervous for the answering click that would be you.

But you never answered and soon the dial tone was one that connected me to an automated machine telling me the number was now not in use. I pleaded desperately to Ian and Joey that I was fine with you writing to me. I just wanted you to talk to me. They looked furtively at each other and a week later scammed a letter to me, but I knew you too well not to know your writing from theirs. They apologised and explained that even though you felt emotionally "punctured", because it felt like you'd been "stabbed and slowly allowed to waste away without seeing me" (dramatic bullshit if you asked me, surprising, especially coming from you), you wouldn't allow yourself to ever be near me again. Toxic, you said, you were toxic.

It was frustrating that no one else saw you. I never understood why you would do this to me but no one had any new answers. They told me to forget you, to hate you if I must, but never to be sad about you. Your updates on Facebook and Twitter stopped all those months ago and you were absent on Instagram and every other social media platform I knew you were active on. You never met any of our friends and you never came to see my parents at the weekends, as you usually did before. My parents also never asked me about you – they were not angry with you as I'd expect them to be and they never brought you up again. I was told that you wanted to "disappear" and that you occasionally saw Ian and Joey but it was "only for a few minutes" or a "drive-by" to drop my things off. I had a new friend drive me to your house once and I watched your window for any signs of movement but there weren't any. Your hideous curtains remained closed and I never saw you pop out, even for a smoke, the entire day. Then a window on the leftmost side of the house swung itself open and your mother, small and always so perfect and well-mannered, appeared and spotted me sitting stupidly in the car. The very next day, I was told that you had moved away to the US to work for a couple of years.

I would sit, accompanied, on the Tube and feel terribly lost. I would think about you, in your new country, sitting on the T-train or subway, and there you'd be, staring ahead at the map, counting the stops till it got to yours, and I would wonder about what you were thinking of as you looked blankly through the moving panels of underground or overgrown marsh. And maybe you'd be like me, staring out into the vast unknown, struggling in thought but all the same thinking about you.

You fucking coward. Why wasn't it you that was hurt instead? I wouldn't have left. I would have waited for you to wake and then I would apologise and beat myself with a bat but I would never leave you.

I was brought up religiously apathetic, but I became a Christian when I was sixteen. A friend of mine convinced me that this was the lesser of both evils and I would have redemption safe in my pocket as long as I remained good-hearted, charitable and kind. Being wonderfully proud of my Christian self, I would take my Bible with me wherever I went, sure to read it openly on the bus, or whilst taking the Tube, always eager to make an impression – me, a follower of God, a good-hearted follower of God. And then your brother died, you fell apart and I stopped following.

Anyway, I had to go to church with my parents one day, months after the accident. Seeing as how I'm hardly the pious sort now, this was a big deal for me. So I got to church and I heard the same pastor preaching. He's been there fourteen years and, this time round, he looked taller, almost elongated, behind the pulpit. He was a thin, well-groomed man with the usual pastor-like trousers and shirt rimmed at the neck by a clerical collar that seemed way too tight for human use. I was fussed about in the usual way – make way for Wheelies, watch it now, be careful. No one actually said it but everyone knew it. They would do Moses proud, parting a way for me wider than the Red Sea. Their eyes were full of pity and there would be the occasional touch on my shoulder, and plenty of aww, you poor thing, written plainly in their manner towards me. I wheeled myself to the front (otherwise I see nothing more than backsides) and just as I was about to give the old peace handshake with strangers I really didn't give a shit about, your parents walked up to me quietly. They pulled their knees in to level themselves with me and grasped desperately at my hands. Your mother spoke first and she was shaking as she said, I'm sorry, dear. I'm sorry about what happened.

This was the first time since the accident that I'd had any

interaction with your parents. I remember feeling both dismantled and anxious at the same time. Is that possible? I dismissed their apology with a half grimace, half smile and said that it was OK and that it would be great if they could relay the message to you that I'm not angry any more, nor do I blame you for anything, and if you could, would you please call me as soon as possible. I looked at them wearily, trying to unearth the truth or mystery behind your disappearance, and my eyes met your mother's and believe me (as you would know), they were a dark, handsome, sad pair of greys carefully hidden behind the warm, gingerbread façade of proper, afternoon-tea invitations. She nodded gently, forced a smile and they got up, said their quick goodbyes and carried on with the peace.

I noticed your mother again later and this time she was staring right at me, crying.

When the service ended, I caught sight of your parents kneeling side by side in the furthest corner of the chapel. The pastor was bent over them, a hand on the shoulder of each, and your mother was still crying. Your mother was always a calm one – a cool cat, you'd say, perfectly indifferent and never at a loss, borrowing wise words from a certain Louisa Gradgrind. I was piqued with curiosity as to what had made her so upset, as this was crazy unusual, but my parents were quick to wheel me off in the opposite direction. I remember looking back and just as I did, your mother looked up at me with such sad anger that I felt momentarily frightened.

I went to the park afterwards. It wasn't rainy out so I decided to wheel myself up to our spot – you know, the one behind the awkward-looking tree and next to that oak-brown bench littered with graffiti spelling out vulgarities in block letters? Yes, that one. I could see a shape-shifting flock of birds scattered in the ocean of a sky – the occasional stray that would fall behind, mirroring the actions of the rest as he struggled back into formation before the wind took him elsewhere. It was chilly and I had my jacket on. I've always been a bit of a stubborn cat so I didn't wear my gloves even though my mother would tirelessly remind me to take them with me.

I shut my eyes and took in the park's kaleidoscope of smells. Chestnuts charring about ten feet behind me, cheesy popcorn, bubblegum candyfloss, pre-holiday-polished cars. It sunk in then that this was Christmas Day, explaining the tinkling of bells on brand-new bicycles, the high-pitched ho-ho-hos. I kept my eyes closed as I overheard a couple quarrelling about how *I Saw Mommy Kissing Santa Claus* was hardly an age-appropriate song for kids to sing. I also heard two children crash into each other and the all too familiar sound of whimpered crying as their mothers gave them a shelling.

I felt someone pull on my jacket and as soon as consciousness hit me in the form of warm light from the bursting rays seeping into the narrowed slits of my sun-seared eyes, I turned to the familiar scent of your bath soap and shampoo. I felt gentle relief, my body a natural catheter, releasing black, bloody fluid that once sat coagulated in my heart.

Hello. It's been months now. Where have you been? I asked as I felt arms encircle my crumpled self into a hug. I hugged back eagerly, my arms stick-thin and pale underneath the now oversized jacket that you bought for me ages ago. You didn't say a word as you slid nimbly onto the bench next to me. I felt you bury your head into my right arm as you sobbed tears of Sorry, I didn't know what to do, I was scared, into the threads of that same jacket. I placed an awkward arm around your shoulders and realised that you too were a skinnier version of your old self. I pulled you in and whispered into your ear as I always used to, reassuring you that all was OK and that we were going to be fine now. We'll be OK, we'll be OK. I closed my eyes into your hair.

A sudden explosion tore through my darkness and ruptured the air. I opened my eyes and saw that it came from the punctured tyre of an unfortunate Ford Focus owned by a gangly twenty-something with mopped hair and a greyish-purple birthmark slapped on his right cheek. I pulled myself upright and found my arms wrapped tightly over my own chest, my fingers now blue from the cold. I sighed, pulled at the ends of my sleeves to cover the exposed parts of my hands, and wheeled myself home as the buttery sun set to the sounds of couples kissing and children laughing.

"I saw the angel in the marble and carved until I set him free."

– Michelangelo

# A Severe Insult to the Brain
## COLIN GRANT

I can't remember now when it first happen, actually happen. Well,
I suppose it make little difference. When the penny drop, it drop.
I did suspect she from time. Where woman concern, is so you must
expect. It actually an insult, just like the blood clot that did insult
my brain. The doctor tell me I must take it easy. But how you gwan
relax when your woman there suck the marrow out your bone?

7.30 a.m. going on 8.00 and the car cold, man it not true. It a
good thing me did have sense enough lift the lid, cover the engine
with newspaper last night, otherwise this piss car not starting
for now. The drizzle like a friend that outstay him welcome: me
remember him from the night before. Adjust the rear-view mirror
and don't forget: decide on a smile as you slide into the driver seat.
This is a new day, after all, and you're not going to tell me a smile
go unnoticed. You may think you alone. My man, you never alone.

Outside the town hall the tramp pick through the Saturday
night, Sunday morning rubbish in a bin. It sick my stomach. Not
even a cup of hot water pass these lip since I get up this morning,
and is a good thing. Why him put on glove first, God for tell. Both
sleeve roll up. The tramp take him time but is nothing but filt' in
there. Last week him still have some pride. Last week him could
still beg a cup of coffee or him bus fare home. This week it the bin.

Just past Teviot Street and you never guess. Not even five
minutes out my yard. Yeah, man, the Blues, the thin blue line. Ten,

twenty yards ahead of me. Unmarked patrol car, nah must. You might ask yourself: "How he know?" Well, Super, no one drive that slow, slow – only Babylon. And yet before I know, them turn and gone.

Yes, bwoi, look into the rear-view mirror. Hold that smile and one thought only: Jess a-catch sight of me out of the corner of she eye as she pass the porter lodge. Where to park, though, when I reach? That is one guaranteed bitch of a question. Under the big sycamore, perhaps? But wait, wouldn't it make more sense to roll through the gate just as she come off the shift? And, surprise! That sweet, sweet moment when she recognise . . . I so tired I ready for dead. Must open the window and hold some fresh air. Must not daydream at the wheel. Must not drift like snow across the open road. Must not drift like snow. Must not drift . . .

Don't ask how I find myself under the sycamore again, and have to reverse back onto the Mile End Road. Me can't take chance and switch off the engine. I liable to knock it off just as she come through the gate. She bound to hear when I start the damn thing up again and realise I been sitting there all along, you dig? I start to think the whole thing mix up, mix up, just a bad idea, to run down woman so. Jess have me well and truly under manners, my frien'. Some serious, serious manners. But then again we are not talking 'bout some little half-dead peroxide blouse 'n' skirt. Man, you will never know a white woman so black. And what I do this woman that she want my pudding so? You tell me! She late this morning, though.

Sleepy Ron in him grey coat peer out from the porter lodge. Every day the same. Ron remind you of one of them silent movie star. Behind the glass screen, the face always vex – red like beetroot – but you can't hear a thing. This morning though the volume turn up high, high and is pure bad word him cuss. As God is my witness. The window shake and the bad word fly. He point to one of them no-joke sign: "Licence to Clamp" or "Tow-away Zone", and before me can even work the clutch the door to the porter lodge fling open.

"You can read, I take it? No permit, no parking. No parking without a permit!"

You ever wonder how these front-of-house diplomat get the job? The grey coat used to be white before the nicotine wash. The face never see sunshine, only rain. The feet rush ahead of the brain. And yet, is this not the same shit me did see stagger out of the off-licence just yesterday? Head back, one gulp of Special Brew and a spray of vomit like you wouldn't believe straight onto the pavement. Bastard pulls back. The beard may be cover in last night vindaloo but at least the shoes are clean.

My mouth dry, man. Can't call up enough mouth-water to let him know how I feel. Anyhow, Jess liable to come round the corner any minute, and how will that look? Keep your eye on the prize, man. A picture-postcard smile, and slip into reverse.

The gear stick almost brock off in my hand. I feel to ram the "You can read I take it" right down Ron craw. I is not a savage. As if him is anything. I know the stroke Whitey play, believe you me. I not going to let no John Bull mess with the strategy. Flick down the sun visor and see it there, in red ink. You same one did write it: "PRIOR PLANNING PREVENTS POOR PERFORMANCE". Everyone must have a code, right? Me live by the five Ps.

Time check? She well late. But me can use the time for one-two last-minute preparation. Perhaps a little mouth spray. Ordinarily speaking I not a great fan of mouth spray but the toothpaste run out. That little squeeze more go on and on but this morning it finish for true and me have for use salt clean my teet'. And where that bush spring from on top of my lip? Take up the clippers, man. A quick trim not gwan hurt.

She take her time, bwoi. And you know what? Is just she and some double-shift African on last night. If ever Tunde try to foo-foo with she . . . She never this late before. I start to wonder if them did put back the clock last night. I must hold a cigarette, just one. Not inside the car, you understand. I don't allow anyone smoke inside, not even she. The little coolie man across the road sell cigarette one at a time. But the trick is this: you have to buy a whole box of match.

If me quick me can keep the engine running. He shoulda open him sweetshop by now. By eight o'clock he shoulda sort out the Sunday paper, ready for one of the cap-in-the-hand old timer that top up the state pension deliver paper round. But the paper still stack up outside the shop this morning, grey by now, soggy round the edge – from some dog piss, wouldn't surprise me. I never really stop to think about the coolie man till now. I actually sorry for him since them catch him sell cigarette to children. And is pure hypocrite. Is the parents same one send the pickney for Embassy Number One. But in trut' you can't feel too sorry for the cha-cha man if you see the way he empty him nose right there on the side of the street.

No sign of life inside him store. Maybe they did put back the clock for true. It can happen without you know. And more than that . . . I wonder if I have the right day. Jess work four night on, three night off – or so she say. All kinda rubbish run through my head: that time I did spy she at a dance and she suppose to be home with migraine. Then there was the saving I take out of the high-interest account lend she. Lend she, you know, and me haven't seen a red cent since.

My spar, Bosey, say ever since the head trouble me have things back to front. That me and Jess was never man and woman. That the brain is messing with me, exaggerating how it was. That it turn black into white. But I ask him how you can feel something about a woman if it wasn't there before. And insult to the brain or no insult to the brain, one thing I know for sure: Bosey always talk tripe – from the day he born.

The mind a funny thing, bwoi. Be cool, my man. Be cool and catch a little shut-eye till she come. I not embarrassed to tell you I push down the safety lock on the door. Too many bad boy out there, give them a chance, cut your throat and take what you got. The hot air from the fan blast away. I feel my eyelid begin to droop. Only when it gone too far now, when sleep actually take hold of me, is funny, I feel say I 'fraid to wake up – not 'fraid that I won't but that I will. Is a funny something. Me wonder say that blood clot have anything do with it. That blood clot a bitch of a thing.

In the dream someone take a screwdriver, bore through the side of my temple. I wake to find Jess rapping on the window with those easy-life manicure nails. Roll down the window nah, man. Purposeful but not eager. Just faster than slow. The perfume a little on the cheap side. She lay it on thick on account of she have to work through the night without no chance even to wash the stench from under she armpit.

"Home, madam?"

Jess make a slow search through she handbag, methodical, real thorough.

"Would you believe it?" she say.

I know what's coming.

"This bag is a black hole."

I'm not saying a word. Let her stew.

"How's my credit?"

She there bleed me dry, man. Don't you think I know? The joke is this: Jess know I know. And I tell you something. You can't ignore the arrow in your back for ever. There come a time you have to clench your teet' and pull out the arrowhead.

"Your credit always" – watch she move she arse inside – "good with me."

Three time already this month I have to take a little squeeze on the petrol money. Every time I reach inside the shoebox for some cash, me have to take handkerchief wipe the sweat from my neck-back. But then again we come back to the same point: this is not some rank, street-walking blue foot. This is Lady Jess. And I choose she as much as she choose me.

"Where to?"

"Just drive. I'll let you know when we reach."

You see what I mean? The way she just lay them lyric on you. Style! This is how it suppose to be: Jess in the back and me at the wheel. That nice, nice feeling, though, never last. She don't do it to spite, but Jess have a habit of drop off in the middle of a sentence when you least expect. Like the street lamp when morning come and it begin to lose the glow, blink and she gone. She don't do it to spite. Is tired. She tired.

She will let me know when we get there but I already know where to go. Let's be honest with ourselves, she don't treat me right. She say it a girlfriend flat but the girlfriend mout' full of gold, a Rolex on she wrist, she locks could do with a wash and she jaw with a shave. Yes, sir, it could be Master D with the BMW or QT with the Merx. Let him stay there warm the bed, dream him dirty dream. This morning that nasty wretch in for one hell of a surprise. Because it not fair when I have sweat after she for so long that another man should benefit, you dig? And I gawn leave *him* with a severe insult to the brain.

A morning-after drunk step out into my path. I have to swerve, almost wake up Jess, not to run him down.

Not long now before we reach. I turn towards Jess as she stir. It not my style but I ask anyway: "Am I coming up?"

"Honey, you won't have to ask."

"When?"

"When the time is right."

When the time is right I won't have to ask but the time is never right. I feel them before I see them – Babylon. They glide up alongside. I slow down, let them pull ahead, but they catch the next traffic light. I can't see them but feel those cold eye on me, take it all in, take in the whole scene. The light turn green but Babylon don't budge. They wouldn't mad. I not in the mood for them this morning. No one or nothing gwan spoil the strategy. Me can't move before them do. It would look too suspicious. Bwoi, them a-take them sweet time. And if them see the monkey wrench that's me finish. Any minute now the light gwan turn back again and how will that look. I must move. I move off slow and – what the rass . . . ? – them follow. But after two, three minute Babylon turn and gone.

J there a-pout at the small mirror in she purse. She take lipstick, add another layer to those full lip. This gal is not easy.

"Left at the corner and first right."

And into one of them street that always look dark, no matter the time of day. We pull up outside she yard. Inside the bedroom – the bedroom, I'm telling you – someone turn the light down low.

"You want I should check back later?"

"Of course if you have something better to do . . ." she say.

Listen how she mock me. I put on the central locking. Take out the monkey wrench and unwrap the paper. I have she full attention now. Have some respect.

"Who you have up there?"

"Just a girlfriend, I told you."

"You're stepping in shit."

"Be nice, now."

"So, if I'm nice you won't flash your pussy?"

I know what I must do. You understand, some black man see a white gal with a brother and think it mean she ripe for picking. Check back with the white sister after rude boy leave the scene. Well, no pudding today. Not today, my frien'. Black man or not, to leave such a man at your back, you would favour an ass. Nah true? But all the practice and the words won't come. The thought scramble in my brain. Can't get it clear. I should tell she to stay put, that I will deal with she later, then walk straight towards the flat. But I fail the test, man. And it frighten me when I look 'pon she. For a minute, I hardly recognise who it is in the back of the car. Jess snap shut she purse and press those lip close to my ear, and sigh just loud enough for me to hear.

"Again, really?" she say. "Is this what I'm going to have to put up with?"

She cut her eye after the wrench and then back at me. "You know, if you show it, you're not going to use it."

She right. Of course she right. Jess lean forward, smooth the back of my head and trace a finger along the scar. "I'm working a double shift tomorrow, babe. I can count on you, can't I?"

Bosey would say she just there a-nice me up. But even when she gone, all through the day, I feel her cool hand 'pon my head, right there where the surgeon put the knife.

"I want to stand as close to the edge as I can without going over. Out on the edge you see all the kinds of things you can't see from the centre."

– Kurt Vonnegut

# Rock Paper Scissors
## MADDY REID

When we get to the front door, I hang back from the step and wait for Lex to ring on the bell.

"So, whose party is it, again?" he says.

"Tasha's," I say.

"And what's she like, then?"

I think about how to answer. She sits at the desk in front of me at school, but I don't really know her. I'm Lutz on the register and she's May. I've spent five years staring at the back of her head. For the first two years she had a bob with a blue velvet hairband, for the next two years she did her hair in a French plait, and now she wears it long and loose, with the ends cut in a straight line. So straight it looks as though it's been done with a guillotine.

"I dunno," I say. "Blonde. Blonde and tallish."

He presses his finger hard on the button.

"Plays a lot of netball," I say, thinking about how she puts her hair up in a ponytail for that, right on the top of her head. "Maybe even captains."

I look at him, standing underneath the porch light. It feels strange for him to be asking these questions. And not me.

He's usually the one with the plans – the friends who have parties and the other friends who can give us a lift there and back, as long as I don't mind sitting on someone's knee and smoking out the window. But this morning when I was over at his house, and he was going on about how there was nothing for us to do, I got to say that Tasha had come up to me on the bus on Friday and told me about this party she was having. "And you can bring Lex, too," she'd said. Someone must have told her I was friends with him.

And so we're here and someone is opening the door and I'm guessing he goes to Lex's school because they seem to know each other and start doing that handshake, man-hug thing. And I just stand there thinking about whether I should be taking my muddy trainers off or not, and how long it would take to undo all the knots and how it would feel in my bare feet – way too exposed. And then I follow them down the hallway, past the umbrella stand and the prints of flowers with their Latin names written underneath, to the kitchen at the far end.

We stop in the doorway. Over Lex's shoulder I can see Tasha on the other side of the room, with a group of boys surrounding her, listening and laughing in all the right places. She's wearing a red dress, and straightened the only kink she has in her fringe. Jake, who plays cricket with Lex, is beside her, his arm up on the fridge so that no one else can join in and she has to slide underneath it when she comes over to say hello.

As she walks towards us I notice how clean the floor looks, with its white lines of grouting. I think about how my dad let me practise riding my bike with stabilisers on it in our kitchen. I would go round and round the table while he played *Bicycle Race* by Queen on the stereo. When it got to the break in the middle he would turn it down and let me do the ringing bit. I had silver-foil tassels on the handlebars and a Mickey Mouse bell.

Tasha smiles at me and I introduce her to Lex. She is wearing heels so high that she doesn't have to reach up to kiss him on both cheeks. They start to talk about the county championships and how much training he does in the morning, before school.

I look at Lou and Jane who are in the corner whispering in each other's ears. They're wearing very low-cut tops, which most of the boys are looking down as they walk past. They're the leaders of a group that hangs out in the loos, by the mirrors, applying sticky Lipcote and rolling up the waistbands of their skirts. I'm not one of them. In fact I don't belong to any of the groups at school.

Mainly because I still haven't worked out what it is I'm supposed to belong to.

I like to think I kind of float between them all, like a satellite amongst the constellations. Or a chunk of space debris.

But in reality you can usually find me walking around the tennis courts, with my earphones in. I did that so much last term the Head of Year made me a prefect with litter duties for the whole area. I was given a blue enamel badge in assembly and all the other prefects nodded at me when I walked past them in the corridors.

In the first two weeks I filled three whole carrier bags with Wham bar wrappers but then decided to hand my badge back in. It turns out I was somehow supposed to stop people doing it in the first place, even write their names down in a book if they were persistent offenders. "I know what they're doing is wrong," I explained, "but I'm not any good at telling them off."

Lex and Tasha are now comparing personal bests. Someone hands me a damp bottle of beer and I pick at the corners of the label.

There's a door leading off from the kitchen, and not too many people to push past on the way, so I take another couple of beers from the table and wander on through into the sitting room, where everything is cream – the carpets, the walls, the curtains – like an empty tub of butter. There are a lot of cabinets. Not trophy cabinets, like at Lex's. But TV cabinets, drinks cabinets, stereo-equipment cabinets. Pretty much everything that can be has been put away.

I stop to look at the bone china display in one of them. There's a statue of the Virgin Mary.

For a while I tried very hard to believe. I went to this charismatic church, at the end of my road, where people were shaking and talking in tongues. The vicar kept asking the congregation to open themselves up to the Spirit of God, so that He could enter them. I asked Him – pretty politely as well. But I remained unmoved.

Some of the girls who went there were very nice, though. One time I was ill with the flu and they called round to see me. They wouldn't explain to my dad what it was about. When they came into my room and saw me propped up in bed, sweating away in a greying vest, they produced this handkerchief for me that they'd had specially blessed in church. It was plain white and seemed to lack any special powers. But they did ask me how I was feeling.

"Well, I've been throwing up all afternoon and watching a film about Houdini. He could escape from a tank full of water, suspended upside down by his feet, fly a plane, liked handcuffs and was cool enough to die on Hallowe'en."

They didn't say anything. I hadn't gone to enough services by that point to know that they totally disapproved of Hallowe'en, thinking it a celebration of Satan and the dark side.

I sit down cross-legged in front of the stereo and flick through all the CDs, not really looking at any of them.

People come to the doorway and peer around the room, nod in my direction or raise their hand, then go away again.

Someone who thinks I'm Luke shouts over. When I look up at them, they apologise.

But it's an easy mistake to make. I've got really short hair, cropped, and I'm straight up and down, with a chest so flat I hardly ever bother wearing a bra. Only when it's games day at school, because we have a communal changing room.

When I was younger I was convinced that I was going to grow up to be a boy. All I wanted to be was old enough to shave like my dad did every morning. He would let me sit by the mirror and lather up his tin of sandalwood soap with a badger-hair shaving brush. At bathtime I would make Rip Van Winkle beards with my Mr Matey bubbles. And I used to practise peeing standing up, until my mum worked out how the puddles were forming and made me sit down.

I lie flat on the carpet and listen to the music. It's shit and on repeat, something I sort of recognise, but don't want to remember. One of the boys comes to the door, and mouths something at me but I can't hear him. I shrug but he doesn't bother getting any closer to tell me.

After that no one comes for a while.

I run out of drink.

I get up and walk back into the kitchen where the soles of my trainers now stick to the stone floor. There is a strong smell of burning because someone has tried to do cheese on toast sideways in the toaster, and all the bowls of crisps have got bottle tops in them.

The back door is shut but I can tell everyone is out there. I can hear them.

I clear a space among all the empty vodka bottles and then pull myself up onto the side next to the window. I take the lid off the bread bin, place it on my knees and start laying everything out – papers, baggie, half a packet of Golden Virginia.

The first one's going to be for me. And the second one's going to be for Lex. He always asks me to do this for him, because I'm much better at it – not that he'd ever admit it. He just gives me that nudge and I agree.

I blame his parents. They didn't teach him like mine did one Sunday afternoon after I'd had enough of hanging upside down from the only tree in the pub garden, holding my dress up so that I didn't show off my knickers. They wouldn't let me use tobacco, so I had to make do with grass and couldn't understand why they were laughing about it.

No. They taught him other stuff. Like the importance of winning. All the time. My parents – they've never even told me to do my homework and my dad once read me this story out of the newspaper about a class of Native American kids. A new teacher came to their school and asked them a question that she knew some of them would definitely be able to answer. When no one stuck up their hand she couldn't understand why. It turns out those that did know didn't want to show up those that didn't. Winning. To them it just wasn't that important.

I bet my teachers would say that I follow this line way too much. Lex, though – when I told him that story recently, he just looked confused, took another bunch of cards out of the Trivial Pursuit box that was sat on the kitchen table in front of us and carried on memorising them.

He's always been like that. The first summer he moved in next door, him and his sister, Emily, spent every Saturday morning having chocolate-milkshake competitions. Their mum would let them use the blender and they'd each try adding different ingredients to the Nesquik mixture – bananas, cherries, fudge, cinnamon, honey. Then Lex would put his hands over my eyes and I would have to test them and decide upon the winner.

The last time we did it, Lex was in the lead by two shakes when he put a carrot and tomato in and pretended that he'd severed his finger. Emily cried for an hour, but whether it was over the losing of the finger or the whole competition, I just don't know.

Now whenever I go over to Lex's at the weekends, we just hang around until he has to go off for training.

He's at county level for pretty much everything. He has a schedule stuck up on the fridge detailing his commitments, surrounded by clippings of his greatest triumphs, photos of him clutching cups and shields, dangling medals. It's easy to take the piss out of him for this, but Lex doesn't seem to mind. He just says that he wishes his mum wouldn't highlight all his top scores in pink.

He was even on the front cover of the local paper last month, below a story about a farmer discovering his entire herd of cows had been killed when the field they were grazing in was struck by lightning. I called him up straightaway when I saw it, and he said, "I've been upstaged by a load of dead cattle." "Yeah, I suppose so," I said, "but when you've got a photo of them on their backs with their hooves in the air like that . . ."

While I skin up, I glance through the window to the patio outside. They're all standing by the pool, with the girls twirling around on their heels, being handed bottles of beer and lit cigarettes by the boys.

I lick and seal the paper on the second joint, then put both of them behind my ear and slide the packets and Zippo lighter into my jeans pocket. I swing my legs out and gaze at my trainers with their dirty laces crossed three times around each ankle, then jump down from the side.

I think it's going to be pretty cold outside so I go into the sitting room and drag a blanket off the sofa, wrap it around me and then open the back door.

The girls are still on the patio, but are now tangled up on each other's laps on the plastic sunloungers that overlook the water, their coats slung over them.

The boys have drifted away and gathered on either side of the pool so they can drag the cover off. It rises like a dark wave.

Someone switches the underwater lights on, turning the water that fluorescent blue. Debris floats across the flat surface.

The girls rearrange their coats, complain about being crushed to death and discuss what perfume they are wearing.

I stay in the doorway.

The boys move on, to the far end of the garden, where they are lit up by the front of the pool house. They huddle together, talking something through, as though they've been given a question and haven't yet worked out the answer.

Then one of them steps forward, already stripped to the waist, his head bent down as he unbuckles his belt. When he looks up, it is Lex. I hadn't recognised him before because I'd never seen so much of him. So much skin.

His shoulders – they look somehow different to how I imagined they would. Broader. And his chest. He has his T-shirt in one fist and throws it over to one of the girls who have leapt off the loungers and are goading him on. Then he pulls at his belt and it slips through the loops. He unzips and starts to push down his jeans and I know I am the only one to turn away.

From the corner of my eye I can see Lou clutching his T-shirt and bringing her hand to her forehead in a mock faint.

And then I remember that I have seen Lex like this before – when we were kids and my dad used to take us swimming together. We went on a Sunday morning, if Lex hadn't already gone to Sunday school. I think about how I never wanted to get into the water, it was always so cold, but Lex would call for me from the middle of the pool where he was waiting, treading water. And then we'd play these games for hours. Doing handstands on the bottom, playing rock paper scissors, and putting our hands together as if in prayer just above the surface, pretending to be sharks ready for attack. We would time each other on how long we could hold our breath underwater and count how many forward rolls we could do non-stop. I did so many one time that I thought the bottom of the pool was the top and began to dive down, thinking I was going to be able to breathe at last. Lex had to pull me back up, his hand grabbing for the thin blue straps of my swimsuit.

Someone begins a countdown, and when Lex finally hits the water I watch him move silently back towards the house.

When he reaches the end he puts out both hands, pulls himself up until he is waist-high in the pool, shakes his head and gasps. Jake leans down to slap him on the back and Lex grabs hold of him and pretends that he is going to haul him in. They wrestle until it looks as though Jake's about to slide in.

Then Lex gets out and walks towards Tasha and Lou, dripping, his arms outstretched for a hug. They squeal and run away, so he turns around and falls back into the water, splashing all of those caught by the edge.

Most of the boys are stripping off now, although some of them are doing it so slowly that I think they're hoping everyone will have forgotten the whole idea and gone back inside by the time they're down to their pants. But eventually they nudge each other into forming a queue, with their hands placed over them like they're facing a free kick. Then they run and leap into the pool, to come up pounding the water with their fists.

I watch them do the butterfly, their arms spread wide and then brought together. Back and forth they go. Crawl. Butterfly. Crawl. Churning the water into foam. Then they wash up on the sides, bent over and struggling to breathe, unable to stop themselves from shaking. A few of them get out and sprint back to their abandoned clothes, their feet leaving wet patches on the stones.

Lex stays in. He is in the corner where all the girls have gathered. Tasha is with him, laughing and rubbing his hair, then flicking the water from her fingertips.

He grins then looks across at me in the doorway. I know that I am scowling at him. He frowns, runs his hand across the back of his head, then turns away.

"One last thing," shouts Jake, who is jumping up and down to keep warm. "Underwater lengths. Whoever does the most wins."

They line up by the pool house, along the edge: Jake, Lex and this other boy I don't know with black hair.

"Go, Lex," says Tasha, and slaps him on the shoulder.

Lou nudges Jane and they giggle into their scarves.

All three of them dive in and almost immediately they are at the side. I leave the house and walk down to the water.

"One."

They turn and disappear back into the shadows.

"Two."

And come back again with Lex just ahead of the others.

"Three."

And the boy with black hair is now slipping behind. He reaches the middle of the pool and emerges roaring into the night air.

Everyone runs past me to see the remaining two at the far end.

I see Jake's hand grabbing for the side, and he is up on the paving stones, coughing and retching.

"Four."

But Lex turns again. He pushes his legs hard against the wall, arms outstretched, then glides back. Halfway through, he seems suspended beneath the water. Unmoving.

All I can think about is how calm the surface has become. How still.

I look at the people around me.

"He'll be all right," someone says.

"Well, we'll know if he floats to the top," someone replies.

And then his arms stretch out in front of him and he is there.

"Five."

There is silence and then everyone rushes forwards and cheers.

Tasha is screaming his name.

And I am somewhere behind them all. And I think I know what to do. I empty my pockets and take off my blanket.

Lex has his elbows up on the poolside and is panting, trying to catch his breath. He is surrounded but I push my way past everyone to get to the front.

I stand right before him and he looks up. Leaves are stuck to his chest like dark handprints.

"So," I say, "you made it to five?"

He doesn't answer. He still can't breathe.

Someone behind me asks what the fuck I'm doing.

"You made it to five?" I say again, bending to roll up the bottoms of my jeans and untie my laces.

His face is so close to mine, I can feel his breath upon me.

"Yes," he says.

We look at each other and there is this moment where he seems to have only just recognised me. I smile. And he smiles back – the one that I have seen in all those photos, when he has won.

"Are you sure about this?" he asks.

"Yes," I say.

So he pulls himself out from the water and sits beside me,

shivering. Someone puts a coat around his shoulders. He is staring at me, and looking as though he doesn't know what to do.

Then he leans over and says, "Stella. Please let me."

He unpicks the knots on my laces, gently unwraps them from around my ankles and slips my feet out of my trainers onto the wet stone. It is rough like pumice. The edge curves around onto the water and for a second I let my toes slide in.

Then I tug at the button of my jeans. I unzip and peel them over my thighs, down my calves, and off the end of my feet.

"She can't really be doing this," says one of the girls.

No, I think. Not like this.

I hesitate, take hold of the bottom of my jumper, pull it right over my head and let it fall to the ground. There is nothing underneath. Bare skin. My ribs strain through. My nipples contract.

I don't hear anyone.

I just hear my own breath now. In and out. Slow. Filling my lungs with oxygen.

When I breathe out I can see it in the air. Like dragon's breath. Like when we used to walk to school together, and I used to try to hold your hand. Plumes of it.

I think about how long you can hold a single breath for.

I breathe out and take a deep breath in. I think about what I am about to do, and try to remember how it's supposed to feel. Weightless. I place my toes on the edge, lean forward and I am gone.

Then I feel myself burst through the cold sharp water, to the bottom of the pool. I feel shocked, hard. Alive.

I look around and for a second I panic. I didn't think it would be like this. Everything is so hazy. I remember it always being so clear below the surface, magnified, the black lines on the bottom of the pool, the regular white tiles.

I push my hands forward, then back, letting my fingers ripple through the weight of the water.

Patches of light bloom from the walls either side of me.

I glide on through. Push and pull. I think about making the movements slow and graceful.

I think about you, somewhere above me.

I count down the turns, one, two, but after the third I feel this pain deep between my ribs.

Everything is telling me to breathe, but I've got to try, try and resist.

And then it comes to me, sliding back into view, the game we used to play. Our favourite game.

I think about how we would stand opposite each other in the pool and shake hands before playing. It was always "Best of eleven". But of course I knew that if we got to eleven and you were losing you would argue again for best of thirteen, fifteen, seventeen. I remember how you would take my goggles from the top of my swim hat, the dark-blue one with the little silver stars all over it, and place them carefully over my eyes. "Breathe in," you'd tell me, and together we would. I'd look at you, with your eyes wide open, the dip in your stomach, and the swell in your chest.

Then we would descend into the water.

As I look ahead I can see us there now, floating cross-legged and facing each other, our arms behind our backs. I swim towards us. We are about to play. Rock. Paper. Scissors.

One movement for the one breath we have both taken.

"Everything you can imagine is real."

– Pablo Picasso

# The Fox
## FIONA MELROSE

I found a fox in a field, dead. I found him at the place in the land where the more prudent crops surrender to the deep, cracked clay, ploughed and then dried like a great adder's back. There lay the fox, dead.

The dogs sniffed him out, but finding no life in him and finding, too, his last great surge out of every orifice not worth investigating, they left him be. I considered strange this indifference from my pack, who, on a different day, would have run him down 'till his legs gave out.

I prodded him with my boot. He was still flaccid, and this being morning and early enough that I could still taste coffee on my breath, I knew for certain he had died in the night.

I kicked him over a bit more, half expecting to find bullet holes or the mottling of buckshot. I found nothing. No snare nor the bite of a predator that let him go free but kept just enough that he would bleed out in the clay. He was in handsome form and, apart from some swelling in his tongue and mud and shit around his rear, he was what you might call a fine fox. I leaned forward; my beard grated on my collar a touch. I examined his tongue a little more closely but even before I completed the investigation I decided to keep him.

I am not prone to hoarding the detritus of the natural world, apart from one autumn when I collected rabbit skulls that littered The Tops like bitter confetti. I was in a bad way then, and contemplating my passage to the grand hereafter formed a significant portion of my ruminations. The skulls were small and clean and offered neat relics through which to meditate the end of my life. Other than these, this fox would be my first trophy.

I decided to wrap him in my jumper, on account of the mud and shit. I escaped the old wool and laid it out like a great crucifix on the ground next to him, then lifted his front left leg and right hind one. He was weightier than I had expected. His nice arrow head rolled back as I lifted. He was an old boy; his undersnout was silver.

He clung to the earth; his back end in particular had conspired with the mud to create a big sucker. His arse seemed to cling to the clay like his life depended on it. Odd, considering the circumstances. I liked him for it.

I straightened up and whistled for the pack to follow. Two in the hedges, one rolling in something, one digging, one watching the digging, and Pup, sitting as usual a few yards from me, all lazy whiskers, gnarly toes, going nowhere.

It was well-nigh three miles home from where we were. The dogs were disappointed we were heading back already, but I didn't want to leave the fox out with the crows getting hungry. My pa had always said, "Funny birds, crows, cleaning up the dead like that. They'd have to have some sense of humour, crows." But I said, "It's their job, Pa. It's not about a sense of humour, it's about work. They take the meat to keep things clean and to eat." "Funny birds," was all he said.

In the end, when his bones were poking out his chest and he had more beard than breath, he passed, quiet and thoughtful, as he would. We had to get the undertakers then, but I did wonder if he'd have preferred the crows. When Dog died, on account of a broken heart those few days later, I took him for the crows, up there to The Tops. It's a good place for crows. They got stuck in to Dog. They cleaned him up in one swing of the sun.

By the time we reached the fences the fox was all lead so that he had weighted into my chest and rested heavy there. I passed the stables as a group of riders let their horses' bell hooves sweep forward towards the valley. There were four. I could see them eyeing up my woollen bundle; I felt greedy about my secret and hoped my fox's great tail wouldn't unfold from the wool and betray us both.

"All right, Midwinter?" the stocky rider said.

"All right."

"Been out walking?"

"Been out walking."

"Been colder. Nights drawing in."

"Mmm, drawing in."

I did think to get the mount he was sat on to tuck his great horse arse under him and migrate with some round and unexpected urgency. Instead, I turned for the cold room, a good place for a cold fox in need of lodgings. I left the pack to clean themselves and drink, and closed the room's door behind me, careful not to bump my fox's head, and leaned on the light switch with my elbow. In here, the light was always disappointing. Still. I lowered him onto the table, and I'm not too proud to admit, undid his shroud with some awkward tenderness. He was all brown and filthy, shedding bits of muck onto the steel top.

I fetched a bucket, filled it with half cold and hot, and got some sponges. New ones. I cut the corner off one and saved it to the side. I touched my fingers to his forehead. Yes, he was a fine fox. I started with the feet, dousing and bathing. His nails and pads showed he was hardworking and old, but strong. I fancied him quite brave. The muck ran in great tides down the side of the table and as I bathed him his colour began to reveal. Even under the light that cast my own shadow over him, his great cinnamon shape emerged. He was a big old fellow. His pelt was soaking from my sponges and made him seem smaller as it flattened with the weight of the water, but his form was still impressive.

I took some time to clean his back end and ran my flat hand the length of his spine to strip the excess water when I was done. I flushed out the bucket and wiped down the table so he lay on a great silver slab. Then I took the blue sponge corner I had saved, and filled and squeezed and filled it again under the tap. I leaned into my fox's face; our noses were nearly touching and his whiskers seemed to awaken in the space between us as my breath passed through them. I raised the triangle and passed it over his sleeping eyes. First the left, then the right. Upwards between his brows then back across one and then the other eye, making sure to clear any mud from the instep of each. I was holding my breath though I hardly knew it. Only when I was done did I breathe out, heavy and straight, so my fox let loose a drop of water from his sponged eye. I stayed there, bent over, nose to nose with him for just a little while.

I fed the pack and washed myself a little. Never too much. "No need to overdo it," Pa would say.

Drinking my coffee, my mind kept turning to the fox. I had all that fencing to fix and wood to cut, but something also needed doing with my fox. I did leave him awhile, busying myself with jobs, but then curiosity got the better of me and I went back out to the cold room.

The bulb hummed up to light. He had mostly dried, and the copper of him near winded me. He was crazy red, like a bonfire, blazing on the cool metal with the light hanging over him like that. It was then that I decided what to do with him. So, I laid out a square of cotton from the cupboard, nice and straight on the table beside him, then lifted my fox on top, making sure to keep him neat. He lay smartly on the linen, paws crossed at the ankles, though he was starting to stiffen a little. I made sure his ears looked good; you'd want your ears to keep their look about them if you were a fox, I figured. Same for the tail. These are the things that define you as a fox. I wrapped him up in the square, and tied the corners together to hold him safely in.

I had a long way to go. I could have slung him over my back; might have been easier, but it didn't seem right. So I held him to me, across my chest as before, and started to walk. Out past the horses we went, across the fields of early beets. Through the gates and across towards the woods. They were good, these woods; honest, too. No hocus-pocus like you get with some. I'm always hearing about woods with troubles. Trouble with the animals, trouble with wildings, trouble with this and that and all kinds of mischief. Not here.

A few times I spoke to the fox. Not loony talk, but I said, "Don't you worry, we'll be there soon enough," and "Oh, mind your head now," and sometimes, "Sorry about that," when I nearly dropped him on account of his weight and the uneven ground and the fences.

At the base of The Tops I sat for a rest, laying my fox down on the grass, still wicked green and deep, and mused at a rabbit skull sitting near the opening of a warren on the bank behind me. Force of habit meant I leaned back to retrieve it and put it in my pocket with my knife and smokes. My arms ached. I did take pause to question my objective but decided to carry on. There can be no half measures with this sort of thing. You need to do a good job of it.

"Come on then, we'll be there soon enough."

The last push before we got through to The Tops required some persistent exertion and by the time I felt we were where we needed to be I was all shaken and sweating. But I knew we were there and that was good. I put my fox down on the rabbit-shorn grass and sat with him awhile. Just sitting and thinking things through a little, as you do, and, I don't mind admitting, letting my breath come back to me in a regular way after the irregular climb. As a boy I would scamper up here every day, hunting creatures, finding this, hiding that. In one afternoon I'd be a pirate, a thief and a king, and I'd get home and Pa would say, "What you been up to, son?"

"Nothing," I'd say.

"Busy up there?"

"Not so much," I'd say.

He'd wink at me and I'd be cagey, say nothing. Then later, when I was eating Ma's stew, all hot and runny and sinking great big bread ships into the deeps, she would say, "Fine day out, dear?" I'd say nothing and shrug and Pa would wink again and I would have to think hard so as not to smile.

Up on The Tops time passes differently. So after a spell, and I couldn't say how long it was, I started to untie the fox from his bundle. I thought he looked a little shrunken but still magnificent. I lifted him off the square and placed him on the rock I had in mind, a nice wide slab. I laid him there and had a thought to cover him up with the linen, like a clean blanket over a sleeping pup. I folded it away to stop any of that. I suddenly felt cold. Up here there were snide winds that came right off the sea. The air could taste of salt come winter. I turned away from the breeze and so too my fox. I knew the crows would come and the longer I waited the longer they would, too, shuffling around on their starfish feet, restless for the feast.

When I got home, I let the dogs out and went to smoke on the wall that looks out over the paddocks and across the woods. I hitched my turn-ups above the tops of my boots so they could swing more freely. I like it still but easy when I smoke. I don't like distractions like chat. The tobacco is enough. I scanned the trees. My smoke was done, and a good one it was. Just enough. He was right, that rider; the nights would draw in soon enough.

# GJ 526.1 A
## DAVE WAKELY

I may not burn with the passion of a flaring sun. Not openly. No public displays. But I'm warmer than the heavens. That's what Adrian tells me. That he understands when I want to spend my birthdays in the old observatory, looking at the stars. Even naming one, once in a while.

Stargazing, everybody calls it. I would rather they said astronomy. Or astrophysics. Does it sound cold to be so pedantic about staring into the night sky and wondering? Spending the night alone with just the heavens for company, distant starlight falling like ancient rain. Wondering whether there's anyone out there. And who will find who first.

Adrian tells me he understands the quietness of it, the sense of discovery. He tells me he loves me, and isn't that the best attempt any of us can make at understanding? Who wouldn't love a man that can say that? The kind of man I never thought I'd snare.

Is that the right word? I didn't trap him. It's always been his choice. A gentleman, despite himself. When he protests, I tell him he must be: he obviously prefers blonds. My little ginger genius with skin as white as snow, but thankfully not as pure. It's our flaws that make us beautiful. How would he feel if he knew I was dreaming about a girl?

"I'm a real bundle of contradictions," he told me the second time we met. Even now I'm still making sense of him, finding new things.

"I'm a scientist," I told him back then, "I love puzzles."

I think that must have been when we both knew – decided two hearts really are better than one. The astronomer and the archaeologist, seeing the world through different lenses.

So here I am. Stargazing alone, as he calls it. In two hours' time, my birthday will begin. Forty-eight years old. He'll email me, remind me he's waiting at home for me, flirt with me. Say something like there's a heavenly body under the duvet, waiting for me to explore its surfaces. Tell me that planets get lonely when they're uninhabited.

Until then, there's just me and my telescope. And that damn song I can't get out of my head:

> *Am I glad my life turned out this way? Happiness is in
> my DNA.*

It's always playing in the bars on Friday nights. Our weekly indulgence: a drink or two in the Goose and a stroll along Canal Street to remind each other how we met. An hour or so with our own kind. Then home to celebrate having each other to go home with, not having to worry about slippery words like "community" or "family". Not needing to define them or defend them. Or defend ourselves. The odd jibe about isn't it past our bedtime, maybe, but it's just banter from the young ones.

The Gay Village, they call it now. It wasn't so jolly back then. No glitzy bars full of hen parties and straight girls being "modern". Back then, it was just rough. We tell them we fought in the wars for their freedom and we're only half joking, but we all laugh together. At least we're free to. We used to be warriors, street-fighters, although it was hardly a choice. Friday nights, a free punch-up with every fourth pint.

We used to call ourselves the Brotherhood of the Goose back then, always ready with the pool cues when the skinheads came calling. When the bootboys waited in the alleys for the bars to close. Ready for when the cops raided, looking to keep the arrest figures up. What was that you said, officer? Easy meat, was it?

A lot of us have fallen since then. I don't mention that planets can turn retrograde. The younger ones wouldn't understand. At least they don't call me Granddad yet. My skin's grown thicker over the years, but it's still sensitive. I only really cringe nowadays when someone says "breeders".

But that song . . . It's everywhere, becoming an anthem. A gentle swirl of electronics, and something in the background that sounds like Morse code. It's hardly there, but it's defiant, beguiling. Something about it just says, "Here I am. Proud." If I ever hear it somewhere quiet, maybe I'll try to make out the rest of the words, see why everyone's adopting it. One day, perhaps. No rush. It's just a song.

So now I have till six a.m. to run the calculations, check the tables and scan the skies. To find new stars. To be entirely selfish. I try to only think about you two days a year. That's what I allow myself. The day after tomorrow, you'll be twenty-five. If I get lucky, make a discovery, I'll name a star for you.

September 21st and 22nd. My birthday and yours. Our special days. The only thing that I didn't think through. That's why they chose me, your mothers. Because I was logical, rational. Being called Adam was just a bonus.

"Calm and intelligent," Livvy said. And Sasha agreed. She was going to be carrying you, didn't *she* get a say? Surely one of us should make having a baby sound like biology and not like manning the barricades. Calm and intelligent completed the square: the four of us.

I was the one who burrowed in the library, scoured microfiche for clues. No one could ever say you weren't planned. Space missions have been more casual. Livvy seemed horrified by it all.

"It's all so bloody technical," she said one night, till I reminded her that it was.

Love is biochemistry. Temperatures, optimum nutrition, sterilising the equipment. We weren't going to be allowed in a laboratory, so we were going to have to create our own.

I was even the one who named you. You're an acronym. Does that sound too scientific? Rob, Olivia, Sasha and Adam – Rosa. Sasha for earth, all things natural. The ecologist, the hippy-kid. The only one of us with parents who might ever approve. I wonder if she ever told them? Livvy for water. The music teacher, the yoga geek. The one who could find a flow to go with while the rest of us floundered on rocks or tilted at windmills. Rob for fire. The activist, the mechanic. Hands-on, and hands that needed to be busy.

And me? Pure air. Between the four of us, all the elements and all the disciplines . . .

God, that sounds like eugenics. OK, all the disciplines except convention. And I was the one who didn't think about his own birthday in the midst of it all. When Sasha realised, she said how much that suited me. And her. And you. To have *one* father who was modest.

That's how we thought about it: two mothers, two fathers. The biological mother would be known. That was going to be hard to avoid. A little beyond us. But the biological father wouldn't. Still isn't, even now. What would it change if we knew?

Two jam jars, a swizzlestick and a cocktail of possibilities. That was the deal, and I've been sensible. Stuck to it. Is that standing by my responsibilities, or running away from irresponsibility? I did it – we *all* did it – out of love. Like the best men do things. Or the finest criminals.

And it *was* love. Not a trace of lust, but I guess you know that much. Or *do* you? Two lesbians and two gay men, having a baby. In 1985. Because that's what your mothers wanted, more than anything. You *were* wanted.

"Fucking with stereotypes? Bring it on!" That's what Rob said when they asked us, the sweet dykes next door. We all laughed at that one. Well, at him, to be honest. Two or three mornings a week, there'd be a blue-eyed, brown-haired boy in the kitchen, struggling to button a checked shirt as I stumbled in to make coffee. Occasionally there'd be two, blushing at me and each other. At themselves. I could no more name them than count them, and God knows I couldn't tell them apart. Fucking with stereotypes, eh, Rob? Bless your memory, you red-haired madman.

No, you were conceived with love. Pipettes and sterilised jam jars, maybe, and thermometers and calendars, but with love too. It was certainly an unconventional Christmas present. But is *that* bad? You were conceived under a snow-covered roof, while Rob and I cooked your mothers' lunch. We'd delivered the present, apologised that we hadn't wrapped it or put our names on it. Not the faintest whiff of God, but enough goodwill for anybody. There was music and laughter. And hope, too. A lot of hope.

It almost didn't happen. I was laughing so hard at the music blaring through the wall from Rob's room I nearly *couldn't*. Some mixtape of club hits. I think the critical moment came halfway through *Slave to the Rhythm*, unless that was just him singing along. Thank Christ it wasn't Christmas carols. Can you imagine? *Oh come, all ye faithful . . .*

Rob said he reckoned he was conceived under the Menai Bridge and the influence of cider. That was his best guess, and his parents weren't telling. Weren't talking to him at all. If my childhood was any clue, I was conceived on a Saturday night under yellow candlewick and an air of unspoken duress.

We thought we were so radical back then, gathered behind our rainbow curtains. Kitchens always full of strangers meeting for some cause or other. Always rallying for this, fundraising for that. Protesting. Still are, in our own ways.

"You don't want to go inviting opinions." That's what Mum always said to me. About almost everything we – *I* – ever did. Maybe I just see the world through a wider lens than she did, but in my experience opinions don't knock and ask to come in. They gatecrash. Everybody's neighbours talk about them. Be honest, open. Leave the door ajar. Let them see the truth so the truth's what they talk about, that's how I see it. But not Mum.

So she never knew about you. I'm not sure she even really knew I was gay. I remember one evening she asked the usual mother's questions. Had I met someone? Was I seeing anyone? Would she ever be a grandmother – not that she *actually* asked that one. I remember I just said that if I believed in convention, I wouldn't be much of a scientist, now would I? We left it at that. At least the job at Jodrell Bank made her proud. Adrian thought it was rhyming slang when I told him.

After she died, my father told me he'd long since guessed. Worked it out.

"Why didn't you ask me? Say something?" I said.

"Oh, I didn't want to cause a fuss," he told me. "You know what she was like."

I wanted to tell him that a fuss is what you make about something that's wrong, that needs changing. Needs starting, or stopping. Not about things that are fine. That just are what they are. I didn't say a word, of course.

So, apart from the four of us, I don't think anyone's ever known about you. Not even Adrian. I swore I'd seal my lips, and I have. Anyway, aren't mysteries romantic? I hope so. Jesus, I don't even know if *you* know. Only that we decided you could know the story, but not the cast. OK, *half* the cast. If you asked when you were an adult, that would be different and we'd deal with it then.

By the time you were born, Livvy's inheritance had come through. They told us you were going to be raised in Portland. The City of Roses, not the city of rain. Livvy had no parents to run away from, but one long hard look at Manchester in 1985 was enough to make her mind up. Home is what you make it and where, and she didn't want it to be there. Not for you. Or for Sasha . . .

This is crazy. I'm sitting here imagining I'm talking to someone. Someone I know can't even hear me. Rational? Logical? Please, it's nearly my birthday. I'm allowed to fail occasionally, yes? Allow me my blemishes. Don't mark me more harshly than the others. Even the diligent fall short sometimes.

I know they told you about Rob. About him dying. I was so scared for you when he got sick. For months, all I could think was *What if?* I'd made him get tested before, swear to be safe. Told him we were giving someone life, not death. Even though I knew that safe is never really safe, just safer.

He knew that was what I was scared of. That I didn't want to tell him, add to his problems. And then one day, sitting on the ward, I just cried and said you were only seven – how could you deserve that? Or Sasha? Or *any* of us? We couldn't allow ourselves to believe that viruses might make judgements. That would be giving in, giving up.

He propped himself on his hospital pillows and showed me Sasha's letter, telling him she'd managed to get you tested, that you were fine. He loved the bit about the doctor, how impressed he was that you asked so many questions. That you didn't go running for the first comfortable conclusion, back away or hide behind her skirts. Just endlessly curious and wanting to know. Said what a wonderful little girl you were, that you must have great genes. Rob looked at me and said, "She sounds great, doesn't she?" His smile would have lit up half of Manchester.

I'm trying to hold back a tear just thinking about him. He was always so fearless, so fucking brave. Writing letters to councillors and organising fundraisers from his hospital bed, for as long as he could hold a pen, till those big bones had been whittled down to sticks. His spirit never got any smaller. "Dignity in all things," he whispered to me near the end. "Even Lycra."

I still remember how he laughed at that one. The wheezing shook him till I thought it was about to kill him. Not that he'd have minded. If there was a last laugh to be had, he was going to have it. Always so unafraid.

They tell me you are, too, Livvy and Sasha. I get the occasional update, little snippets to reassure me that you're doing fine. How you never let yourself get bullied at school. When the other kids tried picking on you for having two mums, you just wrote to the head teacher. Quoted the school charter at him, told him things needed to be done about it. Made a fuss.

Livvy told me that your first partner was a boy, your second a girl. You just said to her there are good people and bad, and categories are for books. That life isn't a library and we don't just borrow people. That whatever you were, you were happy.

Sasha told me that you sing like a bird. How, when you were twelve, you stood on stage on your own in front of a thousand people at a demo and sang a cappello. "She's all girl, but she's definitely got Rob's balls," she said. And I know you helped them make a square for the Aids Quilt for Rob when he went. "Robert the Braveheart, Queen of Manchester. 1963–1994. Best friend of everyone he met."

No photos, of course. I always said no photos. Keep the mystery intact unless you ask otherwise. Just a photo of the quilt. It's still in the hall, with a photo of Rob.

When Adrian saw it, he noticed Rob's picture first. Red hair, feisty-looking, gay . . . No wonder he leapt to conclusions. Made two plus two add up to – no, let's not think about that. I just said that Rob was "family". Laughed when Adrian cracked the old line, the one about how you can't choose your parents . . .

I told him he was no replacement. Spent all night explaining that wasn't an insult. That they were both unique, special. Completely different DNA. I told him I don't judge. I didn't tell him who I was thinking about twenty-five years ago, jam jar in one hand and cock in the other, trying to feel aroused. Some things it doesn't help to tell.

Let him who is without sin cast the first stone. That would put a stop to the fighting. Don't judge what you haven't experienced, haven't seen. I might have a telescope to see further than most people, but it only sees what I've chosen to point it at.

Besides, sometimes you only see what you were already looking for. Or maybe sometimes luck is on your side. What is it they say? The stars align? Tonight, all the mathematics and the computations, all the patience and the head scratching . . . Tonight, it all pays off.

The naked eye can't see it, but it's a pale orangey-pink through the telescope, right where I'd predicted. A young star, still quite small but already shining brightly. Twenty-five light years away, with four planets circling it, two of them further out than the others. One of them more remote, its atmosphere depleted.

A new star to christen in our local catalogue. You will be GJ 526.1 A. Although the scientists won't take any notice, won't give it any authority, I will name it Rosa.

I add you to the database. My third entry. One for Mum. One for Rob. A little anonymous present from me, like those books on science I used to send Sasha while you were growing up. Posted from London or Liverpool so you couldn't trace them. Couldn't trace *me*.

And now it's midnight. I can go back to gazing, to dreaming, to murmuring my secrets to the sky. To imagining how being forty-eight might turn out.

The computer bleeps softly. Adrian's email. Three minutes after midnight.

> *Happy birthday, my wonderful man. Just icing your cake and putting the cava in the fridge. And I've framed that picture of you in Lisbon that you really like and hung it in the bedroom. So now I can point my telescope at a heavenly body and dream sweet dreams. See you when you get home. Enjoy the music and enjoy the stars. A xxxxx*

There's a link. I shouldn't be clicking this, not at work. It wouldn't be anything horrendous, he wouldn't send that to me here. But we have policies. Things you live with and laugh at.

We used to have "don't ask, don't tell". It was OK to scan the skies for little green men, but I had to pretend the big pink ones didn't interest me. Management didn't ask, so I didn't say. But I could still look.

Hips can talk, and a walk can whisper. I don't need binoculars to know that one of the maintenance engineers is always looking back. One man's meat is another man's temptation and even in a boilersuit, a body can dance. Whenever he bends over a desk to update a log, the curves of Harry's arse write erotic poems in my head. I never read them out loud, but my eyes can answer. We may not be naked, but we're all apes.

Adrian sometimes tells me about the latest digs. How once in a while they find two Celts, buried side by side, hand in hand. Maybe even entwined, lying in each other's arms. Obviously both male. How the assumption is made that they were soldiers. Naked warriors who died together. Or brothers, perhaps. He tells me how people look at three-thousand-year-old skeletons and prefer to see fighters than lovers. Casting judgements on the past.

Even with a telescope, we don't really see. Those distant lights are ancient before they reach us. Even if the little green men could see us, sitting alone in their observatories late at night, they'd only see us in history. On horseback or in rough skins, firing muskets. Building stone circles and making sacrifices. Maybe they'd even see two Celts, lying down together. What would they make of that? Would they see carnage, or a kiss?

Fuck it. Just this once. Click the link.

A YouTube video. It's that song. He's noticed me trying to concentrate on it in the Goose. There's that swirl of electronics, and the screen is hazy with CGI graphics. Strands of DNA looping and pirouetting like ice skaters. It *is* Morse code, although I can't make it all out.

O . . . B . . . E . . . R . . .

The connection is slow and the playback judders. I miss a few letters.

V . . . I . . . A . . . S . . . A . . . S . . .

Below its far-off telegraph, just a steady pulse. And then the singer appears. Small, very pretty. Poised and composed. All in white, with long blonde hair.

> *Two and two sometimes make five, that's how come I am alive.*
> *Am I glad my life turned out this way? Happiness is in my DNA.*

I hit Stop. Without scrolling up, I know your name. It's Rosa.

Rosa1986. DNA. The only video you've posted. And the description just says, "For all my parents. Thank you."

I rewind, listen to the Morse code. It's our names. Robert. Olivia. Sasha. Adam. I've found you, without even looking. Or have *you* found me? All those years I've not traced you, tracked you down. Not made it easy for you to trace me.

And here you are.

I leave a message. Online I'm just Stargazer64. I can leave a note. Anonymous. Donate and walk away. That was the deal, and I've stuck to it.

> *You are a star: GJ 526.1 A*

I add a link to a picture of the constellation. A star map. *You Are Here.*

I listen to your song again, understand why the bars are all playing it. Nothing corny. Just obliquely questioning, standing its ground. Calmly knowing. And knowing so much.

The backdrop switches from a circle of fire to a stream to a field to the night sky. The constellation of Virgo. There's an orrery at your feet, a trowel, a book of sheet music, a spanner. A swizzlestick.

Behind you, in twos and threes, people walk hand in hand. Men. Women. Smiling and relaxed. There's not a scrap of self-pity. Just telling the world that it is what it is. And that it's beautiful.

Twenty minutes later, my note gets a reply.

> *Rosa1986: Dad?*

# Indecent Acts
## BARBARA BLEIMAN

## 1944

Pa's hardware store stood in Parow, at the far end of Main Road, the long thoroughfare stretching east to west across Cape Town that eventually came to be renamed Voortrekker Road, after the rugged, tough-minded Afrikaners who had settled the Cape. Parow, in those days, was quite a distance from the city centre, out beyond Woodstock, Maitland and Goodwood. Property was cheap and rentals easy to come by, so Malays and Jews, Afrikaners and English had started to crowd in, and the suburb was growing by the day.

On one side of the store was Irene's, the women's outfitters. It sold corsets and brassieres, blouses, suits and bright cotton frocks, the most glamorous of which appeared on two smiling, painted mannequins in the window. On the other side stood Krapotkin's butcher's shop, its large plate-glass window filled with pallid sausages, mounds of worm-like minced beef and lean joints of lamb hanging from silver hooks. A sticky yellow paper in the front of the shop was always black and buzzing with flies. Krapotkin was a large, pink-faced man, with hands as red and raw as the meat he handled and a voice loud enough to wake the cockerel himself. He was in the shop from early morning till late at night, heaving dripping carcasses and slapping bloody joints of meat onto wooden boards, slicing, chopping, grinding, sawing through flesh and bone, all the while singing, laughing and swearing so

145

loudly that my mother said Krapotkin and his butcher's shop would be the death of her.

The hardware store had a sign painted on the front, with "Neuberger's Handyhouse" in a clear, unfussy style. It stood a little apart from its neighbours, its whitewashed walls yellowed with age, its sloping tiled roof in some need of repair. On one side of the door stood rolls of carpet, stepladders and brooms. On the other were baskets filled with dishcloths and dusters, bars of waxy household soap and boxes of washing suds. A notice in the window said, "Everything you need, from soap and rice to chicken feed!" and "10% off for bulk bargain buys!" A faded red-and-white striped awning was pulled down every morning to provide shade from the hot midday sun and wound back up every evening when the store was closed.

My father, Sam, had bought the store nine years earlier, just before his marriage to my mother. I was born a year later. He worked all hours, either out the front or in the back yard, cutting wood or linoleum, measuring string, counting nails and screws, hanging up strips of biltong or weighing biscuits from the big glass jars that lined the counter. The hired girl, Ada, helped out while my mother moved between the kitchen, the back yard and the shop front, cleaning and cooking, talking to customers, and keeping an occasional eye on me.

* * *

One day Mrs Mostert came into the Handyhouse, bringing her son Terence with her. Terence and I had become friends, drawn together by such deep compatibilities as a love of Dinky cars, an interest in collecting matchboxes and a taste for sherbet dips. Mrs Mostert frequently came and fetched me from the store and took me back to the garage she owned, to play in the flat upstairs with Terence and keep him occupied and out of the way of the oily workshop and the restless bustle of customers and cars.

Standing next to his mother now, Terence was smiling at me broadly and tugging at his mother's arm.

"Ask," he said. "Please, Mama, ask." He flapped his arms up and down wildly.

Mrs Mostert laughed. "You look like you've just eaten a plate of hot and spicy bobotie, Terence! Calm yourself down." She turned to Ma. "Would Jackie like to come for a day out at the beach, at Hout Bay?" she said. "It'll be a long day, but he can sleep over at the garage so we don't disturb you coming back late. It'll give you a chance to have a bit of a rest. It'd do you good, I'm sure – you must be in need of a break, with the baby on the way." She paused. My five-year-old brother Sauly was looking up at her, his eyes big. "And Saul can come too if you like."

Ma placed one hand on her growing belly. She smiled.

"Both boys off my hands for a day . . . And no Sauly waking me up first thing in the morning. Boy, that'd be something!"

But then she saw my crestfallen face. Sauly was a nuisance; he cried and whined to join in all my games. If I refused, he went running to Ma to complain. If I let him play, he invariably spoiled things by ignoring the rules. It always ended up in arguments and tears and Pa or Ma would step in, crossly reminding me of my duties as an older brother and the expectation of greater maturity that rested on my shoulders. In one way or another, Sauly always managed to make trouble. And what's more, he was clearly becoming Pa's favourite, usurping the position that I had once held and now lost, seemingly for ever. Sauly was quick with his fingers, keen to help when Pa constructed paper aeroplanes or little balsa wood boats. He loved weighing and measuring, playing with all the little implements that Pa had made for me when I was small and in which I had failed to show any real interest. Sauly was not my favourite person.

Ma looked at me hard, then sighed. "Let Jackie go on his own. It'll be a nice outing for him. He deserves something good for a change."

Terence and I shared a conspiratorial smile.

Ma packed a little bag with a towel and my grey woollen swimming trunks, a pair of pyjamas and a toothbrush, Sauly all the while howling in the background, "Me tooooo, me toooooooo." I suddenly felt sorry for him and a bit ashamed at the delight I felt at leaving him behind. Should I tell Ma that I wouldn't mind if he came along? No. It was too good an opportunity to miss to be free of him, and free of the rest of the family as well. I didn't say anything.

Ma moved heavily over to the jars of biscuits on the counter.

She unscrewed the lids and filled a big paper bag with a good mix of the best ones. "For the journey," she said. My eyes were focused on the door, watching in case Pa came back in at any moment and caught her at it and said something embarrassing in front of Terence and Mrs Mostert, or worse still, found some reason why I could not go to Hout Bay after all. But Ma managed to hurriedly scoop up some extra fig rolls, drop them quickly into the paper bag and collect everything together for my trip to the seaside before Pa had returned from his errands.

Mrs Mostert gave Ma a quick squeeze on the arm.

"I'll bring him back safe and sound, tomorrow evening," she said, "I promise you."

Walter, the coloured mechanic who works for Mrs Mostert, is driving the Chevvy. I have got to know him well, from my trips to the garage. We have often sat and eaten lunch together at the kitchen table. I like Walter and enjoy his jokes and funny stories. Mrs Mostert is sitting beside him in the front seat. He is singing at the top of his voice, a jazzy tune.

> *Pack up all my cares and woe,*
> *Here I go, singin' low,*
> *Bye, bye, blackbird.*

> *Where somebody waits for me,*
> *Sugar's sweet, so is she,*
> *Bye, bye, blackbird.*

From time to time, Mrs Mostert and Terence join in. I sing along too, but only in my head, not out loud, and the words are a little different. Bye-bye, Cape Town. Bye-bye, the store. Bye-bye, Ada. Bye-bye, Ma. Bye-bye, Sauly. Bye-bye, Pa.

On the back seat, Terence and I are surrounded by bags, beach balls and striped towels. I look out the window as the houses of Parow and Cape Town flash by. Table Mountain looms up, a thin layer of cloud like white marshmallow hanging low above it; beneath it, the gardens of Kirstenbosch are lush and green, with proteas and rhododendrons in full bloom. Soon the buildings and houses thin out and are replaced by countryside: fig and loquat trees, orange groves, grassland, rocky boulders; shacks with corrugated iron roofs and dusty yards with petrol cans, old tyres, goats and donkeys; clumps of thin pine trees; an open, empty road; a leaping kudu; a black man and woman walking slowly, carrying cases on their heads, walking slowly from somewhere to somewhere, with the morning sun beating down on them; a single, candyfloss cloud; the dust of an open-back lorry filled with African labourers, who smile and wave as they go by; a man squatting under a fig tree with a small pile of over-ripe mangoes for sale; a large bird swooping down to catch a lizard in its beak; the wild squawk of seagulls. And then, at last – at last! – flashes of bleached white sand and foamy turquoise sea.

Walter parks the car and we carry everything out over the hot sand which burns my bare feet and makes me hop and skitter down towards the cooler wet sand near the sea. He sets up the big green umbrella, the towels, the picnic blanket and the hamper in a quiet spot, not too close to other bathers. There are coloured families sitting on the beach, under the "SLEGS NIE-BLANKES", non-whites only sign, making sandcastles and swimming in the sea, and there are white families, sitting in a different part, near the "SLEGS BLANKES", whites only sign, making sandcastles and swimming in the sea. We sit on our own, neither with the coloureds nor with the whites, in a strip of no man's land dividing the two.

Mrs Mostert splashes sun oil on Terence's nose and shoulders but not on mine. "You don't need it, Jackie, with your nice olive-brown skin, like a little Arabian prince."

Terence and I fight our way out of our clothes, flinging them down any old where, forcing our legs into tight, woollen swimming trunks, poking them in the wrong way, getting our toes stuck in our hurry to get down to the sea. We race out for our first swim of the day, plunging into the shallow waters and splashing wildly as the waves crash in and suck noisily back out again.

At midday Walter takes our lunch out of the hamper, which has been packed with ice to keep the food cold, and puts the dripping containers on the picnic blanket. He lays the sandwiches out on the plates and, with a sharp knife, slices up a large watermelon. It splashes pink juice and pips onto the white linen cloth that the sandwiches have been wrapped in. He opens cold bottles of fizzy drink, which hiss as he pulls the lids off with his teeth. My drink tips up in the sand and it bubbles and trickles away before anyone can right it. Tears are coming but Walter only laughs and reaches into the hamper for another. Terence giggles. I smile shyly and take a big gulp of soda that explodes in my mouth, like the froth of a sugary sea.

Walter sits down on the big picnic blanket and opens a bottle of beer for himself. I watch him. He helps himself to sandwiches. He is in his swimming trunks, legs stretched out, toes in the sand. He is sturdy, though not especially tall. His arms are strong and muscular, his skin hairless and dark brown. The hair on his head is short. It is springy and black, with just a fleck of grey here and there. His mouth seems to take up most of his face, his teeth a little crooked but white against his dark skin.

I look at Mrs Mostert. She too is watching Walter, a thoughtful little smile on her face. She is plump and pale, soft and large as a cream bun, rolls of fat appearing at the top of her bright-blue swimming costume. Her hair is unpinned from its usual knot, and tangled from the salt and the wind. Without her usual dusting of face powder, her nose and cheeks are spattered with freckles. She's not the same Mrs Mostert who collects me from the Handyhouse in her tidy skirts and dresses, or the business-like woman who serves customers at the garage. Everything about her has loosened, expanded, softened.

After lunch, Terence and I build sandcastles and dig ditches, then run back into the sea, splashing in the shallows, while Walter and Mrs Mostert lie on their towels and doze, close to each other, sheltered by the big green umbrella. The warm seawater rises up and washes over me. I wonder what Sauly is up to at home and am glad that he hasn't come. No Sauly, no Handyhouse, no Pa.

Terence finds a large piece of driftwood, gnarled and knotted and bleached white by the salt of the sea. He wants to show it to Walter, to ask if Walter can carve something out of it with his knife. We run back along the beach, scanning the umbrellas for the big green one that signals our place on the sand.

As we get close to the umbrella, I see that Walter and Mrs Mostert are not alone. They are both sitting up straight, and two men, fully dressed in short-sleeved shirts and cotton trousers, are standing in front of them.

"Stay in the sea," shouts Mrs Mostert, but we are already out of the water and running up the beach to see what is going on.

"Stay away, boys," calls Walter and then, more sternly, "Don't come closer."

Terence and I hold back. We stand where we are, watching, unable to go either backwards or forwards. Now Walter gets up from his towel and places himself in front of Mrs Mostert, standing between her and the men. There is shouting. There are bad words.

"*Pasop*. Watch out, you blerry kaffir-lover," one man is yelling at Mrs Mostert. "We're gonna donner you and that coloured bastard of yours." This man is tall and thin, with an angular face and a long jaw. His face is red with fury.

The other man, smaller and fatter, with large sweat stains on his shirt, is yelling too. He's holding a big stick that he is swinging towards Walter, only narrowly missing him each time, like he's playing a game with him. Walter looks about to see if anyone will come and help them. On towels, stretched out, or under their umbrellas, people are reading their books or sunning themselves. Children are playing ball or digging in the sand. Everyone sitting close by has turned away, facing the sea, or looking towards the ice-cream kiosk and the café in the distance. No one acknowledges that anything is wrong.

Terence is trailing the large piece of driftwood behind him. I wonder if I should grab it and run and hit the men with it. I could bash them on the legs, whack them as hard as I can, hit them and hit them till they run away. But I don't move. I just stand on the sand watching. The tears are coming and I can't hold them back.

The man with the stick prods Walter, stabs at his feet, as if poking at a crab to make it close up tight inside its shell or scuttle away in fright. Walter stands his ground but makes no move to stop him. I don't understand why. Why doesn't he just grab the watermelon knife from where it's lying on the cloth and use it to defend himself? The man grips the stick more firmly. He grunts as he takes a bigger, faster swing which arcs towards Walter, whipping his legs so that he flinches. And now the other one, the thin one who up until now has just stood and shouted, joins in, punching Walter in the face so that he falls back heavily onto the picnic blanket. He falls into the plates and leftover sandwiches and overturns the hamper. Mrs Mostert screams. At the sound of her voice, the two men casually turn away and stroll off down the beach, as if enjoying the fine weather and a relaxing day at the seaside. One whistles as he walks. The other laughs.

Mrs Mostert is weeping and now faces from nearby are turned towards us, watching. But no one moves from their places under their umbrellas. They just sit and stare.

"Don't worry, May. It's OK. I'm all right," says Walter, dabbing at his mouth, testing the damage. He spits out a single, bloody shard of broken tooth and holds it out on his hand. Mrs Mostert passes him the white linen cloth and he presses it to his face to stop the bleeding.

He looks anxiously towards Terence and me, to see if we're OK.

"Let's pack up, boys. It's time to go home."

Slowly we collect everything together and put down the umbrella. Walter carries most of the bags but we help with the buckets and spades and beach ball, which we hand to Walter to put in the boot of the Chevrolet. He takes out the little plastic plug and squeezes the ball, allowing the air to slowly exhale, till the ball is a flat, flabby circle, hardly recognisable any more.

In the car, Mrs Mostert is sniffing into her handkerchief. From time to time Walter pats her knee gently.

"We're OK," he says. "No real harm done. We'll be fine when we get back to Parow."

Terence, who has been sitting quietly next to me, asks, "Who were those two men?" and his mother says, "Just nasty men, silly men. Don't worry, we won't ever see them again."

"Your face is all puffed up," she says to Walter. "Does it hurt a lot?"

"It's OK," Walter replies. "A pity all the ice melted. It would have been good as a little ice pack to keep the swelling down."

"You want to go back home, Jackie, instead of coming to stay the night with us?" asks Mrs Mostert kindly, twisting in her seat to look at me. "You upset by what's happened and want to be with your ma?"

I shake my head. "I want to stay the night with Terence and you," I say.

"Good boy," says Mrs Mostert. She turns back, to face

forwards again. There is a little pause. Her voice is light, breezy, but I sense something important is being said. "Perhaps don't tell your ma and pa about what happened, then, eh? No need to worry them with nonsense like that. Better for them not to know. We're all fine, aren't we? All done with now. I'll make a nice chicken pie for supper when we get back and it'll all be forgotten."

I nod my head. All will be forgotten. All will be forgotten. Nothing will be said.

When I got back to the store the next day, Ma asked me how the trip went.

"Was it fun?"

I nodded.

"Did you swim a lot?"

I nodded.

"Did you eat a nice picnic?"

"Yes."

"Did Mrs Mostert drive you there?"

"No."

"Oh," said Ma, surprised. "So who drove you all that way to Hout Bay? Not Mr Mostert, I suppose. He's still sick in the sanatorium with tuberculosis from what I've heard. Been there for months now."

"Walter."

"Walter?" said Ma. Her face flushed red. "I didn't know Walter was going with you to Hout Bay." There was a moment of hesitation and then, "Does Walter often go on trips like this with May Mostert?"

I shrugged.

"Is he around with you a lot, when you go to visit Terence at the garage?"

I said nothing.

"Does he sit and eat with you at the table, for instance?"

I nodded. Was that the right thing to do?

"And come and go in the house as he pleases?"

I looked at her and said nothing. Why did this matter? Why was Ma asking all these questions?

"How friendly is he with her? With Terence?"

I shrugged.

"What on earth is going on between May Mostert and Walter?" Ma said under her breath.

"Ma, is Walter Mrs Mostert's other husband?" It was a question I had often wanted to ask and it didn't seem to me to be a dangerous one. I didn't think Ma would mind and since I couldn't ask May or Walter or Terence, Ma seemed like my best bet. She would know.

Ma frowned. "What sort of question is that?"

I went on, undeterred. "Is Walter Terence's pa?"

"Of course not, silly boy. What put that into your head? Walter's coloured. He's the paid boy at the garage. How could he be Terence's father? Terence is white and Walter's a kaffir. And anyway, it's none of your business. That's something for you to think about when you're a big boy, not now."

There was a little pause.

"Was everything nice at the beach, Jackie? No problems or anything?"

I nodded vigorously in response to her first question and shook my head firmly to her second.

Mrs Mostert had told me not to say a word. I had followed her instructions. Whatever trouble she wanted me to deny, whatever revelations she was anxious to prevent, I felt sure I had succeeded in doing as she said. I'd not given anything away. As far as I was concerned, Ma was none the wiser and I had done my job of staying silent. Ma's frowns and questions didn't worry me too much. May Mostert had asked me to keep a secret and I was pleased I had managed to achieve that.

# The Twins of Whiting Bay
## JACKIE KAY

They say a dog can hear it a mile off, and it is true my dog was already trembling under the wooden table in the kitchen before the thunder even began its strange and haunting music. Then later, when it boomed and cracked and rolled, as if crying out for war, my dog shook all the more, as only an animal can truly understand the dark threat of thunder. It growled from afar, as if it came from the past itself, then, nearer, closer to me, as the stranger was trudging his way through the gorse on the rough paths along the coast, climbing stiles and staggering through scrub woodland, past the ruins of the old Viking Fort, then stumbling on the stony beach, though I didn't know that then. I'm coming to understand that *what* we knew and *when* we knew it so preoccupies us human beings, it may even be *the* thing that defines us.

I stroked my dog, and said, "It's only thunder, *dinny fash*," but it was as if she knew better; as if she could smell her own death from a long way off. She rumbled at it and the thunder growled back; could she possibly have sensed danger? "Good dog," I said, and patted her black and trembling head.

I was already thinking, as I listened to the heavy rain beat against the tall trees outside our small house, as I watched the wild water swoosh across the window, that it would be terrible for anyone to be "out in the weather". The black rain made the day darken early; it seemed like evening in the afternoon when the

155

stranger arrived at our door.

I can't say that I was frightened when he appeared. I had already told myself I had nothing to fear but fear. My husband and I had an arranged marriage, which I knew for some could bring a portion of happiness, but for me it brought none. My husband was heavyset and had a heavy mind. He was a staunch believer of the Wee Free variety (the name was ironic to me) though he never seemed to believe in kindness. We had both been brought up in the church by the devout people who raised us in this miniature Scotland and been picked to marry and I hardly blamed him and I didn't blame myself. The only comfort I took was in thinking that, in a loveless marriage, at least I knew where I stood. There were no singings of love songs in my ear, no small dances round the hearth, no need to wonder how to put loving words on paper. No words, really – just an abiding sense that we would always be strangers in our own home.

So when the dark stranger appeared at the door the day of the wild storm, with his thick black hair wet through, and his clothes soaked, I expected my dog to bark. She preferred women to men and always barked at strange men. But to my astonishment, my dog licked his hand, a treat she saved for special people. He patted her and said "Good dog," as if he'd known her all his life, and he sat down at the table and put his head on his hands. I realised I was frightened then, actually. I was frightened he might die. There was something in his face I recognised, though it took me a long time to realise what it was. And looking back, I couldn't help go over and over that first moment as if hindsight was something a person could seek. I'd say to myself in an almost inane way, *So, go back a bit. What happened first?* "It was a stormy night." And I felt as if I was telling my story to the one police officer on the island. "It was a stormy night, Officer. I opened the door of our cottage and a man stood there. A complete stranger"– I paused on the word "complete" – "and yet looking back, there was something about him that was so familiar." *What then?* And I'd answer as if I was telling my story to the only vet on the island. "The strange thing was my dog didn't bark and yet she usually barks at strangers." *Next?* And I'd answer as if I was telling my story to the only doctor. "He was sick, Doctor. He was exhausted, his clothes were soaked through, and he looked as if he was at death's door."

*And yet?* And I'd speak as if I was speaking to one of the many poets on the island. "And yet, the minute I saw his face, though he was a stranger, I felt as if I saw my own face mirrored in his."

And then, I'd stop the business of telling the story to the islanders in my mind because I knew the story would be out for real before I got a chance to tell a single soul: folk from Corrie, Brodick or Lamlash; from Whiting Bay to Blackwaterfoot; Lochranza to Sannox would know what had happened and the next time I went out somebody would be sure to say: "I heard . . ." People here were always hearing something. It seemed stories got carried by the wind and the rain, planted in the ground just as surely as if they were seeds, seeds that would take root and become trees, trees that would grow tall as plane or pine, that would fill the place with the smell of the story, like the smell of eucalyptus.

Oddly, I was thinking before the stranger arrived that I had nothing to fear. I couldn't fear anybody stealing from me because nobody stole anything on the island; everybody left doors open. I couldn't fear illness because part of me didn't want to live. I couldn't fear my own origins, since I knew so little. I knew I'd been born a twin; that my twin brother, Strachan, whose name came from the place itself, had gone to the mainland. I knew that my father had upped and left, just as suddenly as a selkie might leave her man, and the story was, that he'd left his hunting furs behind and rowed off in the dark, past Ailsa Craig and on to Ardrossan. "He was a powerful man, your father," people told me. I couldn't fear my family because I was brought up with woodcutting folk in the conifer woodlands of Glenashdale Falls, not far from the Giants' Graves. And though I did probably fear my husband, his tempers and his mood swings, his dark sarcasm and his forbidden desires, his contrite bouts of reading the Bible aloud, I tried not to give him power. And to be honest, I had spirit enough in me. I must have been my father's daughter. I had a gleam to my een; I knew it. Sometimes, I'd imagine I was a selkie, and I'd spend hours hunting for my skin, convinced my husband had hidden it to prevent me returning to sea. But I never found a seal's skin, and I'd have to laugh to think how desperate my marriage was. "Look at you, preferring the idea of being a selkie to an ordinary wife," I'd say on rainy days when I stood in front of the mirror and tried to imagine me as a semi-aquatic marine mammal, sleek-skinned, barrel-bodied. (That was the hardest thing, the barrel body, for I am quite trim and folk sometimes say on a summer's day, "Look at you out in your figure." Well, that happened once!)

Our house was a plain house, a whitewashed cottage with a slate roof that had stood the island's rages from the sea for years. It was a former croft. It nestled in the hills above Whiting Bay and you could see the sea in its seasons' tempers from the square windows. In the middle of our living room stood an ash tree. It was peculiar and the house had clearly been built around it and we never had the heart to pull it up. Well, I didn't have the heart and my husband didn't have the nerve. Though he was God-fearing, superstition ruled him more than anything. The tree stands, he'd say. The tree stays. I often thought of the tree as a silent witness, one that had stood stock still before the croft was built, stone by silent stone, around it, till the slate roof closed in. My husband, Halbert, once told me, gruffly, that the name Halbert meant long and shafted axe! I thought he was cracking a rare joke, but no. Long and shafted axe! Halbert was barely five foot six, and fat. But bedded deep in the tree *was* an old axe, perhaps belonging to a Viking.

That afternoon my husband was out at his butcher's shop in Brodick. Since I married a butcher I'd fair gone off meat, and not a rump steak or a T-bone, a sirloin, a tenderloin, not a rib eye, not a pheasant, partridge, primal cut of pork, nor some of his own sausages, especially some of his own sausages, not even a square sausage, could tempt me. And to think there were people envious of me being the butcher's wife! I once looked up the word in the dictionary and one of the meanings suited my husband well enough: butcher – one that bungles and botches. He'd say, "You dinny know your luck being married to a butcher," when I'd called in. *Look at him – standing proud in his bloodied butcher's apron with his sausage fingers!* And I'd say quietly, "No, I wouldn't know luck if it came and slapped me in the face," aware that the village was listening and he'd look at me swiftly to see if he could catch anything, but he couldn't. Though I saw Sam MacFarlane look guy awkward and Jessie Clarke look as though she was in on a joke. He wasn't quick enough and I was too fly. It infuriated him; a butcher with a veggie wife might as well be impotent. I gave Welsh lamb to my dog, Valkyrie, who wolfed it down, devoted love in her dark espresso eyes, all pupils and no white, such love that I wished I'd been raised by wolves.

Late afternoon, the stranger comes to the door, spent, looking as if he'd been put through the wringer, and yet, Officer, looking so familiar. I sat him by the hearth and poured into the quaich a small measure of Arran malt, and he sipped the nippy dram gratefully and said he must be on his way. "I only bring bad luck to people," he said. "Stay where you are," I remember saying. "Bad luck can't be brought into a house where bad luck already resides." I gave him a bowl of my vegetable broth, which he was glad of. He supped his soup and looked at me and at the kind log fire and I told him to take off his wet boots, to make himself at home. And he said – uncanny this, for his words chimed with my thoughts – he said, "I already feel at home." "That's good." I smiled. "And where do you hail from?" And he told me a long story about a man from Kilmarnock who was after him and so he'd caught the MacBrayne ferry over to Brodick, hoping that the sea between them would throw him off. But on the ferry, he'd suddenly felt very sick. "Don't use up your strength talking to me," I said. I wanted to say, "We have the rest of our lives to talk," but I didn't, for I saw the same thought flicker across his face.

My dog settled herself down and lay at Strachan's feet; she'd found a new master to flirt with, and he looked as though that was a comfort. And he fell asleep at the table with his head on his hands for a dream-like time. And as he sat there, the years seemed to fall away from him and I imagined him as a little boy with thick curly black hair sat at the table with his head on his hands, and myself a little girl, sat there too. And I put my head on my hands and drifted off also to the sound of the rain on the slate roof, comforting now, and the soft snores from my dog and Strachan's shallow breathing. And it felt as if we were all in a fairy tale, a lovely one where we had found our small croft and our bowls of broth and nobody was coming to get us, or put us out into the forest, or make us push our fingers though bars. Time slowed down then; the trees outside swayed and swished and swooned. In my dream, the ash tree inside the house suddenly flowered and filled with light; the green spear leaves appearing glamorous in winter.

It was a shock, then, to open my eyes and see real spring flowers actually outside the window. The meadow was a spread, a banquet I'd have only expected in May to June – in front of my eyes a feast of red campions, daffodils, bluebells, wood sorrel, wood anemones, pink purslane, in the dead mid-winter.

I woke to them, woke to the promise of bluebells, to the hope of the red campion, and my heart lifted and the light streamed in and Strachan's lips were suddenly on mine and we kissed a kiss of sorrel and bluebell before the sorrow ever came. And looking back, Officer, I was glad of that. I was glad of that kiss even though I had worked out by then, by the answers he gave to my questions, that Strachan was my long-lost twin brother and I, Shona, his sister. Before the sorrow came, we had that kiss, and I can't say simply that it felt like I was kissing the love of my life, though it did, but it felt even more natural than that; it felt like I was kissing my own true self, the one I'd lost. Strachan arrived, complete stranger at my door, complete, and for a small moment in time, he gave me my self back; the girl who had years earlier been lost along the seashore, where the seals could often be seen on the rocks. I didn't want the moment to end. I didn't want the butcher to come home and find us. I didn't want the axe to be pulled from the ash tree. I wanted never again to be separated from my twin, my soul, myself.

I remember: I gathered my courage and my few things. My plan was to leave the croft before Halbert got back. But first, I wanted something I'd never had, a small dance round the hearth. I danced with Strachan; I was singing to him an old Burns song, *Ae fon kiss and then we sever, Ae fareweel and gone for ever*, when I heard the front door crash open. Halbert stared at Strachan a good while, unsettled by our uncanny resemblance, and shouted, "Who the hell are you?"

I was too late, Officer, I heard myself saying to the only policeman on the island. I hadn't seen my father for years. My dog tried to defend Strachan, that was the strange thing, barking like a banshee, I heard myself saying to the only vet on the island. He'd lost all his strength, maybe he'd even lost blood, Doctor, I said. Ah, but I loved, I said, to one of the many poets on the island. And love, even for the briefest time, holds up a mirror to the soul, a candlelight to a croft window, an osprey to a sliddery water foot, a sea song to a selkie, water to a fell, a fell to a goat, a fairy to a dell, a leap in the dark, faith, the small beating of my heart.

# The Meadow of the Bull
## DESMOND BYRNE

They managed to get out to the Bull Wall eventually. It had taken some doing to get Fintan out of the Yacht but Niall had persisted; he'd assured Olga that the children would get some air and a run around the beach before they went back for dinner, that they wouldn't stay in the pub long at all. Neville was just a soft bundle in his little new coat and his wool hat with the peak, feeling heavier to carry on your arm but not liking it up on your shoulders, squinting and smiling into the wind and the sun and Niamh charging up and down in her bell shaped check coat and red tights, her lop-sided gallop, feet kicking up behind her. She had wanted to go out as far as they could on the Bull Wall itself before going down onto the beach and though Niall was worried about the time, he had agreed. He was worn out by Fintan and even the thought of Niamh starting to act up was exhausting.

There were families and couples out walking, people with dogs. Niall noticed how Fintan drew the glances of those they passed. He looked even more striking now than he had before he went to England, his upper half filled out, the chest, the thickening of the neck. Strands of hair falling across his brow, blown by the wind; the expensive looking suit. Fintan had left his overcoat in the car and in the light, Niall could see that the suit, which was steel grey, was shot through with fine green thread that shone here and there as it was caught by the sun. There was a name for it, that type of material. Niall couldn't remember it, Olga would know though. Well tailored and well made, Niall could tell. Not even his *good* suit would be as expensive. Fintan was still talking about the boxing gymnasium. The big "darkies", Victoria Park something. Steaks. Eggs. He had turned his collar up and his jacket was misshapen on one side by one of the half bottles he had brought from the car and carried in the hip pocket. Niall had been alarmed at the extravagant takeout Fintan had insisted on buying to have with lunch and he was no less concerned now with the impression they might make drinking whisky from the bottle on a Sunday afternoon. They passed the bottle between them, Niall glancing about, dipping his head for furtive sips, Fintan taking long brazen draughts followed by contented gasps and flexing of his lips.

When they reached the end of the path, Fintan and Niamh continued down onto the half tide wall and capered about on the rocks. Fintan's leather soles slipped and slid and he amused Niamh with elaborate crouching and rocking and windmilling arms.

"Come on and we go out to the end Niamhy," he said. "I can roll up me trouser legs and give you a jockeyback out to the lighthouse."

Niamh looked up at Niall, her feet pressed together on the slanting surface beneath them, legs quivering for balance.

"Can I Daddy?" she said.

"No love, don't mind him, he's only coddin'. C'mon back up and we'll go down to the beach," said Niall. He was anxious to get them on to the beach now, where there would be, hopefully, less people. They walked back and were about to take one of the curved tracks that led from the path down through the dunes, when Fintan stopped and peered across at a man and his teenage son who were sitting on one of the benches. Niall had noticed the pair when they passed them earlier, with their binoculars and text book and notebooks spread out between them; the father a type Fintan would make fun of with his beard and cravat, a *Fáinne* in his lapel, and at whom for an anxious moment he had cast an examining glance then turned away, seemingly, mercifully, disinterested. Now he took halting steps toward them, craning his neck, making a show of diffident curiosity. Niall considered, for a moment, simply continuing on down to the beach with the children and leaving him to it, but instead hovered about at a nervous distance hoping to discourage him from lingering too long.

"What are youse at chaps?" said Fintan. He took up a position at the end of the bench, a buttock perched on its back and a foot planted flatly on its seat next to the boy.

"Bird –" The boy adjusted his position to look up at Fintan. "Birdwatching." He spoke nasally, his tongue tapping against large prominent teeth.

"Very good," said Fintan. "We all like to keep an eye on the birds don't we?" He leaned into the boy, winking, open-mouthed, the mien of gormless curiosity abruptly dropped.

The boy stared, slack jawed; the father forced a smile but his narrowed eyes regarded Fintan coldly.

"Right," Niall announced. "Come on and we get down to the beach because we haven't long before we have to get back for our dinners." He nodded round-eyed emphasis to Niamh and adjusted Neville's position on his arm.

"Can I've a go of your binocks?" said Fintan with a sheepish wince.

The man gave a shallow nod of consent and the boy passed the binoculars to Fintan. He stood, his foot remaining on the bench, back arched, and with frowning caution passed the narrow leather strap over his head.

"Little bit of sun today. For a change," Niall ventured, edging closer.

"Indeed, yes," said the man, glancing curtly at Niall.

Fintan gripped the binoculars evenly; he held them to his eyes and stiffly pivoted his torso back and forth.

"Is that a . . . " he said, urgently leaning into his gaze. He brought his foot to rest on the ground, dropping into a half crouch. "Ah no, it's not," he said, straightening up and relaxing. "It's not." He held up the binoculars again, on his fingertips now, and made a languid arc from the docks, over the bay, coming to rest facing the length of the Bull Wall.

"So it's a good spot is it?" said Niall. "For the birdwatching?"

"The island is a treasure trove," said the man, releasing an amused sigh.

"Right yeah." Niall felt himself colour. "Of course, the island."

He glanced back at the beach. "Do youse live in the area then?"

"We do yes, on the coast road, nearer Sutton."

"Oh lovely. That's lovely up that end. We've just bought a house in Clontarf, just over beyond here like." Niall thumbed the air over his shoulder.

"And where were you before then?" said the man.

"Well my wife is from Howth originally but the last couple of years we've been up in eh . . . up beyond in . . ."

"Menaw," said Fintan.

"Pardon?" said the man.

"Menaw." Fintan lowered the binoculars and nodded in the direction he had been looking. "Down there on them yokes, the eh . . . things for gettin' changed in."

"The bathing shelters."

"That's it yeah, the shelters. Menaw, it says. And fear." He looked through the binoculars again.

The man glanced in the direction of the shelters and back at Fintan.

"That's right," he said, "*fir* and *mná*. It's –"

"What kind of name is that for women?" said Fintan. "I mean menaw, y'know? Honest to God." He lowered the binoculars and let them hang on his stomach and sunk his hands into his trouser pockets. "Menaw." The man made to speak but Fintan continued. "I mean you'd know an' all," – he nodded at the *Fáinne* – "with the oul' *Gaeilge* an' that. Sure I can't remember a word of it."

"I only speak the language, I didn't create it." The man blinked rapidly and made something like a smile, lips stretched and pursed.

Fintan's expression darkened, he squinted at the man then looked blankly away, his head tilted in concentration. The man shifted on the bench, crossing and uncrossing his leg, fidgeting with one of the notebooks in front of him.

"Listen Fintan," said Niall, "we should get these two –"

"I tell a lie," Fintan said, brightening, pointing stiffly at the man. He stood to attention and held up his hand. "An will cad agum dull guh dee an lea'haras, maw shea do hull ay. J'member Niall? Them oul' nuns."

"Oh indeed'n I do, yeah. You wouldn't put a foot wrong would you. So anyway, Fintan –"

"Menaw," said Fintan. "No wonder y'never get a ride ou've any of them wha'?"

"Come on Donagh," said the man. "We should get on. Pack up the things."

The boy began gathering up the notebooks and putting them into a satchel.

"I'm only actin' the maggot for fuck sake," said Fintan.

"Do you mind not using that kind of language in front of my son please." The man stood up, held out his hand and nodded at the binoculars on Fintan's stomach.

"I'm only havin' a laugh with youse. An' I'm sure Donagh's heard worse from his mates at school. Isn't that right Donagh?" Fintan winked at the boy who grimaced meekly, his neck melting into his shoulders.

"If you wouldn't mind please." The man held his open hand in front of Fintan.

"Yeah all right." Fintan lifted the strap over his head. "I'd love a pair of these, take to the oul' gee-gees." He clicked his fingers sharply next to his ear, the index pointed upwards. "That's another one I remember!" He began to sing, keeping time with the raised finger and the binoculars, loosely held in the other hand. "Trup trup a capaleen air on mohair. J'member, Niall, how does it go? Trup trup a capaleen air on mohair, shule go bra agus sudder go ray. J'member it? J'member the bit at the end?" He pushed his tilted face closer to the man's. "Trup trup, trup trup, trup trup trup." Fintan offered the binoculars and they held each other's gaze as the man took them.

"Right, grand. We'd better be gettin' on ourselves," said Niall, "get this pair down to the beach – the island. Are you right Niamh?" He held out a hand to Niamh who was standing by Donagh, watching him arrange the satchel, sash-like, over his shoulder.

As they walked away, Fintan made a face at Niall and Niamh: a little turned down mouth and his eyebrows high, rocking his head from side to side. Niamh stared up, studying the face, about to smile but glancing back at the man and his son who were heading out on to the Bull Wall.

Down on the beach, Niamh found a bit of a crab but she was afraid to touch it. When she showed it to Fintan he immediately picked it up and chased her. She tore off, falsetto screams and gurgling laughter and pleas, slowing down and looking back to make sure he was still after her. She circled and dodged until Fintan shouted solemn promises, stooping with the mangled fragment held at arm's length between forefinger and thumb, a great show of dropping it back on the sand, then pretending it had come to life and pinched him, resuming the chase.

Near the edge of the water Niall put Neville down on the damp, darkened sand and let him walk. He made little abrupt dancing steps and Niall hunched behind him, guiding him with fingertips on his shoulders, watching their squat shadows on the sand. Though the sun was out above the beach, he could see rain pouring from dense grey cloud out on the sea. There was a large ship out there, a tanker or a ferry, Niall couldn't tell which.

"Lookit Nevvy. Look at the big boat," he said. "I can see a big boat."

Neville bobbed and wobbled and pointed at one of the plaited piles displaced by a small creature in the sand.

"Anolimatatong," he said.

"Are they worums Daddy?" Niamh said. She leant against him, peering down, panting still from the chase.

"No, that's only sand love. But I think something worm shaped makes them when it comes in and out of the ground, y'know. There does be little holes there beside them look."

Niamh inclined forwards on one leg, regarding the little mound in the grey-brown sand. She threw her arms out for balance and lost interest in the sand creatures, losing herself in the posture, adding undulations of her head, then falling into a run, tilting and weaving.

Fintan offered the bottle and squatted down a few feet in front of Neville as Niall took a drink. It was nearly finished, he noticed, and considered whether he was feeling drunk or not. Thinking about the pints they'd had earlier he decided he must be, though he hadn't drunk as much as Fintan, despite his coaxing. Fintan had had doubles with his pints and had been on at him to as well and had drunk most of the bottle now.

"C'mere to me. C'mere to me," Fintan was saying, smiling and nodding, beckoning at Neville, his elbows resting on his outspread knees. "On your own Nevah."

Neville's legs crumpled beneath him and he dropped, sitting, onto the sand. He cast his gaze about, then threw his head back, looking up for Niall.

"Odedilioyn," he said.

Niall handed the bottle back to Fintan and picked him up.

"Isn't this grand now. Havin' this on your doorstep," said Fintan. He drained the end of the bottle. "Olga's oul' fella let the moths ou've his wallet in the end wha'."

"He was very good to us, yeah but meself and Olga had a few bob of our own saved as well y'know and we'd the few quid from the house in Coolock an' that."

The high pitch and urgency of his own voice annoyed Niall. He could hear the alcohol as well; words stretched and compacted, honked narrowly from his throat. It occurred to him that he would appear drunk now when they went back to the house.

"Ah sure I know. I'm only coddin' ye," said Fintan. "You owe nothing to no one. You work like a black." On the last word he launched the bottle: the abrupt movement of air, the whip of fabric, the slow arced flight of the bottle into the waves. Neville began to cry. He clung to Niall and pushed his face into his shoulder.

"Aw Nevah, what's wrong with ye," said Fintan.

Behind him, a few feet away, Niall could see Niamh, halted, arms hanging straight by her sides, her foot pointed toward the sea, knee locked. She glanced between Fintan and the spot in the water where the bottle had landed.

"He's very bold isn't he Daddy," she said. The canted soft spring of her knee released and she skipped over to Niall. "You're supposed to take your rubbish home with you, not just throw it in the water." She leaned flush against him and stroked Neville's podgy thigh. "It's all right Nevvy. Don't cry."

"Indeed'n he is. An awful man altogether," said Niall.

"A shockin' bowsy," said Fintan. He was staring out into the bay, rubbing his jaw with the backs of his fingers.

"Can I carry him?" said Niamh. She stepped back and reached out her arms.

"Nodolimpoytilen," said Neville mournfully, pointing at his sister.

"Not now chicken, I think he's a bit tired," said Niall. "We need to get home for our dinner now in anyways."

They walked back toward the Bull Wall where the car was parked. Niall watched Niamh and Fintan ahead of him. Niamh leant against Fintan's hip, holding the tail of his jacket. He rested his large hand on her shoulder, stroking her face with his thumb. As they reached the car Fintan paused and looked out over the water toward the docks and the city.

"Are you missing it at all?" said Niall.

"Missing this kip?" Fintan looked at him and grimaced. "You must be fuckin' joking. I can't wait to go back."

"There must be something you miss about the place, for fuck sake," said Niall, forcing breathy laughter.

"Here, d'you want me to take him?" said Fintan, tipping his head curtly at Neville.

"I mean obviously it'll be different now. I didn't mean . . . I mean y'know yourself . . . I just meant like . . . y'know," Niall said, thinking he might have upset him because of his ma but feeling the panic of recognition as well because he knew it was more to do with the gargle and even without that the slightest thing could set Fintan off. A quiet, sullen Fintan would be as difficult at the dinner table as a rude, argumentative one and Niall cursed himself now for insisting on inviting him. He had felt robust in his generosity, a worldly, down-to-earth fellow whose success didn't mean he was too grand to pass an afternoon with an old friend, one who had just buried his mother, even if his manners were a little coarse. He had seen Olga's objections as mean-spirited and petty when they had argued about it on the way home from the funeral in the car. He had waved her off as a fuddy-duddy when Fintan had arrived, four hours early, insisting on Niall coming for a pint or two before dinner. Having now spent three and a half hours in his company, he was reminded of the Fintan he had known as a teenager. Now, as then, his manner could vault from unselfconscious clowning to unwarranted aggression. Conversation would become absurd, Fintan focusing with unsettling intensity on some word or phrase, insisting on a hidden meaning or intention. He would then become abstracted and indifferent, bored by Niall's protests to the contrary. In a discussion with a man at the next table in the Yacht, which had begun as an exchange of good-natured reflections on the differences between city and country life, Fintan had become aggressive and spiteful, in the end referring to the man as a fucking culchie. Niall had rolled his eyes and smiled at the man, trying, without success, to make light of Fintan's behaviour. The man continued to glare at Fintan, who by then was entertaining Niamh, flicking beer mats from the table edge and catching them between his fingers.

The interior of the car had been warmed by the sun and Niall felt uncomfortable in his jacket. He was reluctant to stop and take it off; the idea of doing so seemed wrong somehow, that to admit this discomfort would betray his irritation with Fintan. The wry smirk and indulgent knotting of his brow that he had managed to maintain most of the morning now felt like an idiot's leer and his face ached from the effort. He wanted to wipe the sweat from his forehead but feared the largeness and whiteness of his handkerchief, its blue embroidered N, would be ridiculed by Fintan.

"We're going back over the rumbly bridge aren't we Daddy?" said Niamh. She clung to the top of Niall's seat and rocked excitedly.

"That's right, we are indeed love, back over the rumbly bridge. Sit back properly in your seat why don't you, there's a good girl," he said.

"We're going over the rumbly bridge Nevvy. Nevvy we're going over the rumbly bridge again. Nevvy. Nevvy." She was hanging at arm's length, still gripping the top of the seat, Niall could tell.

"Bahooh," Neville called out.

"That's right. That's right," said Fintan, bouncing him gently on his lap.

"Let go of Daddy's seat, there's a good girl and sit back properly why don't you," said Niall. "Can you remember the name of the bridge?" He made twitching adjustments of his position in the seat and clenched his fists on the steering wheel. Niamh pulled herself forward abruptly and shouted: "The Bull Bridge," close to his ear. He clamped his teeth shut and flexed the muscles of his jaw, breathing evenly through his nostrils. "That's right chicken," he said. "The Bull Bridge. Sit back properly in your seat now, there's a good girl."

"Mmmmh. Mmmmh," she hummed.

Niall could feel that she had let go of the seat but that her weight was thumping against it. He glanced behind him. She was butting the back of the seat rhythmically with her shoulder, her fists at her temples, index fingers pointed upwards.

"That's the noise the bull makes isn't it. Very good. Now will you sit back in your seat sweetheart, Daddy's driving."

"Mmmmh. Mmmmh. Look Nevvy, I'm the bull. Mmmmh."

Neville was attempting to stand on Fintan's lap and lean over toward Niamh. Wet sand from his shoes was marking the thighs of Fintan's trousers and a glistening vine of saliva trembled now between his lower lip and the shoulder of Fintan's jacket.

"Leave him alone will you sweetheart, he's crawling all over Fintan now, look. Sit back properly in your seat now, there's a good girl."

"He's grand," said Fintan. "He's a fine fellow aren't you baba." He absently patted Neville's buttock.

"He's going to ruin that suit look. Niamh love, give Daddy the box of tissues off the back window please." Niall shot a succession of glances from the road to Niamh and back. "I'll give you a tissue now in a minute, Fintan."

"Don't worry about me. I've other suits," said Fintan.

"Right, here's the bridge now love. If you sit back in your seat you'll be able to see it properly when we go over." Niall turned his profile to Niamh, peering sideways at the road.

"Mmmmh. Mmmmh. Nevvy I'm the bull lookit," Niamh persisted flatly, throwing herself against Niall's seat with greater force.

"We're on the bridge now love. You're missing the bridge."

The brisk muffled drumming of the timber began beneath them.

"Mmmh. Mmmh. I'm the bull Nevvy."

"Niamh, love."

"Mmmh. Mmmh. *I'm* the bull." Fintan joined in loudly. With each bull roar he pushed his face into the crook of Neville's neck and nuzzled and Neville screamed gleefully. He dropped to his knees on Fintan's lap and buried his face in his chest and Niall could see drool and snot gather on the fabric of Fintan's jacket. Niamh lunged forward, finger-horned, bellowing a response. Her elbow dug sharply into Niall's shoulder.

A shudder ran through his neck and jaw and he tightened

his lips sourly. Reaching behind him with his left hand he found the front of Niamh's coat, forced her backwards into the rear seat and aimed five hard smacks at her legs, each one punctuating the instruction hissed through his clenched teeth:

"Sit. Back. Properly. In. Your seat."

Some of the blows missed their mark. Niall glanced back and turned in his seat to take better aim and doing so tipped the steering wheel to the left. The car veered heavily.

"Fuck sake Niall." Fintan braced his legs in the foot well and pushed his back into his seat. He brought a cradling hand round Neville's head and held him closely to his chest.

Niall seized the wheel with both hands and pulled the car out of the swerve. He overshot into the oncoming lane and the long emphatic note of an approaching car's horn was followed by the swears of its driver, muted behind glass and quickly receding. A second horn joined in from the car behind them.

"Fucking cunts." Niall gripped the wheel, his arms and shoulders shook and he ground his foot into the brake pedal. Fintan slammed his palm onto the dashboard. Niall felt Niamh thud against the seat back. He threw open his door and stood facing the car behind.

"Shut your fucking hole you fucking stupid cunt." Niall emphasised the words with sideway twitches of his head and spurts of white spittle, hooking the air in front of his stomach with his fists, full-stopping the whole phrase with a stamp of his foot. He glared round-eyed and panting through the windscreen and his gaze was met by the anxious, bemused faces of the man and his son they had spoken to earlier. He held up a shaking admonitory finger, took a breath and made to speak, but seeing as much incredulity as fright in the faces behind the glass, said nothing, quickly ducked back into his own car and slammed the door.

Fintan had sunk in his seat with his chin on his chest and was shaking with laughter. His face contorted around a pained grin with glances at Niall sending him further into convulsions. Neville sat on his lap regarding him with serene curiosity. He drew saliva soaked fingers from his mouth and offered them. In the rear seat, Niamh lay curled with her knees drawn up, her hands covering her face; staccato breath whistled through her lips between sobs and moans.

"Are you all right chicken? Did you hurt yourself?" Niall reached back and placed a tentative hand on her shoe.

"Go away," she shouted and kicked at his hand.

"Sweetheart, sit up and tell Daddy. Are you all right?" said Niall, craning and squinting.

"No," she screamed, writhing away from him and burying her face in the seat.

He glanced at Fintan, who was watching the car behind as it pulled out and drove away, his lips still pursed and trembling against laughter.

"Niamh. Niamh." Niall attempted a firmer approach.

She looked up at him, scowling and red faced, a deeper red lozenge forming on her cheekbone.

"You hit my legs and then I hit my face on the chair when the car stopped and I'm straight telling Mammy on you." Her voice modulated into a high warble; she flattened her face into the seat again and wailed.

"Listen. Sweetheart. C'mere to me." Niall adopted the tone of melancholy surprise he had used before when obliged to negotiate with her. To retrieve her from her grief was possible but could demand a kind of abject contrition from him that he was reluctant to employ in front of Fintan.

"Sweetheart, Daddy was driving and you were messin' there in the back and I told you didn't I? I told you to sit properly in your seat." He winked at Fintan and winced archly, feigning feigned concern. Fintan's smile faded and he looked away.

"Come on and we all go back for our dinner now," Niall ventured, head tilted for a reply. He started the car and they set off again. "All right? Niamh?" Sweat soaked his shirt, on his back and under his arms and ran unchecked on his brow, his handkerchief remaining folded in the pocket of his jacket.

# The Mainland
## JOEL PEARCEY

Just before I turned sixteen my father got a job working for the Environment Department as its senior water resources manager; a turn of events that resulted in him meeting and falling for a part-time union official of mixed colonial background who lived in a house on a little island about two hours' drive north of Sydney. Within a month, we would be living there, too.

Most kids the age I was then feel they live on an island and the stereotype has it that they go to great lengths to make it plain to those around them, regardless of whether they care to listen. Because I did, I didn't have to. Anyway, even if I'd wanted, there was hardly anyone around to tell: the island was roughly a kilometre in diameter and had only fifty or so houses hidden under its expanse of treetops. There was no shop, no café, no pub and only one vehicle, a communally owned four-wheel drive, which had to buck and churn just to negotiate the island's single scoliotic clay track.

I rarely visited the mainland, only rowing over when I'd run out of muesli or tea. In many ways I've never been happier: blinking to morning birdsong but not rising till late, reading through the evenings and, if I was lucky, sleeping to a verdant soundscape of rain.

Our move to the island followed four purgatorial years in the most middling of Sydney's outer suburbs, only half that time with my mum. She'd never been the same after losing a baby during our second year in Brunei, the first stop in our staggered emigration to Australia. It's not difficult to fathom how enduring a forty-hour labour in order to deliver a downy-haired girl you already know to be dead might recalibrate one's soul, one's capacity for living. From overheard conversations, I had a clear picture of my exhausted mother cradling the still child – her snub nose and round face perfectly formed – my father sitting beside them, helpless, even by his standards. Aside from the lost baby, I hardly remember Brunei. Only the river: broad, snaking, slick surface and turbid depths; my mum complaining that she'd rather risk being swept away than continue to live on stilts.

It would fit a tragic narrative to say that she'd taken to drink after losing the baby, but the truth is that even in my earliest memories she's a six o'clock drunk – the kind for whom alcohol is not simply an addiction or a way of passing the time but a liquid fugue. A disappearing act in which you not only drink the bottle, but the bottle drinks you. That she was usually drunk and screaming when she threatened to leave made it seem like she never actually would, so that she did go and managed to be sober doing it, came with an aftershock of unreality.

At the time I thought I took it well – that I was relieved, even – but when I recall the months after she left and see my worried eyes and full, gormless mouth staring back at me from her dressing-table mirror, not daring to touch the tin containing the lock of my sister's hair, I'm not so sure. It was more than a year until I saw her again. She was wearing a yellow leather miniskirt and riding pillion on her drug-dealer-boyfriend's motorbike; the beginning of a two-wheeled road trip of Australia, which, fatefully, would eventually encompass Southeast Asia, the ruin of her maternal beauty, nearly a decade of mother-child estrangement and a stint in an Indonesian prison. Still, there would be two more torpid years in the suburbs, before my dad and I finally upped sticks and left them for good.

I don't see how we would have come to know of the island's existence, let alone moved there, had my dad not met Dorothy a few months earlier, at a union conference. I was introduced to her during the early summer. We'd spent the morning watching the annual jetty-to-jetty dog race between two of the larger islands in the little archipelago – an anarchic event made up of dog owners in tinnies trying to steer their outboards and their swimming dogs to the finish line, with the winning dog receiving an eighteen-ounce steak and a bottle of whisky. We'd been on for tea at Dorothy's house and were returning to meet the twice-daily ferry when my dad saw a For Sale sign staked on the edge of the track, a pitched timber roof just visible through the treetops. Within an hour he'd called the estate agent from the island's single callbox, met him on the jetty, barely looked at the house and put in an offer, for the full asking price.

We hardly kept any of our possessions, most of the furniture being too bulky or too heavy for the clay track. For the first few weeks on the island, while we were still settling in, we spent nearly every day at Dorothy's, with my dad practically gurning at me from her cane furniture, stupid with all his unconsummated projections and the intense, summer heat, while she made lunches and teas. I remember feeling like his ambassador, perhaps there to testify to his paternal gift, or, if I were to be unkind about it, a mere accessory to help him pick up women, the way some men drive fast cars or take cute dogs to cafés.

We'd eat together then sit on her back step smoking a joint, while my dad waxed lyrical on the social politics of her chickens or listened earnestly to Dorothy's take on shiatsu massage theory. The last occasion we were there together was the day of my sixteenth birthday. Dorothy baked me a cake and gave me a card she'd drawn herself. It was just a bit of folded paper, really, with a light pencil sketch of a watchful bird on the front. Inside was a message: *Jay – Love, however you want it.*

Looking back, I struggle to convince myself that I was insensible to its meaning; she'd even posted it down the front of my shorts. Did I really believe it was just a slip of the hand, an unfortunate ambiguity? Something, though, prevented me from showing my dad, so I must have had an inkling. Not that it mattered; within a couple of weeks, he'd finally faced, incredulously, Dorothy's rejection. He wrote her a long and vitriolic letter. "It's a real character assassination, but she needs to hear it," he told me before reading out the juiciest bits. I still remember gleefully composed phrases such as "Indian giver" and "new-age prick teaser".

Without the prospect of laying Dorothy to keep him on

the island, my dad became much more involved in the liaison and travel side of his work and began to spend large chunks of time visiting important water resource sites in Queensland and Northern New South Wales. Soon I was hardly seeing him at all.

Technically, I was meant to be at school, but pretty soon I stopped making it in. Instead I'd wake early, seduced by the sound of the air, which was thick with the music of kookaburras, currawongs, cockatoos, lorikeets, butcherbirds and always distant ravens. Still blinking, I would look into the treetops, which would be silhouetted by a slow-bleeding sun, and try, hopelessly, to find the authors of this song.

Most mornings after breakfast I'd go down to one of the two little beaches and strip off and swim, wading through the shallows, trying a few strokes, tasting the salt on my tongue, then floating, trance-like, on my back. Seldom would there be another islander doing the same; most days the only human life I'd observe would be a single-engine aircraft droning as it passed overhead or the idle traffic of sailing boats and tinnies, wind-carried voices skipping disembodied across the water, and the occasional speedboat unseaming the surface as it zipped by faster than a reflection. The afternoons I would spend reading, listening to music and smoking the occasional joint. Once or twice a week I would speak to my dad, who was dividing his time between rural sites on his water rounds and the ministerial department in Canberra. He'd met a new woman and made no secret of his infatuation. "She's beautiful," he said. "Totally unlike anyone I've ever known."

One cloud-covered morning just past my first summer on the island, I was taking my usual swim, treading water, just watching raindrops plash the surface, when I looked up and saw Dorothy standing on the shore of the cove, dark and watchful under an umbrella. As I came out of the water, my skin feeling the chill and sting of the rain, she walked towards me, and offered me a towel, telling me it was no longer warm enough to just let myself dry in the air.

After that she'd come regularly, always bringing me a soft, clean towel, sometimes even helping to pad me try – "You'll catch a chill, daydreaming. Here, let me," she'd say. Then we'd walk back to her house, often not speaking a word for the length of the journey. I'd use her shower – there was no running water on the island, only rainwater tanks, and my dad had still not got round to installing a hot-water system in our house. Afterwards, we'd drink tea and have a small lunch. When it got cooler still, and I stopped taking my morning swim, she'd slip a note under my door, often leaving two or three eggs and some freshly baked bread: *Come see me this evening, Jay. I got a beautiful fresh bream from the ferryman. D.*

She had no television in her house, not even a stereo, just a big old radio she called "the wireless", on which she sometimes listened to the World Service or Radio France Internationale. She always steamed the fish – it was never cooked any other way – and after our meal we'd drink herbal tea and share a single-skin joint. She'd usually have a book ready – Nabokov, Chekhov, Hesse and Laurie Lee – and we'd read aloud to each other; she, always slowly, deliberately; I, often stumbling over words I'd only previously had to shape inwardly, shyly mispronouncing them. Having just come from the western suburbs where a failure to show sufficient interest in a sport that involved glorified hugging and clutching at short shorts was, to borrow a barbarism from my Year Nine PE teacher, "incontrovertible proof of poofterism", I was just glad of the opportunity to bring the solipsism and insubstantiality of the page into the world; to hear how words sounded when shaped in the mouth, how they travelled in the air. As she watched me read, the beginnings of a smile flickering at her lips, I was only dimly aware of how complicated it might have been for her.

I knew she'd been born in Kenya, that during her infancy her landowning parents had fled the Mau-Mau rebellion for Zimbabwe, but there was something else in her voice, a wilful reach for the sound of another unplaceable place, something girlish, a forced musicality, that always left me feeling uneasy. It was strange that this sound dissipated only when she read aloud.

Sometimes while we read or stepped outside for what she called our "post-prandial puff", she'd hold my hand, and although it did inhibit me at the time, making it impossible for me to speak, in recollection it excited me and I would feel, in her absence, a physical longing that I could neither summon nor act upon when we were together.

The first time she returned from her shower and let her kimono fall open, I was so unprepared for it that I experienced it more as reverie than reality. Yet now, after decades, I see her with absolute clarity: her body, so poised and youthful when clothed, was, to my adolescent eyes, somehow timeless, weathered; her breasts, small and pendant; her skin dusky and finely, almost imperceptibly, wrinkled. Perhaps from her early years under the African sun. I remained motionless, wordless; sunk in the cushion of her cup-shaped armchair, wanting to spare her embarrassment, certain that it was an accident, that she would regather and retie it the moment she realised it was unfastened. And she did, eventually, but only after she'd held my gaze, held it with a look that was as calm as it was bold. But, as with my reaction to her card, in my initial dissonance I set a pattern, and little slips like this – sudden glimpses of nakedness when looking up from the pages of a book or turning from the doorway above her back step – became an insistent but unexplored motif of my visits.

Occasionally my dad would come home for a string of four or five days, but mostly it was just the odd weekend, to say hello and to refill with cash the envelope he kept in the egg rack of the fridge door.

I enjoyed the company. We'd sit on the porch smoking bongs and he'd tell me about his meetings with government ministers and the environmentalist and farming lobbies. He was particularly fond of the farmers; something about their parochialism, their placedness, appealed to him, perhaps because he'd grown up all over North Africa as well as Singapore, finally setting foot in Letchworth just in time to fail his eleven-plus. "They're really special people," he told me. "The blokes are straight-up. Doers. Not like us. But they lack our latitude. Sure they're rednecks, to a man, but they appreciate me because I'm not just another shirt telling them they're sucking the rivers dry."

Mostly, he'd talk about his sex life. The woman who followed his prevaricatory and projectional dalliance with Dorothy was called Harriet. She ran her family's motel out in remote Western Queensland, in a town at the centre of an important site in the area's agricultural irrigation flow. I knew my dad was serious when, on the occasions I needed to call to tell him I'd run out of money or wanted a signed letter supporting my reasons for continuing home education, I wouldn't need to look any further than the motel to trace him. Sometimes he'd even answer the phone.

"I've been with some interesting women and I've had some great fucks," he told me one night before leaving yet again. "Even your mother and I used to like doing it. It's how we ended up together. But there was never any love. With Hattie, it's different. I'm not just cunt-struck – you know, I'm the first man to make her come and that's really got to mean something. You should meet her, I'm sure you'd get on."

Towards the end of the autumn I doubled the number of people in my social life on the island when Dorothy introduced me to a Bangladeshi Rastafarian called Sonit. He was a carpenter and craftsman with a large property and private jetty. He had a labyrinthine and well-cultivated garden which needed tending, so thinking I might enjoy the work and the opportunity for some independent income, Dorothy suggested that he take me on for a few days a week. I knew nothing of gardening but she was eager that I have something to do while she took long-service leave to visit her parents in Zimbabwe. They were both ill, approaching the end of their lives, and although she didn't want to go, she considered it her duty. On the evening of her leaving I rowed her to the mainland. She sat at the prow of the little boat smiling minutely in that way of hers while the wind stole the substance of the few words we offered each other. "Sonit will look after you," she said, as I lifted her bags into the back of a taxi. "Keep reading and don't smoke so much dope that you forget to feed my chickens." I don't know if it was my gaucheness or her design, but in saying goodbye and awkwardly moving to kiss her cheek, I received, for the briefest moment, the moist imprint of her lips on mine.

I did not become an accomplished gardener. I did a great deal of arbitrarily cutting back the encroaching bush. I also remember harvesting chives with their wan little flowers, and bringing in the vegetables, all varieties of bruised reds and purples: amaranth, aubergine, chard, beetroot. As well as paying me in cash, Sonit would tip me choice buds from his cannabis crop or take me to his kitchen where he'd cook up dahl, fish stew or a vegetable curry for me to take home.

His house was an extraordinary and eclectic work of artifice, from his front door and its elaborate, erotic chinoiserie carvings to the line of Gothic candelabra along his hallway to his decadent front room, where I'd usually find his young and beautiful girlfriend reclining on an over-sized cushion, half-clothed and draped in the diaphanous rags of the East. Always, the air would be piqued with spices, incense and sandalwood, and she would look across at me with a cannabinoid glaze in her eyes and a flushed strawberries-and-cream complexion. I never saw her on her feet and I never learned her name.

My dad reacted strangely when I told him about Sonit's girlfriend.

"I think she's the most beautiful girl I've ever seen," I said.

"I reckon that under all those dreads he's no different from any old curry muncher," he replied. "*No*, I'm not being racist, I'm being *ironic*: it's the Bob Marley effect that gets him laid – he doesn't mind profiting from a bit of racism, so long as it's of the *inverse* kind. You won't find an impressionable little hippy anywhere on this coastline who wants to shag Mr Patel from Tandoori Nights, but give her a bare-chested Rastaman living in Xana-bloody-du and just watch her wet her knickers."

It was the middle of my second summer on the island. Dorothy was still away, although I knew I was to expect her back soon. The radio weather reports said it was the hottest January in several decades. I'd wake in the mornings to a house already panting with heat and although I had resumed the routine of my morning swim, it was so hot that on the walk back I felt I had to physically part the air before me, air dense with heat and the pulsatile sound of crickets and cicadas. Once home I would go straight for the shower, now grateful for the cool water from the outside tank, then lie in the hammock on the porch, alternately sleeping and waking, only to drop off again, letting my book fall to the floor.

Right in the middle of the heatwave, my dad arranged for me to visit him so that I could see "another Australia" and, more importantly, meet Harriet. I was greeted at the little airport on the mainland by one of my dad's farmer friends. He owned a two-seater Cessna and as a favour had agreed to fly me up to Northern New South Wales, where I'd connect with my dad who would then drive us north into Queensland. I watched the plane taxi out of the hangar as I stood on the runway; the tarmac had become a sump for heat and was practically viscous with it, almost melting the soles of my shoes.

I knew that my dad was now regularly staying weeks on end at Harriet's motel, and that it was all on business expenses, even though he was meant to be working and travelling across an area larger than one million square kilometres. I'd begun to tease him. Were the farmers in Harriet's town now getting every drop of river? "I thought the whole place would be underwater by now," I said. "That we'd be travelling by submarine."

We drove to the motel alongside the Balonne River, which was cast under the brilliant spell of a magenta sunset, an aesthetic effect my dad made a great deal of, overselling the motel before we'd even got there. The building was typical for that part of the state: square, dull brick, concrete porch; low, shaded awnings.

The drinks and dining area was painted a garish parody of the sunset that had just greeted us. I sat on a high stool while my dad went behind the bar and confidently poured us each a cool beer from the draught taps. Behind me, at a table in the far corner of the room, echoed the emphysemic cough of the only customer.

Harriet appeared from a door just to the side of the bourbons. She was all dusty-seeming: auburn hair, auburn freckles. It was clear that she was nervous, although she had wits enough to work a wry smile into her awkward but not unattractive mouth. I liked her immediately, but just as soon feared for my dad. I sensed that although she was fond of him and humoured him, this was unlikely to be enough.

"Isn't she lovely?" he said shortly afterwards. "Isn't she?"

The next day we went to her parents' house for a barbie. "Her old man is great," my dad said. "The classic cotton farmer."

The television was on when we got there and her dad, Yabby, was sitting inside on an electronic recliner, with the back doors open onto the acres of farmland behind him. He was drinking a stubbie while watching a current-affairs programme that was detailing the failed Native Title Act application of some indigenous people in another state. The judge had ruled that their right to the now pastoral land of their forefathers had been "washed away by the tide of history".

"Know why them call 'em boongs?" he said, nodding in the direction of the native Australian land-rights campaigners on the television.

"No," I said. "I don't."

"Coz," he replied, "that's the sound they make when they bounce off your bull bar: boong, boong."

To my eternal inner shame, I conjured a laugh, half out of politeness, half out of embarrassment, all while my dad looked lovingly on.

The next day he took me to see the Jack Taylor Weir, an important feature of the area's water management system. On the town side, where we stood, it was full, but downstream of the concrete spillway there was little more than a murky rock pool surrounded by dry, cracked earth.

"Where's all the water?" I asked.

"In the fields, mate. Growing the cotton you and I wear. And in the farmers' storages – you saw one at Yabby's."

"Yabby's a real racist," I said.

"You can call them racists, but that whole discourse hasn't even arrived here yet. They're beautiful people. Salt of the earth. The old fella was probably only winding you up. Took one look at you and realised you were ripe for it. You'll get used to him. He's a character."

"No need," I said. "I don't imagine island life would suit him."

"Perhaps," he said, smiling broadly. "But Hattie's pregnant. She only found out this morning."

"Wow."

"Yeah, she's still getting used to the idea, the poor girl, so let's keep this between me and you. But isn't it wonderful? Isn't it, mate? It's going to be beautiful. I've got a feeling this is all going to work out really well. We're going to be a family."

The drive back to the airport the next morning was exhilarating. A highway practically deserted, just the odd ute or road train quickly disappearing into Doppler sound, a speedometer ecstatically oscillating at the two hundred kilometres an hour mark.

"Couldn't you be arrested for driving this fast?" I asked.

"Not likely," said my dad, turning to me, still drugged with his happy revelation. "Cops are like hen's teeth out here. Everyone does it. They call it low-level flying."

On the flight back, the farmer agreed to make a detour along the coastline, banking low over the island. There it was, thick with trees, but for the jutting matchsticks of a few jetties, scarcely a sign of habitation. I thought of Dorothy, who would surely be back now and waking to rising birdsong. Curiously, the outline of the island seemed to me an almost exact miniature of the Australian mainland.

As we came into land at the little airport, the stall alarm sounded.

"Perfect landing," said the farmer. "Just on the stall."

It was ridiculously hot when I got back. I was restless – too restless to read or just sit and daydream – but, even though she'd been back several days, something prevented me from going to see Dorothy. She had left me a few notes in the letterbox inviting me round, but I had neither been nor replied. Slowly, I began to understand why I would not go. It was what I had known all along but had not been ready to understand: she had been making me an offering. Now, I determined, I would take it.

I replied with a short note in which I apologised for not visiting her sooner. I would be swimming the next evening at the cove, I said, if she wanted to come and meet me. I thought I would not worry if she didn't come, knowing that she sometimes had to travel to her office in the city, but as I pushed off the sand underfoot and moved into a rhythmic breaststroke, occasionally looking for her figure on the shore, I worried that I would remain there idly swimming until dark, harbouring something that had at last progressed beyond a latent longing.

She did not come, but when I got back to the house, there was a note for me: *Saw you swimming. Didn't want to disturb you. I have a fresh salmon. Come and see me. D x*

When I arrived at her house the door was open, her dark hair was wet, and she was wearing the familiar sheer kimono, black and scarlet. She looked sad, resolute. I walked towards her and brushed her smooth, cool lips with my thumb. She led me to her bedroom where I kissed her neck as she ran her hands through my hair, treating my body without haste or hunger. She crossed her arms and pushed the kimono from her shoulders, then drew me down onto the bed. Our love-making was intimate but it was also rich with all our silences and long separation. Even now I think of it as more caesura than sense: a physical disquisition on loneliness, love, and dissociation.

My dad came home that week, wet and muddy from trudging up the clay road. It was early. I'd risen before dawn unable to sleep because of the sound of the rain battering the tin roof in undulating torrents.

He turned the television on. "Look," he said. The pictures juxtaposed dying crops and emaciated cattle with, upstream, flooded roads and farmland, footage of topless kids paddling boats down residential streets. There had been a massive rainstorm and a vast slug of water was moving down the river, breaking its banks, rising over rooftops, shimmering like snakeskin. But it would not move downstream of the Jack Taylor Weir. It would not reach the floodplains of the lower tributaries.

*There are allegations that farms upstream have been diverting thousands of millions of litres a day to their huge storages,* said the voiceover. *A single pump can take the equivalent of eighty-six Olympic swimming pools a day, and some farmers have dozens of pumps.*

My dad's face appeared on the television. He was answering questions from behind a walnut desk in his department's media room. *This is not about the greed or morality of individuals,* he said. *This is the failure of past policies: a classic tragedy of the commons.*

"Shit," I said.

"Too right," he said. "And it's over with Hattie. She's had an abortion. I only found out because she was refusing to fuck me. She had it done weeks ago. Now she's fucking well going to South America. God knows how long she'll be gone. Doesn't want me to come. She made that clear enough."

He looked across the water, towards the mainland. The sun was spilling from behind the clouds and settling into the day. He then turned and smiled at me through his tired blue eyes before looking back at the mainland again, now squinting like a blind man pretending to see through cataracts.

"But we'll be all right, mate. We'll be all right. About time we got off this fucking island though, don't you think?"

"In order to be created,
a work of art must first
make use of the dark
forces of the soul."

– Albert Camus

# Tunde
## LOUISE CHRISTIAN

Tunde's family had all been killed in one night. The memory of that night had become a surreal slow-motion sequence of events in his head, which replayed itself on innumerable occasions, despite his constant strenuous efforts to blank it out. He could just be waiting to catch a bus on a busy street or watching football on the telly, when it would come back to him. Now that he was standing in a courtroom what felt like hundreds of thousands of miles away, it was more like a pain buried deep inside his body, a sliver of sharp metal, which he could not locate or explain.

He was in the witness box in the Immigration Tribunal at Rosebery Avenue, Islington, and a polite but sceptical audience was analysing his every word. The pressure of not being believed was like being hurt all over again. He had never imagined being questioned like this, trying to remember details, to explain to white men in suits. He blinked back tears.

"I put it to you that you have concocted this story, when you know full well that your family are alive, and sent you here for economic reasons," the Home Office barrister was saying. "You were too young to get here under your own steam."

He had been eight years old when they came for his family, and living in his home country, the Democratic Republic of Congo, although the name was like a sick joke, of the kind his sarcastic old school teacher had once relished. He saw again his father's crumpled body, the thick blood oozing down his mother's legs beneath her flowered skirt, and heard his sister's screams as soldiers dragged her away. A severed leg lay discarded in the yard among the chickens – he didn't even know whose. A flashback of the bloodshot eyes and foul breath of a soldier who pushed him into the latrine put him back in the smelly darkness of it, too terrified to come out, petrified by the acrid smoke seeping under the door, fearing he would be burned alive.

He remembered little of his subsequent flight out of the destroyed hut into the bush, except for the shaming guilt when he realised he had lost his whole family, and that he had hidden himself as they were slaughtered. And he could scarcely recall how he had survived afterwards, hiding in the villages further south as a surrogate son to a series of families who hoped he would find food for them. Or how he learned to catch small animals, kill birds with a handmade catapult, and forage for edible roots and nuts.

"It was hard for me to survive after the soldiers killed my family," he told the barrister, whose sneering disbelief was all too apparent in the questions he was asking,

"So you really expect us to believe that the whole of your family were killed and yet you managed to find the money to leave and come here?"

He had a better memory of what happened some years later – he would have been about twelve – but there was still a fog in his head that obscured the small things. He knew he had been seized by rebels in a night raid on the village, but he did not know if they were the same group who killed his family, or how many there were, or where he was exactly when they came, or what they said.

"It was at night so I did not get a good look at them. But there was a lot of talk about boys disappearing to go and fight, even quite small boys. They were wearing a sort of khaki uniform but not like the army's. They did not give me a choice. They just shook me awake and pointed their guns at me, and forced me to get into their truck."

When they got to the camp in a mangrove swamp many miles away, there were hundreds more boy soldiers and they told him that he would not be allowed to stay unless he passed an initiation test. They gave him food but also insisted he swallow some white pills. Afterwards he became weak and feverish. That night he and other young boys lay on the ground, dormitory-style, in a huge tent, but he could not sleep. When they took him to the open ground for the test, the next morning, he simply did not have the strength to kill a kudu deer or wrestle with another novice, as required. He found himself in a small group of the skinniest and weakest-looking boys, who were led to a different tent; one of them had spindly legs and could hardly walk the short distance. He was still feeling ill, so did not care that they were given only a watery stew to eat.

"I assumed they would let me go now and was relieved I would not have to fight," he told the stern-looking Judge, who had interrupted to ask what he thought was happening.

The next day it was airless and humid, and he remembered looking up to see that the sky was covered in black clouds spitting rain, like large animals threatening to pounce. But he felt better. He spoke little to the others in the group, and when soldiers arrived and announced they were to go on a hike, he assumed they were going to the place where they would be released. The march turned out to be very long and by the end of it everyone was exhausted. The boy with spindly legs and a couple of the others had to ride in the truck but Tunde walked on, even though his legs and back were aching unbearably. It took the whole day to reach a torpid muddy yellow river, above which was a mosquito-infested camp, managed by real adult soldiers.

The barrister asked another question.

"I was so tired when we got there, I was more pleased that there was food and shelter than disappointed about not being set free," he explained. "I only realised later why there were not more communal tents."

As he spoke, he visualised the never-ending arrivals of wounded, sick and skeletal people and shuddered at his initial puzzlement about where they all went. After a while, he'd noticed that every day, the soldiers marched a large group of people further down the river, away from the camp, forcing them to wield shovels, which some of them could barely carry. Then later the same day, the soldiers carried the shovels back, but the people did not return.

"But why didn't they kill you, too?"

"I did what I could to make myself useful to the soldiers, gathering firewood, fetching, carrying and lifting everything they ordered. Eventually, they let me help in the kitchen tent. And then . . ."

There was a silence. Tunde suddenly stopped speaking and dropped his head. He stared at his feet perplexedly as he recalled the next part of the story. Although he had a vivid memory of it, he felt that it would be better not to say too much. He had been quite vague when he gave a statement to his solicitor, Charlotte, because he thought she would not believe him. It would after all be difficult for anyone to credit what happened next – he could scarcely trust his own memory. So he tried a summary.

"When I realised they were killing the people down at the river, I decided to escape. A soldier helped me because I had done work for him."

The barrister produced a case report and spoke with the Judge and the other barrister, pointing something out, but Tunde was not listening. He was thinking about what he was not telling them; what he thought they would not understand.

There had indeed been one particular soldier, whom he had started to look out for and help at the camp. He was a big, placid, slow-moving man in his thirties, with folds of extra flesh, short dreadlocks and one dead eye which had a milky film over it and oozed pus. He was the least mobile of the soldiers, and Tunde was able to help him keep up with his own tasks in the camp and lessen the problems caused by his failing eyesight. Eventually, Tunde learned that he was called Bolo, although it was unthinkable that Bolo would ever know his name. He called him "You boy" as harshly as the other soldiers, but never whipped or struck him as they did. Tunde tried to help Bolo, even when he was also doing another job, because he saw that Bolo had difficulty carrying hot water, cleaning his gun, or lighting a fire. Bolo never said anything to him. Nevertheless there were times when he indicated, just by a pat on the head, or pressing some scraps of food into his palm, that he appreciated what he was doing.

One day Tunde was carrying a heavy pile of firewood down from the forest, when he saw Bolo approaching with a frightened look on his face. Bolo put a finger to his lips and then pulled him down under the cover of the intense lime-green palm fronds. Then he pointed further back, down the hill. They left the pile of firewood and went towards the river, away from the camp. As they squatted on the marshy ground and watched the red sun sink behind the trees, casting a strange eerie light on the foliage, Bolo told him in a whisper that it had been decided Tunde would be among those to go down to the river the next day.

"Even the boys that do work like you go there before long."

Tunde was shaking. He knew what it meant.

Bolo said hesitantly, "I have an idea. What happens is they will ask you to dig a big pit. Then they tell you to come up from the river for water. After that they take each one separately back down to the pit. But you won't leave the river. Stay in the pit and pretend you're dead. I will tell them I shot you." Out of his pocket he produced a grubby white T-shirt with dried bloodstains. "Put this in your trouser pocket and put it on when the others leave the pit. Lie face down and do not move. I will make blood go on you."

Tunde felt tears fall down his cheeks, but he was too frightened to say anything.

Solemnly Bolo took a large key out of his other pocket. "This is a key to my house in Akan – fifteen miles to the east. It is empty. My wife and baby are dead. There is valuable jewellery in a big saucepan on the top shelf in the kitchen. It is no use to me any more. Take it, sell it and go to the people smugglers to get you out of this bad country."

In the dark light, Bolo's face was expressionless, his eyes half closed.

"But what about you?" Tunde said, startled.

"I will be taken to the river soon," Bolo said sadly, his eyes averted. "Not because of you, but because I am weak. I can't run. I think about this and I want you to go away. That will be my consolation when they point the gun at me."

Tunde wanted to argue with him, but Bolo put his hand gently over his mouth and whispered, "No more talking or both of us will die and I will have no consolation. Stay here till I am gone."

The ingrained habit of doing as he was ordered kicked in, and Tunde watched as Bolo lumbered to his feet and staggered back up the hill. They spoke no more words and barely saw one another until the next day, when Bolo bent down in the newly dug pit and smeared fresh blood across Tunde's face as he lay rigid in the far corner, petrified of moving even one muscle or making a sound. Later still Tunde did not breathe when a soldier turned him over and inspected him.

Once again Tunde wondered what had happened to Bolo. If only he was still alive, he would go anywhere or do anything to rescue him. He imagined bringing Bolo to London – the NHS fixing his bad eye.

"How did the soldier help you?"

Tunde came out of his reverie at the question being barked at him by the Home Office barrister. He was still in the courtroom being cross-examined and they were talking to him again.

"He thought of a way for me to escape and told me to get some jewellery at his house in Akan, fifteen miles away."

"How did you get to this place called Akan? Fifteen miles is a long way."

The sudden feeling of panic was like a weight on his chest, stopping him from breathing. His mind was dissolving in his head and he had no words or pictures about himself. He could not remember what happened after he had played dead in the pit for so long. He could see the jewels in the rough metal pan, coiled like a glittering snake, but he could not visualise himself in the house, lifting them from their hiding place, let alone remember details about how he got there. Now he was giving evidence, the barristers did not let him consult the statement that Charlotte had taken from him, and he could not remember what was in it. Had he walked to Akan, or had someone given him a lift? If he said something different, he knew they would say that proved he was lying.

"How did you get there?"

"I am sorry. I don't know."

"I put it to you that your family were never killed, you were never in a military camp, and that this soldier who rescued you is a figment of your imagination. You came to the UK to get work and you came illegally on a false passport, which your family paid to obtain."

The barrister had all but turned his back on Tunde and was speaking scornfully to an audience that did not include him. He did not appear to be interested in a reply, but Tunde tried one, even though he could barely articulate the words. "It's not true. My family are dead." His speech came out lumpenly, as if without conviction, but inside him there was a torrent of anger thumping against his ribcage.

"I was in the camp. They would have killed me, if it had not been for the soldier."

The Judge in this immigration tribunal – they called him an Adjudicator – looked down at him with an exasperated air. He looked freshly scrubbed, red-faced, and had a distinctly military aspect. His suit could have been a uniform. His hair was aggressively short.

Just another soldier, thought Tunde. The anger welled up inside him, choking his throat. He looked beyond the barristers to Charlotte, sitting at the back. She had told him that his inability to describe everything was not unusual and now she nodded, encouragingly. Remembering her instructions, he said, "I was very young at the time and afterwards, I just tried not to think about it."

Tunde followed Charlotte out of the court into the massive entrance hall. It was even more crowded than when he had arrived. Every seat was filled and there were queues of people, nearly all with black or brown faces, waiting patiently to get information from staff behind counters with bars, to sign up and be told where to go. Despite the numbers of people, there was an unconvincing semblance of calm.

Charlotte pointed to an area at the end of the hall where there were flimsy interview booths in which people were seated with lawyers scribbling in notebooks.

"That used to be the kids' area and they even had some toys for them. No such luxuries now."

She led him to a café round the corner, the sort of place where lorry drivers went. She bought both of them sandwiches and steaming mugs of coffee.

He could not eat his but bit off the tiniest corner to show thanks, then tried to conceal the rest under his paper napkin.

"I'm afraid we are bound to lose. Mr Richards, the Adjudicator, is known for his determination to get as many people out of the country as possible. He's on some sort of mission, which is disgusting. Just imagine if he let everyone stay. He'd never last more than a few weeks. But look, Tunde." She leaned over and patted him on the shoulder. "Don't worry. We can take it further. This is not a disaster, just a setback."

He was not used to being patted on the back by young women, let alone by one with brightly coloured streaks in her hair, or of such an unconventional appearance, despite her trouser suit. At least he felt she was on his side, even if she did seem to be saying strange things for a proper lawyer.

"I have bad thoughts inside my head when I look at the people in court, even my barrister," he confessed to her. He was thinking of how they all seemed to be in cahoots. The young Asian guy who was putting forward the arguments to support Tunde's case, and who had seemed friendly enough outside court, was using pompous, unfamiliar terms like "my learned friend" and seemed to know the Home Office barrister. He had spent more time talking to him before the court started than to Tunde himself.

"Haroon is a good advocate," said Charlotte, "and very thorough. He will make the best of our medical report, which says you are suffering from post-traumatic stress syndrome."

He decided not to tell her just how mad he was feeling. The rage was icy now; later he would want to smash his fists into something – anything – to get rid of the constriction in his chest.

# Quicksand
## JACQUELYN SHREEVES-LEE

Three mice lie dead on the glue mat. Picking it up by the corners, Teapot avoids the sticky patch in the centre. He's been caught out like that before, glue sticking to his palms or fingers. After dumping the mat in the black bin liner, Teapot places a new one near the back door. The mice creep in from the playing field, finding cracks in the petrol-station walls. "We're lucky," his younger brother Kaz tells him, "it could be rats."

Teapot has spent the last few hours cleaning the shelves and surfaces. He keeps a big yellow bucket of warm soapy water at his side but doesn't bother changing it when the water turns a dark, metallic grey. Dragging the mop over the once cheerful yellow floor tiles, now defeated by time and reduced to dismal beige, Teapot sighs. Kaz will moan that he hasn't rinsed the floor properly and Kaz will be right. Corners have been missed and thin lanes left unwashed but Teapot returns the bucket and mop to the narrow cupboard where the cleaning materials are stored. Dulled by the drudgery of selling petrol and mini-mart odds and ends, his eyes scan the assortment of pointless have-a-nice-day knick-knacks on the counter – the tacky key rings with smiley faces, the 60s CDs that never sell and last Easter's Easter eggs, going cheap.

The central aisles are stacked with groceries and the corner area near the door is filled with bottles of deionised water, brake fluid, anti-freeze, tow ropes, blind-spot mirrors, emergency puncture-repair kits, L-plates, turtle wax and myriad other car-maintenance materials. There are cardboard air fresheners, from "Old-Fashioned Vanilla" to "Hot Sticky Fudge". Teapot can't believe anyone would seriously want a car smelling of hot sticky fudge. It isn't a best-seller; customers prefer "Lavender Fields", of which they frequently run out of stock. Men who've forgotten to buy flowers for their women stop on their way home to scavenge amongst the sad bunches left in the bucket beside the newspaper rack. Some customers, like Mr Pettigrew, the polite old boy, with skin the colour of mushroom soup, come to buy a Lottery ticket before the 7.30 p.m. deadline. Mr Pettigrew told Teapot that he wants to leave London and return to his childhood home of Devon, where he'll end his days with sedate clotted-cream teas and views of a predictable, unhurried sea. Others are hooked on what they could do with a cool fifty-four million rollover.

Tariq Ali, better known as Teapot, and Kazim Ali, known as Kaz, have worked in the petrol service station since leaving school. Their father calls the family business "a good little earner". He hopes his sons will continue with it but Teapot has ambitions and dreams above the stink of petrol and carloads of unhappy families. His father tries to keep it going but Teapot's mind isn't set that way. He likes lippy, hell-bent kids and can spot the glimmer of hope beneath their bravado. Five years earlier, just after he left school, Teapot found a job with a summer play-scheme and enjoyed it even more than he'd expected. During the first week, one boy, Gary Tribe, inserted a small plastic peg up his left nostril and two days later managed to wedge his head between some railings. "Crying out for attention," the lead youth worker decided. Teapot found a way in and over the following six weeks, turned Gary around. The youth worker told Teapot he was "a natural" with the kids.

And for a while Teapot played with the idea of training to be a youth worker or teacher, until his father said, "Forget it. No one makes money helping sad kids."

When Teapot returned to college, Kaz asked if Teapot was being serious, remarked that he needed his head tested. Kaz isn't academic; he prefers fast cars, women and the sliding, steamy rush of night clubs.

Teapot checks his watch: nine o'clock, Friday evening. Only the feisty, keen-eyed foxes patrol the local streets at this time. Teapot likes the night, catches the edgy coil in the air, the scent of risk, of most people heading home but others intent on breaking whatever rules and taboos they keep in the day.

The door opens. A young black woman enters the shop. Donna Flint.

"She walks in beauty, like the night". Byron's words could have been written for her. Her black skin fleeced with the buff of midnight and the startle of her dark, baleful eyes. Each time she walks in, Teapot feels something new moving inside him. She comes in all weathers, arms either loose and swinging or tightly folded beneath her breasts as though she's been bracing against a harsh wind or cramped with period pain. Donna reminds him of no one else. She is purely and wholly herself, but in a trapped and belligerent way.

As she walks past the mounted, curved mirror in the corner, Donna's figure stretches and spreads as she cartoons in and out. Teapot sees her lips move, her tongue hits the roof of her mouth and softly she sings dubadubaduba. She picks up one of the awkward metal baskets and hooks her arm through its red handles. She never buys petrol. As far as Teapot knows, she can't drive, hasn't got a car.

Teapot had gone to school with Donna's brother, Danny. In Year 10, they'd bunk off school, head down to Tottenham Marshes, smoke weed and fish in the nearby River Lea. All they ever caught were small, blue-grey minnows which they always threw back. After the Tottenham riots, Danny got sent down along with Eddie and Big Mikey, his cousins. It was Danny who had coined Tariq's nickname, Teapot. Other kids had called him half-breed, mongrel or half-caste but with Danny Flint he was just Teapot. Teapot was never given full membership by black or white kids; too black for some and too white for others. Pushed to the periphery, Teapot tried not to let the other kids matter, but Kaz carried a small, ivory pocket knife.

Donna walks along each aisle, armoured in her bomber jacket and narrow jeans. Multi-coloured bracelets reach up to her skinny elbows and join the jingle-jangle percussion of metal basket and high-rise heels. She hovers over the jams and marmalades and stoops to rummage through the biscuits, her fingers fluttering over the Jammie Dodgers and Jaffa Cakes. After tossing a packet of Viscount chocolate cookies and a bottle of Irn-Bru into the basket, she quickly wedges two packets of custard creams, her favourites, into a jacket pocket.

Sometimes she steals small loaves of bread, bottles of shampoo, bars of soap, or packs of processed cheese from the fridge. A couple of times a week, in this small fluorescent theatre, Donna performs her deviant ballet and a watchful Teapot wonders what she'll steal next. She reminds him of a bad magician he saw as a kid at a friend's Hallowe'en party where nobody clapped and everyone spent most of their time on their knees hunting for a lost white rabbit.

Up her left sleeve, Donna swiftly tucks a stick of Cadbury's Flake. She's needle thin and Teapot wonders what she does with all the food.

Some years ago, he'd gone to Danny's eighteenth-birthday party and there had been a very long kiss that in Teapot's head ran into miles and hours. Teapot had slowly opened his eyes to better believe Donna's glorious face and there she was looking back at him. She broke off and left him in the hallway, confused and stranded. Later he got it. You don't peek when you're kissing. It raises suspicion that your motives are elsewhere or that you're second-guessing. Teapot, however, had been fully present; so present he thought he'd combust. Donna continued to ignore him for the rest of the evening and he assumed he'd been filed under "mistake".

Afterwards when they passed one another on the street they'd mumble awkward hellos that drizzled into sheepish, barely-there nods. A handful of years now cordon them from one another. Teapot has emptied the time away in the petrol station and Donna disappeared for a while. People said she went to stay with family in Derby.

Crouching by the fridge, she squeezes a small carton of milk into another pocket.

Local gossip reported that she wasn't well; something whispered, half caught, "women's problems", or something "mental" when the world went wonky or she went wonky in the world.

Teapot wonders whether life has stolen so much from her that she wants to snatch it back. She's a bit strange in her inwardness, he thinks, but she's also a bit of wonderful, torn-tinsel Tottenham. He doesn't know when Donna's fingers became so light and nimble but he guesses there are empty inside pockets that she needs to fill.

She lands the basket noisily on the counter. Each time she moves her head, her large hooped earrings sway across her cheeks. Teapot scans the items and punches the keys in the cash till, aware that behind the beaded scatter of dark dreadlocks she's watching him. He wonders what she sees, worries about his unsatisfactory efforts to grow a "poet's beard".

"Suits you," she comments, staring at his chin. "I like it."

She's chewing gum, her mouth slack, giving him a flash of white teeth and pink tongue.

"That'll be five fifty," Teapot says, looking up and locking his eyes on her face. His voice softens when he speaks, shrinks to the back of his throat and he coughs in the hope of restoring some authority, but his voice buckles and breaks.

Donna counts out loud and gives him a handful of coins. The dark cupboards of her eyes are filled with secrets and Teapot senses something broken despite the temporary mending of a smile.

"Four eighty, that's all I've got," she says, wrinkling her snub nose, sizing him up, square in the eye. "Can I owe you?" she asks.

"How about you and me hanging out together?" He coughs hard and his Adam's apple bobs like a stone he can't swallow.

"You mean like a date?"

"We could carry on from where we left off."

"You mean at Danny's party?"

"Yes."

She swings her weight over to one hip and rests a hand on her waist. Pushing out her chest, she smiles and slowly a gate swings open.

"OK. You got yourself a deal. Took you long enough to ask."

She laughs and he laughs with her. She brushes her nose with the back of her hand and he glimpses the polished nails, chewed at the edges. It's the brew that gets him every time; the bric-a-brac of trial and error in her presentation; the worn high heels, buttons missing, locks tucked up and locks breaking free. And the sweet, musky perfume she wears underneath the cigarette smoke.

"Next Friday. Seven. I'll pick you up." He wants it to sound like a decision, a done deal, but it comes out like a question.

Her face breaks into a broad smile and she turns to leave.

"I'll be back later," she calls out, without looking over her shoulder.

Her hips work a swing in the way that some women walk when they know they're being watched or believe they've hooped a good thing.

Kaz strolls through the door just as Donna leaves. He doesn't acknowledge her and saunters up to the counter, tugging the slim cords of loud, pumping sound from his ears. Dark shades balance on his head. He's been to the gym, working out, dense muscles bulging like they might pop.

"Check this." He grins and flashes Teapot a shot on his mobile phone. "Potts thinks she's out of my league, that I'm punching above my weight." Kaz brings his mobile phone nearer to Teapot. "Fit, innit? Met her at the Black Cat. You missed out there, bro."

Teapot thinks it's easier to agree and nods, but he notes the quiet fretfulness tugging at the young woman's eyes and her limp, unconvincing smile.

Like wolves, Kaz and his friends hunt in packs. Teapot knows the sleight of heart Kaz plays with women's emotions, how he zeros in for the kill.

"I'd cut my hand off for a slice of that," Kaz adds before he presses Save and inserts his mobile in the back of his jeans.

Teapot heads for the toilets around the back where the floor is always wet with piss because some people are lazy and can't be bothered with accuracy or hygiene. Washing his hands, he glances in the mirror above the small sink; his father's face, minus the odd gold tooth, stares back at him. He knows his father imagines him treading too closely behind; the weak-kneed, undeserving usurper. He reminds Teapot that he could still show him a thing or two, and that "There's life in the old dog yet."

Back in the shop, Teapot removes his paperback of poetry tucked beneath the counter. From being cramped in his pocket, the book refuses to lie flat and turns inwards. He has homework: an essay on the Romantic poets, Byron, Shelley, Keats. John Keats once lived just down the road in Church Street, Edmonton. Teapot visualises Keats living in the present day, hanging out with the brothers. Swaggering with a jerk in his jeans and boasting along with everyone else about things he'd never done or sitting there quietly in the corner, committing them all to paper. Old J. K. Teapot likes poetry and stories, and while Kaz preens and parties, Teapot shoots up on literature.

Reared on his mother's bedtime stories of wailing banshees and the mighty giant, Finn McCool, Teapot revels in folklore, and even in adulthood still holds out for a happy ending. In particular, he likes the story of how his parents met. Many years ago Farouk Ali met their mother, Maureen O'Sullivan, when they worked at Thompson Electrics. Teapot's mother worked in the canteen. She never used to charge Farouk for tea and regularly gave him free sandwiches and that's how he knew she liked him.

Farouk's relatives opposed the marriage, warning him that he would "heap hot coals on his head", but Maureen's parents welcomed Farouk's moneyed presence into their family and trod any private doubts underfoot. Maureen didn't work after she married Farouk. The understanding was that he would take care of her and that she would take care of their home and their children.

Teapot's distant grandfather had helped clear the dense Guyanese jungles for tea cultivation and then worked on sugar plantations. When Teapot's father talked about the suffering of the Indians, his mother dredged up the Irish potato famine and the plight of the "white niggers". "That's what they called us," she announced proudly. Teapot wanted to tell her to stop showing off. Competition for the crown of the most oppressed would follow and then Jews, Palestinians, Africans would be poured into the mix. "Blacks? My dad used to call them porch monkeys," his father said. Kaz laughed out loud, Teapot left the room.

Teapot tidies a box of tights that has toppled from a shelf and recalls his earliest memories of things intimate and warm. He remembers a Christmas, long ago. The laughter stopped when seven-year-old Teapot entered the kitchen, the couple springing apart as though suddenly scorched. His father said that he was helping Aunty Loll with something and dropped the mistletoe to the floor. Teapot thought his father had been eating his aunt, devouring her pretty doll face.

"Mummy told me to get a plaster." The young Teapot held out his thumb.

"It's just a scratch." His father shrugged and walked out of the kitchen.

Bending down, Aunty Loll took his small hand and led him to the sink where she ran his bloody thumb under the cold-water tap. She wrapped his brown thumb in a plaster. Teapot wanted her to kiss it better. Aunty Loll had been soft, warm and made a kind of petticoat music when she moved. After that evening, she never returned to their house and his father began talking to Teapot without looking at him, sentences barked like slammed doors. Nowadays Teapot finds it hard to remember a time before the doors were closed.

He places the box of tights on the shelf and settles on the stool. Kaz returns from checking the petrol pumps on the forecourt.

"Studying again?" Kaz asks, peering over Teapot's shoulder.

"Homework."

"You need to live more, bro. There's a world out there and you're in danger of being left behind."

"I'm gonna be a teacher, Kaz. This" – Teapot points at their surroundings – "and all that clubbing ain't for me."

"I got other strings to my bow too, bro," Kaz replies, winking and turning to his mobile.

Teapot opens his book on Byron.

A little later, Kaz asks, "Did you fix the coffee machine?"

"Yeah, the wires at the back got tangled."

The coffee machine pumps out coffee with three simple commands: Pull, Pour and Go.

Teapot continues reading, aware of the boom-boom base of teenage cars surfing the streets and puncturing the late-night silence.

The heavy door pushes open. Donna stands in her high heels. Her toenails are painted in stars and stripes and Teapot suspects that this isn't about the United States but a fashion statement, a nail thing. Her eyelashes are heavily draped in mascara and her lips purple and pouty with gloss. This painted face all for him. Offering Teapot a warm smile, she reduces him to something mushy. He smiles back but on spotting Kaz, Donna quickly turns her attention to the bread and pastries. Kaz glances over at Donna, pulls a sick face and mouths, "Skank." Slowly she walks over to the refrigerator topped with large unrealistic toy tigers and lifts a nine-pack of beers. Swinging round, she stops and gazes down at the cosmetics.

Teapot studies her every move so as not to miss anything, however slight. She could take it all – the liquorice allsorts, the chocolate fingers, the loo rolls; the petrol could run out, every car could stop, and Teapot would still look on, hanging on to the poetry and promise of her dubadubadubas. Below the slip of skirt, her dark-brown legs are bare and thin. The muscles in her calves; sinewed and taut. She is a gazelle, graceful and lithe, even though Teapot worries that in her high heels she might topple and break at any moment. He wishes she'd kick off her shoes and come slow-dance to whatever music she hears, his arms tightly wrapped around her like strong rope.

He waits for another smile.

Donna walks towards the counter and looks directly at Teapot, fixes on his shy, Malteser eyes and the sleeping snake of his black ponytail. He scans the nine-pack and holds her gaze. He could never wink properly and instead offers a soft grin.

"Eight quid, please," he says.

Donna produces a fiver and some change.

"It's OK," Teapot says.

Kaz's eyes narrow and he shakes his head. "No, it ain't OK. No wonder the figures don't add up, if you're giving stuff away."

Ignoring Kaz, Donna looks at Teapot. "Thank you," she says and turns to leave.

Kaz blocks Donna at the door, watches the smile falter on her face.

"Where do you think you're going? I think you've got something else to pay for."

Donna hesitates.

"Well?"

Gripping an arm, he shakes her. The nine-pack falls to the ground along with two bottles of purple nail polish.

"You think you can come in here and take what isn't yours?

You know what my pop calls people like you?" He digs his fingers into her arm.

"Fuck off." Donna pulls herself free.

"Sewer rats. Dirty. Filthy. Sewer rats." Kaz thrusts his chin forward, hardens his eyes and sniffs the air like he smells something bad.

Leaping over the counter, Teapot runs towards the door.

"Enough," he says. "Just leave it."

Kaz looks at him, struggles to believe what he's just said.

"Not fucking likely. She's a fucking tea-leaf. And it ain't the first time, is it, bitch?"

"I said leave it."

Kaz stares long and hard at Donna. "Go on, get out. Don't show your face round here again. I mean it."

Teapot pushes the heavy door open.

"You OK?" he asks softly.

Donna's eyes are wet and she bites down hard on her lip but manages a faint "Thanks." Slowly, she walks out into the night where heavy, low-lying clouds choke the moon and stars from the black London sky.

Closing the door behind him, Teapot turns to Kaz. "What is it with you?"

"With me? The woman's a thief. The world don't need no thieves. Her whole family's trash. Everyone knows it. Her brother's inside, her mum's a crack-head."

"I said, shut it."

Kaz starts pointing a finger at Teapot, stabbing it in the air.

"I don't get it. Don't tell me you're soft on her. Donna Flint? You've got to be kidding me. The woman's a thief."

"And you're so different?"

"This ain't about me."

"So the speakers don't count?"

"The riots were something else. You don't get it. This place is ours, our yard. She was stealing from *us*."

"That's where you're wrong, Kaz. I do get it. The people on Tottenham High Street are us. Mustafa. Dennis. Faizal. Mrs Parker. The guys in Body Muzik – who you and your mates stole the speakers from. *They're* us."

"No. They're not us. I know where to draw the line."

"The line? What line? Do you seriously think the politicians and the police see a line?"

Kaz doesn't answer.

"Well they don't. In their eyes we're all the same. You. Me. Dennis. Mrs Parker. The guys from Body Muzik. Donna. We're the small, unimportant people. It ain't about this poxy little petrol station, the picture's bigger than that, but you don't see it, do you, Kaz? You don't see how we're *all* in this *together*."

"I'm not one of your small, unimportant people."

"I'm trying to say we're on the same side. You, me, Donna. You think working in this petrol station makes us bigger pieces on the chessboard? Gives us any kind of real power, do you? Then you're more lost than I thought."

"Fuck you, Peter Perfect!" Kaz shouts and turns away. "Don't preach to me, I know how this society works."

"Yeah, sure you do."

Turning back, Kaz's eyes bore into Teapot. "*You* think you know how it all works but *you* don't know *shit*."

"*I* know who *I* am, Kaz."

"You? You know *fuck all*. You think your dead poets and your dumb A levels are gonna change anything? Well, newsflash: *they ain't*."

Looking around, Teapot draws in a deep breath, his voice raw and ragged. "This place ain't gonna amount to a pot of piss. It's just money, petrol and more money and more petrol and that's it. It don't mean anything and it ain't ever gonna mean anything. You. Dad. Look at it, it's just quicksand. That's what quicksand does. It pulls you under, leaves no trace. If you're not careful you'll sink along with everything else around here."

"Quicksand? What the fuck are you talking about? Your problem is that you think you're better than me and the old man, with all your poetics, your clever words and your big ideas."

"I never said that."

"You didn't have to. I know one thing: you can become the biggest fuck-all poet of all time, it ain't gonna change a thing."

"Who said I wanted to change anything? I just don't want to be like you or Dad. I want my life to mean something."

"Well, you can dream on all you like, but the petrol stink's in you, like everything else around here. You need to wise up, Teapot. It's dog eat dog out there. This is us. This is what we do."

Flecks of spit dart from Kaz's mouth and he keeps his eyes firmly on Teapot's face but Teapot looks out at the endless trail of night traffic. Without meeting Kaz's eyes and with a dry mouth he says, "And like I said, quicksand."

As he returns the beer to the fridge and the bottles of nail polish to the cosmetics shelf, Teapot's steps sound loud on the sticky floor. Slowly he sits down on the stool, its leather seat split open like a busted lip. Releasing a long breath, he forces the exhaust and petrol from his lungs but his heart still hammers. Kaz throws on his jacket and storms out of the shop, bad blood and anger raking through his face.

The following morning Teapot can't find the two boxes containing the speakers Kaz had hidden in the lock-up at the back of the petrol station. He makes no comment and leaves Kaz talking to a customer. Teapot knows where she works – Munchies on the High Street. He glances in, sees her in her sure-footed flats, dreadlocks pulled against her scalp, eyes dull with yesterday's menus. Donna looks short without her heels. No high-rise views here, her feet on firm ground. The dubadubadubas silenced in her mouth and saved for later. Teapot sits at a window table, facing the full heat and glare of the late-morning sun. Blocks of dark, autumnal paintings dot the walls and although the leather seats are comfortable, the tables are worn. The café is busy and the wallpaper of soft rock music blends with the chatter and clink of cutlery. Donna watches Teapot enter and slowly approaches him.

"About last night," she begins. "I want to say I'm sorry."

Teapot shakes his head and stops her. "I'm sorry all round," he says.

Neither speaks for a while.

"What can I get you?" she asks.

"Egg and chips."

"Fried?"

Teapot nods.

With a small black biro, Donna scribbles Teapot's order on a tiny notepad. She catches sight of his book on the table.

"Poetry?"

"Yeah, I'm doing English A level."

"North London College?"

"Yeah."

"My mate Debs goes there. She's doing hairdressing."

Teapot looks at her. "What about you? What do you want to do?"

"Dunno." She fiddles with her fingers. "Still trying to work that one out." She replaces the biro and pad in a pocket. "Got to go. The boss will think I'm skiving."

"Next Friday, then?" Teapot asks.

"Yeah. Friday."

Walking to the kitchen Donna hangs Teapot's order on a small metal hook, alongside a row of other metal hooks hammered in the wall. The kitchen is hectic with spluttering appliances and orders being called out for collection. In her arms, Donna balances four all-day breakfasts for the long-distance lorry drivers seated by the flat-screen TV.

From his pocket Teapot produces two slender bottles of purple nail polish and places them on the table beside a packet of custard creams, a five pound note and some loose change. While Donna works her way around the tables carrying trays of hot food and warming drinks, Teapot catches and throws back the tentative smiles she sends his way. He knows that while poetry drills away at the marrow, it is other people who make people better.

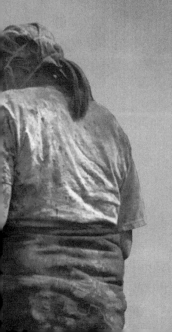

"Anxiety is the handmaiden of creativity."

– T. S. Eliot

# Goat
## EVIE WYLD

### Winter 1999

Pete's wife left him as he stood smoking his own good mull on the veranda of their home which faced out onto the highway, with the vast bush behind. Hen, the old white goat, tooled around on the end of her tether – he'd have to move her peg soon – the grass all gone from her circle.

Deb swung the last bag into the boot of the car – their car. She was taking that and leaving him the ute, which was, he supposed, fair. The muscles craned out of her biceps. She'd got thin in the last year.

"You sure you're heading off?" he asked her. His voice was hoarser than he would have liked, but only a fraction.

Deb turned to him and put her thin wrist to her forehead, wiped the sweat, then took her hand to her hip. She breathed deeply – the suitcases were heavy.

"Yes. I am heading off, Pete," she said and they stayed like that, her eyeballing him like he was the sort of bloke that might chase her around the place with a soap in a sock, him letting smoke fill the space between them. Even now she was trying to make him something he was not, and he couldn't change, not for any man or woman. He'd always known that about himself.

In the end it was her lack of interest in life, Pete reckoned, that made her go off him. He had sworn as a grommet the first time he'd run away from home. He'd never get a real job, not him. He'd live off the land, go under the radar. The closest he'd come had been six months of labouring on a building site, but he'd learnt a skill there. He'd made their mud-brick house himself, shaped the bloody mud bricks and baked them in the sun.

"This place is full of fuckin' redbacks!" Deb'd shouted at him once years ago, when the summer plague of them had hatched. But when they met, her with the cheesecloth and the tanned dusty feet, him with his hair that floated around behind him like a live animal, it had been all about the living with nature. They'd drawn the house plans together, they'd sketched the bread oven, the rainwater chute, the space and space and space to plant and to be lost in. The bread she'd used to make him with the aniseed taste, and the thick crust that made your gums bleed. Fuckin' awful, but he'd loved it, loved her making it for him. And her father, the big know-all at Knob Creek with his hard and silent stare. Even at the wedding he'd taken Pete aside and said, "I just need the smallest reason to break your legs, son," and Pete enthusiastically shaking his hand while he said it, smiling and feeling the grip tighten, the old man's hand like a buzzard's claw, while flash bulbs pinged off around them. And she'd framed one of those, and chosen not to see her father's face, ground out like a shaped stone, in contrast to Pete's boneless flat nose – or maybe she'd kept it up there all these years as a warning. He hadn't thought about that before.

She disappeared back inside, passed him without looking. He heard her scraping together the last things that she owned from the side table. The chime of her keys, the noise of the few cents that lay next to her cigarettes, being slid across and into her palm. *Can you reckon it?* he asked himself. *Smoking those cancer sticks when there was pure golden mull they'd grown themselves?* She hadn't, of course – had been five years since she'd shown any interest in the crop. Since she'd had the turn, vomming into the dunny and crying till a blood vessel went in her eye. He shoulda known then – the slow burn of rage that was in her. Her insistence on the wireless Internet. Her purchase of a phone with a keypad. Her promotion at work.

Hen was straining at her leash to get to a tissue that had blown out of the car. The wind obliged her and shunted it closer and the goat ate it.

## Summer 1965

It wasn't as if it hurt that much, getting punched in the face. His nose had been broken before, when he was a nipper. Some drunk bloke arsing about with an oar at a Rotary picnic had cracked it right into his face. It had hurt that time, he remembered it: the bone, the blood, his mother screaming like a gibbon, his father giving the drunk a beer in reconciliation a few moments too early.

At the circus, though, when a drunk bloke paid five dollars for one strike, Pete knew his nose didn't have all that many places to go. And it made friends of the carnies, who shared their drink once the lights went down.

"Not many young blokes can take a punch like that and keep smiling," a wiry-looking fella called Mick told him, and it made Pete warm inside and he wobbled a back tooth with his tongue, enjoyed the heady shock of it. Was amazing, the human body really. Just amazing.

Some nights he'd have a sackful and sleep right there on the fairground, wake up bitten by fire ants, with not enough water left in his body to piss with.

Carmen was Mick's older sister with long black hair from a film. "Meet me by the fairy floss after closing," she'd told him on a night Mick and the boys had started early and were already laying into each other, proclaiming all over the place that this bloke was a sworn enemy and that bloke was the truest friend that ever lived and then swapping the blokes around and back again. Behind the fairy-floss shack, the smell of caramel in the air, she gave him his first smoke of mull.

"Know what'd happen if Mick found out I smoked this?" she asked, a black eye glinting.

Pete had wrinkled his nose, holding it in while it was hot. He let it out, felt his lungs sprout wings. "But Mick smokes all the time. You're older too – I thought you must've got it off him?" Disappointment leant its elbow into Pete's throat. He'd thought they'd met round the back of the fairy floss for other reasons.

"Ha!" said Carmen. "Not our way, mate. Not our way."

Carmen had a sharp upper lip and a large lower one. She had a tiny dark mole in the very centre of her nose. Pete dreamed about her hair the summer through, after the carnie left and right around until the next year, when he had bulked out, flat nose and all.

But the next year some evangelist preacher had his people parked in the spot the carnies usually took.

"What happened to the circus?" Pete asked a man with a clipboard and white socks who was selling tickets.

"Not been a good year for the circus, son – all these animal rights-ers making a song and dance," he said, "but fair dinkum, this bloke'll knock your socks off." He pointed to a photograph of a man who looked like he was glowing out the back of his head.

"You'd better hope he can knock yours off, mate," Pete said.

The man looked at him and said, "'S only four dollars."

Pete hung around anyway until the crowds came in and listened from outside the arena to a man blabbermouthing about serpents and Jesus while people cheered. It didn't sound like they were the kind of folk to pay five dollars and then only get one hit in.

## Spring 1955

The mother broke her ankle getting off the bus and if someone asked after how she'd done it, she'd say "Skiing," and then watch triumphantly the look on the person's face. They were not the type of family to go skiing, even if they could afford to get to the snow.

Because Pete came up just above her hip, she used him instead of a walking stick when she moved about the place. She planted a wide hot palm on top of his head and squashed his neck down into his shoulders. She'd not been fat in the first days Pete could remember, or in the photo of his parents' wedding that hung in the toilet. But she said the backs of her hands swelled in the heat, her wrists became puffy and ran with sweat. But if it was just a problem with her hands then the rest of her body got the hang of it pretty quickly. They sat on the sofa together, watching *Wheel of Fortune* and eating icy poles. She'd mouth the answers to the questions, never say them out loud, but she'd move her lips just before the contestants spoke, slap her hand down on the sofa if they got it wrong.

That October while the buds opened on the bottle brush that marked where the Mcnullys' place started, with their big horned goat with a long tether, Pete knelt on the sofa and watched out the window. Older kids played chicken with the goat, seeing how far they could creep up on him before he chased them out, his hooves making the sound of a dog eating bones. From the window, Pete could see them sometimes, tumbling back onto the pavement, laughing, their eyes wet, faces red, the noise of them that came in through the closed window. Before long Mr Mcnully always came out waving a shovel and roaring like a hog. He shouted down the road at them, for teasing his goat, but Pete knew the goat was there so that Mr Mcnully could wave his shovel and scream at kids. It was a good joke. *Everyone needs a goat*, Pete thought, watching Mr Mcnully shake his head and start back up his driveway with a smile on his face. *Every single person needs a goat with horns.*

"I need him with me, I can't move about otherwise," his mum said over and over, and no one offered her a walking stick in his place.

## Autumn 1979

They went together to buy the goat. Pete had his heart set on a big angry one like they'd kept down the road from him when he was a kid. The one with horns painted red as a warning, after a kid in the year above'd had his back opened. But Deb hadn't liked the look of the buck's balls. "They look like me dad's," she'd said, nodding to a pair that stretched their leathery way to the floor. He'd loved her in that moment, more than he ever had.

And so they'd gone for a nanny goat, with her big pink udder looking to Pete just the same as the balls. They'd be able to get milk from her, even if she'd give them no occasion to paint her pointy little horns.

"I'll make you goat's curd," said Deb. "You can eat it on me bread." The thought of it turned Pete's stomach at the same time as making him smile. "We'll call her Henrietta," she said, without knowing it was his mother's name. He wouldn't mention it. Too late now. The goat looked up at them with its yellow eyes and Pete wondered how long it'd live. They'd get a billy goat after this one was gone.

"Let me live, love and say it well in good sentences."

— Sylvia Plath

# Transformers
## JULIUS PASTEINER

I'd seen him at school and heard the rumours – Mike James, the boy who witnessed Craig Ingram, the hardest of hard kids, drown in the smudge of Little Whyke Reservoir. It went that Mike didn't do anything to help, that he watched him go under. Everyone saw him differently afterwards. He changed from a scrawny estate kid with a cowlick and a wonky smile to a legend of sorts. But not the kind you clung to, the kind that gave you the shivers, set you walking in the other direction. Who'd look into those sunken brown eyes and ask how he was? Not the Ashmill lot. Not us. I guess he'd glimpsed a sort of realness nobody was ready for.

\* \* \*

The day started normal. I woke early and sniped Nazi heads with my carbine on Medal of Honour until Dad left for his late shift, then I showered, tried various hairstyles in the mirror, gave up, and stretched out on the sofa for a session of *Midsomer Murders*. A dire episode. Chief Inspector Barnaby caught in decoys while the killer flutters her lids. I couldn't make it to the end, told little Sis to tell Mum I'd be home after dinner, and wandered down to meet Jim.

He was fixing a joint sat on the bench that perched over the twinkling millpond. As I pulled up, he bent round, squinting. "Stan boy," he said, sounding unusually eager to see me.

"Yeah?"

"What do you reckon?" He twisted a shiny Nike-clad foot in the sharp light.

"Quality," I said, not giving away an ounce of my jealousy. "Quality," I said again, taking a seat.

"Mum got them." He passed a lazy eye over the Nikes, his mood changing. "They might grow on me," he said. Liking then not liking, that's how he kept our interest.

I switched tack. "Liam coming?"

"'Course. What else is he going to do?"

He passed me the joint. I took a giant heave on it. Ridiculously giant. Before I could breathe out, I felt sandpaper at my throat and spluttered like a lightweight.

"Easy, Stan." Jim snatched the spliff back. "We've got the whole afternoon to waste."

"Something's got me craving."

"That's how it goes," he said, all mystical or something. Then he tapped my shoulder. His voice hushed and somewhat reverent – still tripping on mysticisms. "Listen," he said and peered forward.

I strained my ears out across the pond to the plump rhododendrons on the far side, to the shaggy weeping willow hanging over the reeds to our left.

"Nothing."

"Seriously?"

"Nothing!"

"Listen! The buzzing. Over there." He pointed to a dragonfly. Big eyes on a static black dash hovering over the water. "Amazing sound."

When I heard it, it was like suddenly realising a lawnmower was going in my head.

"Potent shit," I said.

"Manu's new batch." He grinned.

The dragonfly then twitched, careered towards us, grew large, and disappeared over our heads trailing wakes of fuzzy sound. We both got the fits immediately. Couldn't help it. The dragonfly seemed suddenly such a mad, jittery little creature.

Liam arrived next. He stood in front of us, head just over ours, mouth open, gawping distaste into our smoke and giggles.

"What's so funny?" said Liam, who was shaped like an oversized teddy bear. Features packed tightly in the centre of a pale moon-face. He wore a Bath rugger shirt, sleeves cut short, battered grey trackies and never jeans.

"You are," said Jim, and we giggled some more.

"Dickhead druggies," said Liam.

"Joint?" Jim said, and flipped his wrist.

"Nah."

"It won't kill you," I said.

"Nah," he said, and sat cross-legged on the earth in front of us, pulled out his Nokia 3310 – his pride and joy – and started a marathon Snakes game.

\* \* \*

Mike James worked at the only off-licence in Ashmill village. It was at least a half-an-hour walk from the rough part of town, White Eagles estate, where he lived. We blamed fate and luck and various disgraced football players for being forced to buy baccy and king skins from Mike. Of all the shitty jobs he could have done, what were the chances?

I'd spoken to him for the first time a few months earlier, the day it fell on me to purchase a new pouch of Golden Vadge. It was the start of the summer hols, baking outside, a joyful stretch of caning ahead of us. I dressed in my newest clobber, Nike Cortez, Next polo neck, Firetrap jeans, spanking Casio. I pushed the offy door open smooth as you like, strutted up to the counter, slapped down my dad's spare set of keys.

"Tough day at the office," I said, letting my voice drop low as it'd go.

Mike didn't even look up. Not a glance. Carried on staring at the security-camera monitor. A hint of a sweat-gleam on his pasty skin.

"Golden Virginia, small pouch."

He slid it across the counter. "Anything else?"

"Not today."

I paid. Left slowly, making sure to swing the keys in an arc as practised. Boom. I strutted out seven feet tall and packing mercurial new weaponry in my Firetraps.

When I got to the millpond I handed over the goods, told Jim and Liam that I stared right into Mike's eyes. "I didn't blink," I said.

"Liar," said Liam. "Piss bucket."

"He's dead inside," I said. "Nothing there."

So that afternoon, when he first moseyed up dragging his duffed Reeboks and sat on our bench, my brain cogs ran with all sorts of blackmailing opportunities he might have in store. Say everything we'd ever bought off him was on the spot his. Tell us the police were coming to search our houses for narcotics. Force us to jump in the pond or he'd rinse all the shrapnel from our pockets. He said nothing – nodded, sniffed the air and wiped his nose, looked dimly around.

We followed Jim's lead and forced nods back.

"What you up to?"

"Watching the wildlife," said Jim. "Liam's in a sweat over Snakes. He's got the best score in Sussex. You know they call him Snakehead on tinterweb?"

"Snakecharmer," Liam said, slipping his phone back into his trackie pocket just in case.

"Worse, Liam. You're such a loser," said Jim in his tetchy voice he reserved for Liam.

Mike cut through it. "S'pose I can have a go on that?"

Jim passed the spliff over.

"Ta," he said.

His drag was massive. Leaned back as he inhaled. Kept the spliff between first and second finger, hand cupped. He held his inhale for what seemed for ever, then let the smoke spout out his nostrils in long almost sculptural twists.

"Ace dragon," said Jim.

"Wizard," I said.

There'd been a kid called Ben or Benjy or Benny or whatever that hung with us lot at the beginning of the summer. He was, like Mike, a tad bit older than us. Fifth Year. A tall kid with Air Max on his feet who seemed untethered to any particular group. He sat on the bench and Jim shared with him. We made small talk about the baking heat, the way the sky appeared far wider and bluer than any of us had noticed before. He walked off one afternoon and never returned.

That's what we hoped from Mike James, too.

After that first toke Mike started appearing each afternoon. He'd finish work then trundle down to the millpond. We'd go quiet, pass him the joint. He talked about his boss being a big man and a nonce. That work wouldn't give him minimum wage because he wasn't eighteen, which was funny, he explained, because he was the best worker they had. We listened and let Mike hog the spliff beyond his turn. In fact, he often puffed down a whole airy-one to himself while we avoided his gaze and searched out patterns in the pond ripples.

Jim made an effort. He told Mike about the ducks. There was a skinny one we called Posh and a frantic one that never ceased doing laps we called Becks. You got one point for hitting Posh with a stone and five for Becks. Head hits were a straight ten. Mike flinched acknowledgement, perhaps chuckled or maybe coughed, it was hard to tell. He took a few turns and sunk a few lily pads, but lobbing stones didn't hold his attention for long. It made me think he was only here for Manu's new batch.

Our discomfort fell on Liam heavy.

"How's the tractor?" I'd ask.

"Stan, you know it's buggered."

"Farm's going under, is it?"

"Don't be harsh," he'd say. "Don't get on me."

"Isn't your dad an alcoholic or something?" Jim would ask.

"From a druggie, fuck off!"

"Want a puff?" Jim would say, turning the screw. He'd push a burning spliff towards Liam's face. So close one time Liam leapt up and swatted the air like he was under attack from a swarm of killer bees. "Fuck off," he yelped again, and bundled towards the water's edge, where he teetered like a fat penguin. It was the first time we heard Mike really laugh. A shifty and oddly high laugh. Brought to mind small, pointed creatures – elves and leprechauns. Jim and I joined him, because it made us feel careless and bad or something more interesting than we were.

We never asked any questions and he never asked any of us. I reckoned we were just kids to him, same as the next, something he could use or get used by. It must mash you up, I thought, to see someone like Craig drown. To actually watch it happen, your mate, the one you bunked school with, who'd only just begun to raise your status. See, Mike wasn't exactly intimidating before Craig took him under his wing. He was one of those dappy boys who took an age to realise that ankle huggers and brandless, gypo school shoes was a look literally worthy of stick. With Craig, he became something. Now he was something else.

He stayed about the same length each day. A long hour, never more. Chip away at Jim's cling-film wrap and then say "Laters," or "See you round," and stagger towards the weeping willow. We'd watch him part the branches, phase into another world. To the estate and whatever went on there. You could hear the tension break, like the whine of a firework lifting off. Jim would start talking about something messed up and evil he saw on the Internet. Generally porn-related. Midget stuff was his favourite. Liam would ignore us, start another Snakes game, and for the rest of the afternoon we'd feel somewhat blessed to be in the sun with nothing to fear.

Of course, we didn't mention Mike after he left. What were we supposed to say? Yeah, that Mike's a solid lad, I should ask him round for tea . . . ? Truth was we didn't want to meet him on the level – eye to eye. If we did, we'd have to acknowledge he was real. That he was more than a rumour we didn't want to get to the bottom of.

\* \* \*

And come dark we'd all drift off home as bleary as Mike. I'd slip up to my room and avoid the parents, which wasn't difficult. Things had gotten pretty strained of late. Dad was working through the night at St Peter's hospital and rising around eleven, while Mum left early each morning to teach at the summer school. They barely saw each other and always appeared in a rush. I don't think we'd sat down at the same table for weeks. One morning little Sis knocked on my door.

"What?"

"Dad's downstairs shouting at the washing machine," she said through the door.

"I heard," I said.

"I don't think it's the washing machine," she said.

"No."

She pushed the door open and stood, head just over the handle, wearing her favourite stripy dress. She asked with a brave and childish face on, "What shall we do?"

"Wait for him to leave. He'll be gone at twelve." I turned on the Playstation, waited for Medal of Honour to load up.

"I'm going to help," she said, and pattered along the landing. Light strobed her dress through the banisters. She was the only one who wasn't ignoring the hole in the middle of our family, like she saw how big it was but still believed she could plug it.

\* \* \*

Friday – always Jim's Big Night – and Mike was still kicking around. It was gone six and we were all at the millpond, several spliffs down and beginning to twiddle thumbs.

"Let's go back to yours," I said to Jim.

"Not yet," he said in a pleading tone he knew only I'd noticed.

"I'm thirsty," I said. "Aren't you, Liam?"

"Yeah," said Liam. "Miguels till I die," he chanted. "Miguels till I die –"

"Don't sing, Liam," cut Jim.

"I'll sing my lungs out if I want. Miguels –"

"Gay, Liam. It's *gay*. Gays sing like that," said Jim with satisfaction.

Mike toked and handed me the spliff. "Let's go," he said.

A sticky quiet smothered us, clung to our throats. Nobody knew what to do. I inhaled and listened to a dragonfly flitting uneasily in the warm air – that electric buzz, which rose through me and trickled out to my fingernails. Jim or Mike, it was in the balance for a moment. Who was going to give the final word? The shadow of the telephone pole ticked across the pond. Then the ducks flew off.

Jim got to his feet. "Come on, bitches," he said. "Back to mine."

On the way past the Sunrise pub Mike did the kind of thing we had expected him to do. He hopped the picket fence and pulled us over to the window.

"Bigots," he said.

It was the usual crowd, four or five paunchy blokes with boozy red faces, wealthy farmers and local businessmen, sitting around the ale pumps trying to trawl the past into the future. I heard them once joke about the death penalty and culling immigrants like rabbits, but they didn't mean it, they were just disappointed. From what I could see everyone was pretty safe. Very safe. Families in huddles, bored kids, dogs by the fireplace.

"They like the banter," said Jim, whose dad's face glowed redder and more often than most.

"They're lazy," said Mike. "They're posh, lazy bigots."

"Don't you work at the offy?" snapped Jim in a cruel voice. "That's got to be a bent job."

Mike ignored him, as if he hadn't heard, and gambolled ahead. We caught up, Liam and I in the middle, Mike and Jim on the ends.

We stopped outside Jim's, probably the plushest big-windowed barn conversion in Ashmill. Jim dialled in the code and we stepped through the small porthole in the front gate and crunched up the drive.

"Not a bad place," said Mike.

"Wait till you see the inside," someone said.

Jim's parents were amazingly generous. Basically open house all year round. So when we rocked up needing refreshment, we raided the two-door fridge for bevs and sat about playing Medal of Honour on a plasma the size of a pool table. Jim slaughtered everyone as normal, taking Liam down with a magnificent headshot from across a canyon in the semi-final and Liam nearly wept, would've broken the game pad if his pudgy arms weren't in fact full of sausage. Mike was hopeless. Destroyed time and again and barely noticed. He sat on the white tiger rug, back against the corner of a leather chair, his expression a bit askew, like a lost dog who'd just arrived in a home full of cats.

For the final round, Jim's dad joined us, Miguel in hand, to watch his son take me apart. No mercy. Shot in the back while I hunted a decent sniping point. They all lofted beers and cheered. Jim's dad told us he'd have never got anything done with a machine like that to waste his time on. I thought he was joking. But he wasn't. Suddenly he looked concerned by something, said, "See you, lads," and left the room, swinging heavily.

By now it was pitch-black outside and we took our third or fourth Miguel to the patio, sat around in the garden furniture, and Jim sparked us another joint to admire the shrubbery with. It was his mum's pet project. The whole area a tropical paradise lit by spots set into bamboo paths and lanterns tucked behind ferns and cacti. It had a dreamy atmosphere, kind of magical of an evening, like the inside of an aquarium.

At first, I thought the noise was the ringing in my head from staring at the plasma for too long. You kind of get locked in after a while, like you're actually in a different universe, lining up shots and running for cover, the rest of the world curving off into a sort of nothingness. But the noise was all around us and there was a soft thud to it.

"What's that?" said Liam.

"Shit," someone else said.

We hunted the garden for the source of the noise. Liam was on all fours looking under the giant Colocasia leaves and sticking his nose between the baby bamboos. The rest of us craned our necks to get a better vantage on the sounds but were too drunk and stoned to shake the mystery. Then, from far off, a louder noise, a kind of rushing pop, like a gym mat falling to the floor, followed by a dying crackle. The lights in the house fizzed, then the garden lights went, and we disappeared from each other.

Mike cracked up. Something had got to him, he just started going with his spiky leprechaun laugh and soon we were all at it, filling the darkness, which carried on until Liam tapped my side. And there Mike was opening the rear gate, cutting a route for us across the rising wheat fields shot with spooky glimmer from a high fat moon.

The less I thought the more my excitement grew. Wheat beards well over shoulder height rustled madly and tingled across my cheeks as we went. Ahead, silhouetted against a starry sky, was Oak Island. It always looked like a mistake, a chunk of mossy earth no bigger than Jim's dad's Range Rover sat in the middle of a field. Above it grew a single grand oak. We didn't know why the farmer had never cut it down. But because Jim had discovered a rope scar on the thick branch several summers ago we told ourselves it was a hanging tree. For witches and such. We imagined it would've been bad luck to remove a tree with a hanging branch. Crops would fail. Wells dry up.

Up on Oak Island we had a good view back to Copse Lane. A bloke in overalls was lumbering, toolbox in hand, across the headlight beams of a parked van. He struggled with the gate and the creepers, which concealed most of the Copse Lane substation, and forced his way in using his shoulder.

"What d'you reckon?" whispered Liam.

"Fuck knows," said Jim.

Mike moved again, no longer bothering to be stealthy. Quickly we were down the slope and level with the substation. We stood together and watched from the road. The bloke fiddled with a panel plastered with yellow DANGER stickers. He was a foot taller than us, sort of humpbacked, and telling from his gut the type to sneak a kebab between jobs.

Jim still had the joint in his hand and the bloke must have smelt the ganj because he swivelled. His eyes blazing like a badger's wild stare in the headlights until he raised a hand to make a visor.

"You local boys?" he said.

"Nah," said Mike. "We're from White Eagles."

He looked puzzled, perhaps a tad irritated, shook his head, and in a sterner voice said, "You better stand back. Far back."

We waited in silence. The space between us shrank. He pulled something, flipped something else, then pumped a lever. There was a flickering noise, which flattened and coarsened into a thudding drum.

"Bugger," said Liam.

"It can make quite a racket," said the bloke.

We listened closer. The sound all over, altering the air, rolling in then out with our breathing. I couldn't stop the smile, everything went soft and flexible. My organs reverberated with the sound, like I was the source. Mike was the same, smiling. Not thinking. Just letting the sound collect inside.

We stood dead still for ages and I wanted the sound to not stop, and yet it stopped somehow and the bloke pressed some other thing, and there was this manic crackle, which quickly faded to nothing.

"It's the transformer – sensitive on these old ones," he told us.

"Power should be back in an hour or so, once I replace the circuit breaker. Best you lot went home."

Mike was closer to him by a step, not moving, just standing there, his finger hooked on the fence. And we must have looked pretty zombie-like lingering with all the bevs and ganj in us and the beams slanting in from behind. And from where we stood he did look a bit like a zoo animal, what with the shadow of the fence griddling him.

"Best if you lot went," the man said again, stepping towards us.

His face was patched in light and I could see how knobbed and acne-scarred it was. My heart stiffened.

"What?" Mike said.

"Are you done?"

"Do it again," Mike said flatly. "Make the noise."

"Melt your brains elsewhere, I've got work to do." He spat and a blob of glistening saliva clung then oozed from the fence. "Go on, fuck off to the estate," he said, and did a snappy little shoo-off wave.

The bloke turned his back to us so we faced his weird hump. Mike, still holding his Miguel in his hand, stepped through the gate and swung the bottle hard down onto his head. It exploded, shards showered out, caught light, and made a beautiful tinkling sound off the fence and the substation. "Fucking hell," Jim spurted. We stood dumb. Then the man was on the floor holding his head and rolling. Dust billowed. His shouts came out garbled, like he was swallowing his own tongue.

Mike kicked him in the stomach and he went quiet.

For a few seconds we watched the still body, so much like some dead guy in a film I half expected Mike to say, "Let's bury him in the woods." Of course, nobody said a thing. The man began to whimper and we scattered into the field.

At Oak Island, heart chafing my throat, I stopped running and climbed the mossy bank. Jim stood under the thick hanging branch, his face blocked in shadow. Liam was next up, bent over, drawing heavy breaths. "God, bloody banger," he wheezed. "God, bloody banger." Mike came last, jogged out of the gloom, sat on a root and stared into the unlit air.

Liam was saying we should ring an ambulance and held out

his phone for someone else to use. The man was already on his feet, though, his eyes searching the field like a demented guard dog. I expected Mike to take control, to give some instruction, to at least say what he was doing, but he was elsewhere.

"I'm off," Jim said. He nodded and twitched, flicked his eyes between us. "I'm off," he repeated. "Tomorrow, yeah?"

A second later his head bobbed above the gleaming wheat. Then Liam left.

I got the idea to climb the tree once it was clear neither Mike nor I was going to leave. It was easy enough, and soon we were on the thickest branch, legs dangling, gazing out over most of Ashmill, some of town too, all swamped in darkness. Only the glasshouses shone silvery.

"It helps," Mike said.

I looked across at him and caught something new in his face, a release of tension, his skin slacker. He was less cut off.

"Yeah," I said, knowing that in some way he was talking about Craig.

"I felt I could kill someone once," he said, and looked across at me. "Level things up, you know? But I haven't got an enemy, not a proper one."

For a long time I pretended to understand while we both concentrated on the no-light, medieval view of Ashmill. Honestly, I had no real idea what Mike was feeling – I wasn't sure what I was feeling either – but I was content to sit and listen and see. Soak up whatever mood we were in. Then Mike pushed himself off the branch – not a word, not a "Laters" – and disappeared into the wheat and I felt I should have said something, talked about things that bothered me, at the very least let him know I didn't care what he did.

* * *

The parents were throwing plates early that morning. I heard several smashes followed by several yells and counter yells, then a huge crash. A harsh sound. Had to be the porcelain serving bowl they were given as a wedding present or something bigger. It was not the kind of noise you want to be woken from your dreams by. I lay in bed, listened to their lingering tug of war. I imagined little Sis was on the other side, wide awake, thinking up ways to fix them.

Hours later, when I arrived downstairs, Dad was at the table staring vacantly into his reflection in the conservatory window. A grey film had formed over the bowl of cereal in front of him.

"Mum," he said.

"Yeah," I agreed.

Sis crept in, skipped over the wood floor and gave him a big hug.

"Toast?"

"Thanks," he said warmly.

"I'm going to be in my room," I said.

I played Medal of Honour for a solid five hours before meeting Jim and Liam at the millpond. I'd been thinking a lot, was ready to say Mike was an all right lad, and if it came to it, put the bloke in the spotlight, say he had it coming. But when I sat down, it was clear that last night was the last thing anyone wanted to talk about. I should have known that it was just one of those things that never happened.

"Pills are ready for Friday," Jim said. He pulled out a Jiffy bag from his pocket and put it up to the sun. "Litre of voddy at mine first," he informed himself more than us. "Massive night before school starts."

I nodded.

"You know," he said, "our bodies are pretty much chemical sacks. Ganj, MDMA, powder. It only alters the amount of chemical released into the bloodstream. There's nothing unnatural about doing that. If anything, it's more natural. Like traffic lights that stay green for longer."

Jim was back to being the mystic again. "Liam, does that make you want to try?" I asked.

"Sounds like hot hippy piss."

Liam was cross-legged, mobile in hands, hunting down a pixel apple with a spiralled snake, his focus-face at constipation level. The sky above us was blue all over, the scant clouds stunned out to the edges. The pond looked slick and a nice green. Posh and

Becks were doing circuits around the lily pads like Scalextric cars. I watched the sun sink lower and light bleed through the weeping willow so it looked like a strange old man with a fiery beard. I hadn't seen the dragonflies all day. Couldn't hear them, either. Somewhere not far away a lawnmower droned. Mike was never going to come back.

"You think things are all right here?" I asked Jim.

"Yeah," he said, fingering the pills in the Jiffy bag as he counted. "How many do you want for Friday?"

I couldn't sleep. I churned the duvet, changed the pillow position a thousand times, studied the curtain wafts for hours. I heard rabbits squeal in the rhododendrons and cars growl off into the distance. On the Net I hunted porn. Midget stuff, animal stuff, milfs, anything to knock me out. Nothing worked. When Dad came home from his shift around 3 a.m., I heard the shower go and waited until he was in bed before going downstairs, where I fixed a mug of Nesquik and watched reruns of Jeremy Kyle to make myself feel better. There was a boy wearing the same Reeboks as Mike, same oily skin, too. He'd had some massive barney with his girlfriend, wasn't speaking to his alcoholic father. He kept telling Jeremy that he couldn't trust anyone, that he didn't know what to believe.

I thought about Oak Island. Wondered if it was true, if witches were seriously hanged from the thick branch. I thought about Mike. It bothered me how little I really knew about him and at the same time I just wanted to not-think at all. If I could force myself to forget, then it would be all right. I tried my best to remember Mike never being there, never smashing the bottle over the bloke's head. I pretended the weird noise was my own invention.

And each night I heard footsteps creaking on the stairs. The switch in the bathroom would click and a spear of light would appear under the door and the shower would rush. There was no more thrown kitchenware. Not a shout. The ringing of a silent house. I tried to remember when my dad wasn't doing the late shift. I couldn't. One night I rolled over and looked at the ceiling, the fuzzy darkness. I pictured two houses on either side of town. I pictured two Christmases. I felt the earth tremble.

\* \* \*

School started and Mike was nowhere to be seen, lost in the crowd, or maybe bunking. Who knows? He was in the year above, so any chance of crossing paths would happen at break, which was getting more segmented the older we got. Sport boys, townies, boffs, emos – everyone had their corner. Then one afternoon I came home and Mum had this dire face. I thought finally she was going public about her problems with Dad. She shook, her hand literally flapping a tissue like a white flag. She told me a plane had hit the Twin Towers in America. "What a tragedy," she said. I looked into her frightened face and didn't understand what she was saying.

Later that week the family were eating at the Sunrise. I listened to the regulars giving opinions on the attack. For days now it was all the world was talking about. A farmer in a wax coat and heavy wellingtons had it that World War Three was brewing. Jim's dad was weighing in too. He downed the last of his pint and informed the men that London would be their next target. His argument had something to do with jealousy and general laziness. I think he was probably off his nut on English ale and had lost track of the topic of conversation.

At our table the atmosphere had turned. Dad pulled apple crumble around his plate with a fork and Mum stared at him without flinching. In the beer garden Sis waved from the top of a shiny pink slide then launched down.

"You should be the one to tell him," said Mum, swaying slightly.

Dad glanced over at where Jim's dad had stood. "That man should shut his mouth," he said. "What he doesn't notice is what an idiot he is. He doesn't see how mixed up things can get."

"Don't deflect, darling."

Dad threw daggers at Mum and worked his crumble into islands. "Everyone has to do late shifts. It's policy."

"I can tell him?" she said, pretending to be calm.

"Your mother believes in imaginary things," said Dad plainly. He looked out the window and gave an overenthusiastic clown-smile and wave to Sis who was at the top of the slide again.

Mum gulped on her wine and theatrically wiped her lips with her sleeve. "I must be mad then," she said hysterically. "How does it feel to be married to a mad woman?" Dad carried on looking out the window, blowing air from swelled cheeks, so Mum turned to me. "Stanley, how does it feel to have a mad person for a mother?"

"Brill," I said, and feeling something big and impossible fall from the ceiling, lifted myself from the table. "I'm leaving now."

"Where?"

"Jim's."

I walked through the curtain of weeping willow, rounded the millpond, but made for the estate. There was a shabby snooker hall near Londis, just north of the park, and I went in not caring about the hard kids drenched in hoodies at the door or the bloke in gold chains using his cue like a Samurai sword. I found Mike sat against a scummy wall. Above his head somebody had written a note: *I'll Suck For Cigs*. He watched the air, glazing out.

\* \* \*

A year ago I would've never gone to a place like that. It was always Jim and me then. We'd pack our things before the bell and peg it out early to avoid the mash of blazers at three fifteen. We'd buy bags of Pop Rocks and trek up to Oak Island to talk about the girls on TV we'd like to fuck and how and where, and I'd get all fizzy, just thinking. Then we'd head to our separate homes fogged and dreamy, lock ourselves up with the family computer and search for the perfect fuck. And it was all forgotten in the morning, on our walks through town to school, scared shitless of the girls in their short blue skirts streaming towards the Girls School, of every kid with an eyebrow piercing or a dense stare, of Craig and Mike and the horror stories.

\* \* \*

"All right?" I said.

His head spun. "What?"

"Want to go to Copse Lane?"

He shrugged, shook himself, and then we were off, taking jaunty steps through side alleys, minding we didn't bump into any

of his friends or any of mine. He told me to wait at the rear entrance
to Woolworths, and a minute later returned with sagging pockets.
On the way up, past the theatre and the rugby club, towards Ashmill
we chewed through a feast of Whams and Drumsticks and foam
bananas. Then, at the corner near the secured well and the rickety
chapel of St Margaret's, he asked if I wanted a hit and showed me
the placky bag and what looked like a can of value hairspray.

Under the oak of Oak Island my head was a soaring blimp. I
rubbed my stung eyes which felt a mile from my body and asked
Mike if he wanted to hear the noise again. He didn't make a sound
but I knew his answer.

We waited for the sky to darken before going down to the
substation. I took my time over it, ambled slowly through the
wheat fields now cut to stubble length and beginning to glow
in the half-light. I imagined I was in fact walking over my dad's
oversized face on Sunday before he shaved. I heard the cables hum
over our heads and imagined they were strings, and the pylons
masting the Downs, frets, as if a massive instrument was tuning
up. I saw a giant, edge-lit nimbus cloud phase and wrinkle into the
face of Craig Ingram. Then another twisted into Mike's sad face,
and others into Jim and Liam and the parents and Sis, even the
Sunrise men lofting bevs.

Mike broke the lock with a blow from a boulder. His eyes were
huge and glossy. Red-rimmed.

"It's the same as any fuse box," I said. "All you need to do is
short it."

While I told him how I knew what I was doing, about the
insomnia, and how great the Internet was at finding stuff out, he
stood there taking hit after hit on the aerosol. I went on, told him
my parents were probably going to break up, that the world was
headed for a third war.

Mike watched on, not a list to his face.

"Sorted," I said, and moved to his side. "Use this." I handed
over a long crooked stick.

He nodded like someone who wanted to shake his head.
"Ain't it gonna pop?"

"Do you care?"

He shrugged.

I moved my eyes from Mike to the substation. My head brimmed with a kind of black throbbing sea that might as well be nothing at all. It was an awesome feeling when the drum sound started, better than the first time, the air slipping away as the sound grew and low-angle sunlight cut in. I saw the fence shadow stretch along the ground and rear up, making the world invert somehow, as if it was us behind the fence and everywhere else was blocked off. Then, tearing up behind the drum, came an insane crack, and sparks spat out, flickering up from the substation, showering the trees which stood around like bystanders at an accident.

"Let's scarper," Mike said.

The leaves of the nearest tree caught and the fire spread, blazed into the dry foliage. I shook my head. "There's no point if they don't find us," I said.

And when the sirens rose from town and the fire engulfed half of Copse Lane, when Mike finally grabbed me, flushed and wild with panic, emergency lights colouring his skin, I began to see. "What the fuck is wrong with you?" he said, no longer caring to know. His hand clenched my T in a fist. He drew me so close I saw into his eyes, the huge dark concaves reflecting what was around, my eye square in his, a fire burning beyond. Adult silhouettes building.

"They're coming now," I said, when I knew he wasn't there.

## Paradise
### SARAH ALEXANDER

**2005**

The pier looked identical to the old one – the wood, flimsy; great gaps between the warped planks – but Ellen knew it had been rebuilt. She had seen the pieces of it strewn about in the water, sliding recklessly out into the Indian Ocean along with overturned longboats and shreds of smashed up furniture, corrugated iron roofs and kitchen utensils.

It was gone now, all that churning debris. The sapphire sea glistened as it had before.

The pier bounced beneath her as she was swept along by a flood of passengers returning to the island. When she reached the end, she paused and looked at the wreckage on the land. The reports she'd seen, but hadn't really believed, were true – the narrow strip that formed the main village on the island was a desolate, smouldering wasteland. Everything had disappeared, sucked out by the wave or burnt to the ground. A row of bungalows had slid carelessly into the sea, their green felt roofs wet around the edges where water seeped in. A few empty shells of the more sturdy buildings loomed out of the yellow haze, surrounded only by piles of rubble and small dusty craters where palm trees used to stand. The air tasted of salt, burning wood and rotten flesh. Ellen realised then, as she choked on the smell, that it had been a terrible mistake to return. This was not the place she remembered.

From her hospital bed in London, Ellen had thought of nothing but returning. She'd spent endless hours searching for the names of anyone she'd known, reading survivor stories and examining before-and-after pictures trying to piece it all together. None of it made sense – the timings, her injuries, her survival. Her memory played tricks. Sometimes she thought it had never happened; other times her dreams disturbed her sleep, sharp fragments of memory forcing her awake – tumbling, bricks crashing down on her, trying to get to the surface. Her mind replayed the hours she'd perched on that roof – or was it only minutes? She'd felt trapped in an alternative reality. And then there was Paul. She'd been almost sure she saw him, touched him. But then again . . . Those tricks. She'd typed his name in the search box, Paul Fraser, over and over again but nothing came up. He wasn't on the dead list either, but that didn't mean anything. She'd trawled through hundreds of photos of bloated bodies laid out in messy rows, examining each one, heaving as she did. But the pictures weren't enough. She had to go back.

Now, standing at the gateway to her answers, Ellen wasn't sure if she had the strength. Looking around she could see only locals. They gazed at her as they walked about in the dust. The pain and loss were in their eyes and the way their arms drooped. Perhaps tourists were no longer welcome here. What if the islanders thought she was just here to see the damage – a disaster tourist? They couldn't know she had lost, too. Her scars were covered by her clothes and buried deep inside her. Looking down at her Western clothing she suddenly felt like a fraud. She hadn't lost anything, not really. She hadn't lost her home, her business, her whole family. A few photos and superficial cuts were nothing. She didn't belong here.

Ellen turned to run back to the ferry and slammed into the solid chest of someone much taller than her. Steadying herself, she took a step back. The man in front of her was blond with a weathered, creased face. He seemed out of breath and distracted; his hands shook as he lifted them in a kind of apology.

"Sorry," she muttered. "I've got to get on that ferry."

"Didn't you just get *off* that ferry?" His eyes focused on something behind her.

"Yes, but now I'm getting back on it."

"You can't," he said, finally drawing his eyes to her. They were brilliant blue. "It's not going anywhere."

Ellen hesitated, trying to place his accent. He sounded Swedish but she wasn't sure. *Something* about him was familiar but maybe it wasn't his accent. Before she could answer he turned to a small, hunched man sitting in a red plastic chair nearby and garbled something in Thai. She understood "today" and "tomorrow".

"There's only one ferry a day now. You'll have to stay overnight," he translated.

Ellen felt the weight of her rucksack pulling her down. The air was suffocating; hot and humid. Sweat trickled down the back of her neck and the scars on her feet and legs started to itch. Her left thigh, still slightly swollen from the bruising, throbbed.

"I need somewhere to stay then." She didn't recognise her own voice. She sounded like a small, scared child.

"I know somewhere. I'll show you." He nodded for her to follow. "I'm Erik, by the way."

He guided her along the mostly deserted main strip. A few makeshift shops were back in business with handmade signs saying "Souvenirs for sale". Peering into the stalls she saw empty shelves and tidemarks. As they trod through the dirt Ellen could tell Erik was broken inside. She saw it in his legs, the way they sunk into the ground with each step, never quite straightening. His shoulders, too, were sunk, slumped. And she saw it in what no one else would've noticed – the tiny involuntary shift of his ears when the wind picked up. He held his breath for a moment, listening.

"It's just the trees," Ellen whispered, although she wasn't sure herself.

Erik cocked his head. "You were here, weren't you? I remember you."

Ellen nodded carefully, not quite ready to talk about it. "I worked at the bar on the hill. I think I remember you, too." Her voice cracked.

"Fuck! You're the English girl. They all think you're dead! Come on, everyone's up there now."

Ellen threw her hands over her mouth and blew into them, adrenalin surging through her. The air caught in her lungs as she tried to breathe.

"Everyone?" she gasped, trembling.

He didn't answer but she thought she saw him shake his head as he wandered off towards the hill.


The Hilltop bar was actually only halfway up the hill, but the steps were steep. Out of practice, Ellen had to keep pausing to catch her breath. Erik seemed to struggle, too, clutching his side and wincing every now and then. She'd made this journey every day for the last two weeks of her stay on the island. It was Paul who'd got her the job. He managed the bar and seemed to know everyone. Each day he introduced her to a new friend – and no one ever seemed to leave. At first, she didn't understand how anyone could stay on a tiny island for so long, but six weeks later, she'd almost known; it was something to do with the way time fell away, yet never moved. Occasionally she had an urge to leave, but Paul just winked and said, "Stay a bit longer," and for some reason she couldn't resist. But slowly, the hole inside her that made her constantly move on got bigger and the island got smaller. There was nowhere to hide any more. Finally, she made her decision. The ferry had been about to leave with her on it when Paul called from the pier, "Do you want a job?" She didn't really want to spend Christmas alone, or spend it without him. She had in the end, though. After waiting over an hour for him on the beach, she'd finally retreated to the solace of her tiny cramped bungalow and watched the waves from inside.

The open-air bar was as packed as it always had been. People were sprawled out on bamboo mats and perched around the tiny counter inside the shack. The trees cut out most of the remaining afternoon sunlight and long shadows streaked across the ground. Ellen followed Erik through the crowd, scouring for familiar faces. Warm bodies knocked together and beer bottles were passed through the air.

"These are all the volunteers," Erik shouted over the music, "taking their afternoon tea break. They clean up by day and party by night."

Finally, Ellen saw three people she knew, clustered together behind the bar. Daeng saw her first and launched himself straight over the counter, almost knocking her down.

"Are you real? Are you real?" he said over and over again,

sweeping her off her feet in a painful bear hug. Ellen tried to keep it in but a small yelp escaped.

"Are you hurt?" he asked, letting go.

"A little," she replied laughing, tears falling.

Viktoria and Anders appeared by her side.

"I can't believe you are here," Viktoria said, reaching for Ellen's arm, her eyes brimming. "We kept trying to find out but there were just too many names."

Ellen smiled, unable to ask for more details.

"Who else is here?" Ellen was afraid to say Paul's name.

"Pretty much everyone," Anders said. "Except Paul."

Ellen felt the blood drain from her head. All her visions from the past few months came crashing down around her.

"No, he's OK!" Viktoria quickly added. "He's just on the mainland. He'll be back in a couple of days. You are staying, aren't you?"

Ellen exhaled as slowly as she could. "I'm not sure. Maybe just a day or two. Is he OK? Was he hurt?"

"No, he wasn't even here!" Viktoria exclaimed. "Didn't you know? He missed the ferry the day before and got stuck on the mainland. You have to wait for him. He went round all the hospitals looking for you."

"Oh God, I was so sure he was dead. I thought I saw him in the water."

It made sense now. She should have known he wouldn't have stood her up without a reason.

Erik placed a beer in her hand. She hadn't even noticed he'd disappeared. "Survival," he said, clanging his bottle against hers before downing it almost in one.

That night, Ellen lay alone under a thin white sheet in a drunken haze. As the fan above shuddered and trees outside creaked, she recalled it all again. The torrent rushing around her, the searing pain as twisted hunks of metal clawed their way through her skin, the semi-naked bodies bobbing past face down, a hand rising from the water – her fingers brushing it before it was swept away. The water had whipped around her legs, trying to pull her down, and she'd clung to a rooftop so tightly that her arms began to shake.

She'd touched her left side to feel the damage and her hand had disappeared inside her body. Through soft, sticky flesh, she'd felt the hard substance that must have been a rib. For a brief moment she'd wondered if she would be eaten by sharks.

Ellen traced with her finger the scar that ran from her hip to just under her armpit. After the operation she had examined it in the mirror. A long scabby red line, criss-crossed with thinner horizontal lines from the stiches. Like a zip, she had thought. A zip that was holding her together. It was smoother now but still puffy. She turned the fan off so she could hear the island; held her breath and listened to the sea, the waves gently landing on the sand. The sound she used to love.

The next day, Ellen went in search of her bungalow and the rooftop that saved her life. She clambered over broken glass and blackened patches of sand rimmed with flakes of silver ash. Her feet were quickly coated in a fine soot. The stifling air made her sluggish and she kept her eyes on the sea, examining it for any movement. It was hard to tell, though, through the shimmering heat waves. Everything seemed to quiver. Ahead, she saw a bulldozer, a trail of sand blasting from the back of it. She heard a low rumble as it rammed into a ruined building, sending bricks and dust into a monstrous cloud. Her heart thudded slowly, dully, like a faraway long drum. Her palms became sweaty and something constricted her throat, suffocating, strangling. It dawned on her that if the wave came again, there would be nothing, nothing to slow it down. As her breath quickened she pulled her throbbing legs over the rubble, back inland, towards the hills, scrambling, stumbling, not fast enough, not fast enough. It thundered behind her.

Over the next few days it got even hotter. Every morning Ellen met Viktoria and some of the volunteers at the tool shed to collect shovels and wheelbarrows. They spent five days cleaning up the reservoir, sifting through the debris for scraps of people's lives – photos, documents, shreds of clothing. They bagged everything else for burning. The volunteers laughed all day long and talked about how good they felt to be able to help. Ellen stuck close to Viktoria and when they were far enough away from the others, Viktoria told her about Daeng's sister, Mara. Anders had found her and carried her back up the hill. She'd survived most of the night, with Daeng and Anders looking after her, but died just before dawn.

"Anders carried fifteen people up the hill that night," Viktoria said quietly. "Erik was one of them."

In the afternoons, when the volunteers sought refuge in the shade, Ellen wandered around the island. First, she checked the incoming ferry and when Paul was not on it she tried a different route through the rubble in search of her bungalow. Before, she'd known where the path had forked. The building next to hers had been blue with a manta ray painted on the side. By her front door was a palm tree that bent the wrong way, leaning towards the hills rather than out to sea like the others. Now, there was nothing to guide her.

As she walked, there were things that made her pause. The carcass of a fish three hundred metres inland, its scales hard and dried; an upturned speedboat in the wreckage of a storage room, life jackets strewn about; and the frame of a rotting bungalow with a mattress wedged in the rafters. But it was the lone flip-flops brought in by the tide that made her stomach turn. She walked in slow, unsteady circles until the sun went down.

Despite the darkness and the wind rushing through the trees, it was in the evenings that Ellen felt the safest. She could sometimes pretend that nothing had ever happened. That she had stumbled upon this beautiful island, far away from any kind of reality, and that it would always remain perfect. But even though her new friends called her brave and crowded around her to listen to her story, they fell away quickly when their favourite songs came on. Viktoria and Anders seemed relaxed but restrained. They talked quietly and laughed gently but Ellen saw them huddled together at times, faces scrunched up and fists clenched, riding out a moment. Ellen did not feel she could interrupt. She didn't know what it was like to carry the dying up into the hills. Another Anders had carried her.

Erik made her feel uncomfortable, the way his eyes lingered on her, and other times he got so drunk he forgot who she was. He muttered often and incoherently about a girl and white sheets and more than once Ellen wanted to run away from him, but in the end she was the one who walked him home, slept beside him and held his hand when he woke in the night sobbing. She reminded him that when the ground shook it was just the bulldozers and when they heard screaming in the distance it was just the monkeys. Her words provided her own comfort.

"Bones fix," he said one night as they sat together on a bamboo mat. He pressed two fingers into his temple and Ellen saw the tips of them go white. "It's up here that it hurts so much." He was the only one who knew what it was like to be under the wave. He had the same fear as her – that it would come again.

On her sixth day back, Ellen walked past Erik's room on her way down to the pier and heard him screaming. When he didn't answer her knock, she pushed the door open and saw him hurl his phone against the wall. His face was screwed up tight and his hands were around his throat. Ellen ran to him and held him by the wrists while he howled. She could smell beer on his breath and his saliva was thick and stringy in his mouth.

"My stupid fucking mother," he spluttered. "She calls me every fucking day, three times a day. She thinks I want to kill myself and I swear, if she calls me again I will."

"Why does she think that?" Ellen asked, trying to keep her voice low.

"Because I tried to kill myself," he stated. And then he snorted.

Ellen let go of his wrists and sat on the edge of the bed. The air con was almost too cold and she shivered, but Erik sat there, naked apart from his boxer shorts, sweating. His scars made her stomach twist. They weren't dainty like hers. It was as though huge chunks of his legs and chest had been gouged out and the papery skin stretched thinly over the missing bits of flesh. It seemed a miracle that he was even alive. Erik finally released his throat and sat up.

"In the hospital, I stored up all my medications and took them one night. She was crowding me all the time, fussing over me. She never let go of my hand in three months, not even when I went to the bathroom." He looked up with red eyes. "I lost everything you know. Ten years this was my home."

He began to mutter about the girl again.

"Slow down a bit. Tell me about her," Ellen said, knowing that she would miss the arrival of the ferry.

Erik stared at the wall.

"She was on top of me when I woke up in the reservoir. Her hair was in my face, damp and hot. She wasn't moving – she got really heavy. I turned her head so she could face me and I talked to her. Some people came, wearing bright-orange jackets, and they were all so small, I didn't think they'd get me out."

He sniffed and rocked.

"But they did get you out."

"They lifted so many men and women before they got to me. They had white sheets. They covered them. When they got to us, they covered her, too."

Ellen looked at the tiles on the floor and on the wall of Erik's room. Everything was new and shiny and yet it smelt damp. She wanted to wipe away Erik's scars and mend his fractured ribs. She wanted to pull his chest apart and climb inside and wrap her arms around his heart. But even that would not be enough.

She stroked his arm until he fell asleep, weaving her way around his scars. While he slept, Ellen retrieved the bits of his broken phone and found the number she needed.

Ellen stood at the pier, breathless. Her legs were streaked with dirt, sweat and blood, her feet completely blackened. She hoped no one had seen her run from another imaginary wave.

"Ellen!" A voice behind her.

She knew it was him before she even turned around.

"Paul Fraser," she called, as he walked towards her. "I've been waiting for you."

His hair was cropped shorter than she'd seen before, his skin a golden colour. She'd imagined this moment so many times and yet she was still unprepared. When he finally wrapped his arms around her she cried.

"Don't let go," she sobbed into his neck.

"Darling, I'm so sorry I wasn't here. I'm sorry I wasn't there on that day. I'm sorry about everything," he blurted out. "Viktoria called me. You must've been going through hell. Christ, I can't even believe you are alive."

"It's OK, I promise. It's OK."

Ellen let the time slip away as she savoured his hot breath

against her neck. She didn't even care that it hurt so much when he squeezed her.

When she finally pulled away, Paul's grin was nearly wider than his face and just how she remembered. His eyes fell to the blood on her legs.

"Look at the state of you. You look like you've stepped straight out of a disaster zone."

"You idiot." She poked him in the ribs. "I need to get cleaned up."

Paul pointed to the sea. "In you go, then."

Slowly, and with Paul by her side, Ellen moved to the shoreline. She waded in up to her knees. The silky blue liquid rippled around her and it was warm and beautiful.

"You made it just in time," she said, rubbing the dirt from her feet with her fingers. "I was about to leave."

"Stay a bit longer. The heat's about to break and everyone's coming back now. It'll be just like before."

Ellen didn't dare look into his eyes.

"One more day," she replied, smiling, her heart in tatters.

They sat together on the beach and watched the waves trickle in and out.

"Did you have fun on the mainland?" she asked, although she wasn't sure she wanted to know.

Paul quickly shook his head. "I was at the Swedish embassy, about Erik. We got him on the ferry a couple of times but he kept coming back. A consul's coming over tomorrow to escort him home."

"That's good," she said quietly, wondering if she should have done more for Erik. "I've got his mother's number if you need it."

Paul leaned into her shoulder. "Do you remember our trip to Monkey Island?" His stifled laugh instantly lightened the mood.

How could she forget, it had been her favourite day.

"That monkey stole my donut. And then ate it in the tree just out of my reach!"

"You should have seen your face," he guffawed, and rolled back onto the sand. "I wish I'd had a camera."

"Let's take a walk up to Viewpoint," Paul suggested the following day when Ellen showed him her ferry ticket. "For old times' sake."

The ticket in her hand felt so light, as though it might fly away. It fluttered in the hot breeze.

Slowly they climbed the hundreds of uneven steps up to the highest point on the island. When they reached the top, Ellen turned around and looked down on her paradise. It was yellow and dusty and bare. There in the distance was the faded-green tennis court where the rescue helicopters had landed, where the bodies had been piled.

Only a few days before the waves, she'd looked down on a lush green forest surrounded by sparkling blue waters. She hadn't been able to see the rotting bungalow frames, the filth buried just below the surface of the sand. But it had been there just the same, she knew that now.

"There's my old room, what's left of it." Paul pointed to a building with a red roof not far from the pier. "It was completely flattened."

"Lucky your timekeeping is so bad, really." She nudged him, waiting for his infectious laugh, but when she looked at him she saw a single tear fall from his face.

"I wish I had been here," he whispered. "I don't know why, but I do."

Ellen knew exactly what he meant.

He quickly wiped his face. "Keep in touch, won't you."

"You can come and visit me in Australia, if you want. If you need to get away."

"Try and stop me."

For a brief moment Ellen imagined walking with Paul across the Australian outback, a thousand miles from any ocean, just walking and walking. Perhaps one day, she thought.

"I never found my spot. It was somewhere near the reservoir. I thought I'd stood in the right place but it didn't feel right."

They both stared down at the big empty hole that used to be the reservoir. Ellen found it hard to believe she'd helped clear the debris. It seemed an impossible task.

"Maybe it's better not to know," he said.

He was probably right.

Paul raised his arm again. "That one there, next to the water tower. That's the remains of Erik's building."

Ellen followed the line of his finger and when she saw the half-collapsed building with the blue roof her chest tightened.

"It's being pulled down tomorrow," Paul continued. "You know, before you came back he used to go there every day and just sit inside."

She scanned the area, trying to make it all fit. There it was. Her bendy tree, right next to Erik's building.

"Are you OK? Ellen?"

His voice suddenly seemed far away.

"You want to go down?"

Each breath she took seemed to last for ever. The ground around her melted away and the trees rushed towards her. She felt her legs give way and put her hands out to save herself, but when she looked down she was still standing.

"Ellen?"

"Where's the sun gone?" she murmured. The sky had turned charcoal.

"The rain's finally on its way." Paul jumped like a gazelle down onto the steps and turned back.

"Are you coming? I'm desperate for a drink."

Ellen crouched down and removed her flip-flop, shaking it to get rid of a stone that wasn't there, stalling.

"Just a minute," she called. "I'm almost ready."

# Creative Writing
## MAGGIE WOMERSLEY

It was the second week in January and the snow had been falling all day like soft dirty feathers.

In seminar room G1, on the ground floor of the Julian Fellowes block, Erica Savvy flicked to the back of her notebook and wrote "snow falling like dirty feathers" on a blank page.

The deafening silence as the rest of the class pretended to consider her short story about a grieving woman buying a pair of inappropriate shoes made Erica feel nervous and hot. To distract herself she searched for a less clichéd adjective than "deafening", but couldn't find one because deafening was exactly what twelve human beings sitting round a table *not* talking about her story sounded like.

At last somebody said, "'She looked out at the clotting dusk' is good."

It was look-on-the-bright-side Melanie, deputy headmistress of a failing primary school in East Putney. Melanie's shy glances darted like swallows from under the eaves of her fringe and Erica found herself fighting the urge to write "eyes like swallows" under the thing about the snow.

"Yes, I *loved* 'clotting dusk'," added Jacintha, who always wrote in the first person in the present tense about what it was like being Jacintha.

A few of the others murmured their agreement, and then

the noisy silence descended again as Erica sank deeper into despondency. Out of the corner of her eye she could see the Wunderkind scribbling away on his copy of her story, his arm curled freakishly as he filled the margins with black biro.

At last Simon cleared his throat. "OK, everybody. Let's unpack what Justine's trying to do here with the dead mother."

Erica felt herself flush with embarrassment and irritation. Simon had been calling her Justine since halfway through the last term. It wasn't as if the group was that big, or Erica one of the quiet ones. She'd corrected him the first couple of times, but she'd had the sneaking suspicion he wasn't really listening. She curled her toes up inside her sensible shoes and imagined suspicion sneaking round the room like a rat in the wainscot.

Nobody spoke so Simon continued. "For example, what do people think about the protagonist's need to assuage her guilt through buying increasingly kinky footwear?"

There was some fidgeting from the person sitting next to Simon. Erica braced herself.

"It's probably because I'm not a woman, yeah? And my mum's still alive, right? But I just didn't get it," said Skuzz the prose-hater.

Skuzz – she couldn't remember his real name any more – worked for a train company scrubbing graffiti off railway hoardings. He had an MA from the Camden Consortium of Oriental Studies and Sex Tourism, but he preferred an outdoorsy life to academia. The book he was working on was a graphic novel about Bangkok ladyboys. Simon seemed very excited about Skuzz and his cartoons; he'd even helped him come up with his ridiculous pen name at a getting-to-know-you session during freshers' week. Skuzz sprawled in his chair with his legs apart, and shrugged at her. She fought the urge to speak out in defence of her heroine's right to buy slut shoes, but the first rule of workshop was don't talk during workshop (when your work was being discussed). So she chewed on the inside of her cheek and nodded thoughtfully, as though mulling over his remarks.

The seminar dragged on for another twenty minutes. Simon talked about her story a little bit, but mainly about the changes to their course venue for the rest of the term.

"So next week we'll be in the east tower of the Russell T. Davies extension. Everybody know where that is?" He glanced around the room and a few people nodded.

He is terribly handsome, Erica thought wistfully, and of course a published novelist in his own right. Then Simon gave out some questionnaires about what they thought of the course so far, a map of the Russell T. Davies extension, and a reading list made up entirely of novels with one-word titles. Skuzz threw his straight in the bin and high-fived Simon on his way out. Erica stuffed her hand-outs into her bag and got up to leave.

In the narrow corridor that linked Julian Fellowes to the main building, Melanie caught up with her.

"I really liked your story, Justine," she said, bouncing along just behind her, because the corridor was too narrow for two to walk abreast.

"Thanks, Melanie. I liked yours last week," Erica replied, half-heartedly.

"Alice," Melanie corrected her, a little huffily. "My name's Alice."

Which was weird, because Erica was good with names and she was sure that Melanie had been called Melanie all through the previous term.

They reached the end of the corridor and Erica pushed open the heavy security door. The cold air whooshed around her like peppermint mouthwash, swilling and cleansing, unabashed by the inappropriate simile she had attached to it. The others fanned out around her and made for the gates, all except the Wunderkind who hung back, and seemed keen to get her attention.

"Here," he said, thrusting his heavily annotated copy of her story towards her. "I made some notes."

She tried to thank him but he was hurrying off, probably rushing back to his semi-detached crypt in a crumbling Victorian cemetery, north of the city. She watched him disappear into the snowstorm like a ghost – no, more like a wraith. Wraiths were darker than ghosts and the Wunderkind was a prolific wearer of black. Erica put "ghost" on the backburner; she'd get a chance to use it eventually. Then she dived into the swirling flakes. .

Four years earlier Erica had been a well-paid executive at a TV production company making cookery programmes. Through her work she had met a lot of interesting people, travelled the world, and eaten a great deal of restaurant-quality food. But Erica had aspirations to be a writer and so she'd given up her job to spend a year in a rented cottage with only a dicky septic tank and rats for company. After her money but not the novel was finished, she moved back in with her mother (who was in fact alive and well and not at all happy about living in parentheses) and found that the TV industry had wizened and shrunk. Her old company had gone bust and everywhere the story was the same: people were writing now, not watching telly.

So Erica had got a job at the all-night garage on the Caledonian Road. It wasn't particularly well paid, but it was close to college and it would look good in her author biogs. She had initially wanted a job in an old people's rest home – all those life stories, ripening on the vine like soft summer fruit – but when the manager discovered she was a creative writing graduate he had requested that she sign a confidentiality clause. Apparently they already had a Writer in Residence, and they didn't need another. Then he handed Erica a brochure detailing the home's Writers' Adoption scheme, whereby – subject to passing the relevant police checks – writers could hire old folk by the hour.

Horrified that her own mother might end her days being plundered by vampiric writing students, Erica had rushed straight home and begun tape-recording her mother's memories herself. But in the end she'd had to admit that she was probably too close to her mother's story to be able to see a viable three-act structure. So she had put the tapes on eBay and sold them to a graduate of the Danny Boyle Academy of Bucolic Engineering. She'd had to sign over foreign rights and all residuals, but the money had paid for a couple of writing courses so she figured it was worth it.

En route to the garage Erica had to pass a row of speakeasies touting for business. Each offered live readings and open-mic slots seven days a week. One place had its name, Ink Stain, splattered like squashed spider legs across a whitewashed wall, while the sandwich board outside promised free entry to anyone accompanied by a card-carrying literary agent. Another, Harry's Flash Fiction, promised twenty different writers a night all reading five hundred words on the theme Bad Hair Day. There was also a confessional poetry slot called (Un)Happy Hour, during which all drinks were half price. Erica shuddered and pulled the collar of her coat closer to her throat. Joints like these were springing up all over the city, pimping the authors of uncollected poems, barely begun novel extracts and, most common of all, short stories.

With the snow falling more thickly than ever, smothering the noise of traffic and flattening the contours of buildings, Erica's own lack of publishing success felt like a necklace of lead weights pulling down the balloon of her hopes and dreams. She felt adrift and lonely – even her metaphors were running amok.

Still, there was always the chance that Mandy the Prostitute would come into the shop tonight, and the thought of being able to stare at Mandy, talk to Mandy and ask Mandy what it was like being a prostitute lifted Erica's metaphorical balloon just high enough for it to sail clear of the bleak trees of unpublished-author despair. With a lighter step, Erica pushed on through the snow, strode across the garage forecourt and in through the staff entrance. In the locker room that smelt of Pot Noodle and windscreen washer she put on her uniform before taking up her place behind the bulletproof glass of the counter.

Hours passed and the snow turned the world outside to white oblivion. Erica felt oddly vague and ill at ease, as though somebody somewhere was talking about her, and not in a nice way. Then at around half past midnight, Mandy came in. Despite the snow, her skinny legs were bare beneath the short denim skirt she always wore, and she had pushed up the sleeves of her pink leather biker jacket to reveal bony wrists jangling with bangles. Mandy's hair was the colour of weak tea and she wore it scraped back in a tight ponytail that Erica liked to think was designed to hold the features of her face in place while she chased the dragon with her drug-dealer boyfriend. Surreptitiously, so as not to spook Mandy, Erica reached for her notebook and wrote "Chasing the Dragon – idea for a series of young-adult novels set in a dystopian megacity". The pen hovered over the paper, waiting for her to give it something more to do, but her mind had gone blank. She added the words "Maybe watch *Blade Runner* again" and closed the book.

Meanwhile Mandy sauntered around the aisles shooting glances in Erica's direction. Erica knew that Mandy was shoplifting, but that just made the whole encounter more authentic so she never said anything. Mandy came up to the counter and asked for cigarettes, and while Erica's back was turned, leaned over the counter and noisily helped herself to cigarette lighters and packets of Trojans.

"Busy tonight?" she asked, in her sharp-as-lemons cockney accent.

"Nah, you're the only person who's been in," Erica replied, trying not to wince at the thought of a mouthful of freshly squeezed lemon juice. "Suppose the snow's keeping everyone inside."

Mandy gave her an odd look and glanced out of the window.

"Are *you* busy?" Erica asked, trying not to eat Mandy up with her eyes – there was something a little bit different about her tonight, something not quite in keeping about the "Keep Calm and Carry On" badge pinned to her lapel.

Mandy raised her eyes to heaven and said, "Punters! You wouldn't believe it. All they really want to do is talk about their wives and kids."

"Yeah," nodded Erica, "I can imagine." And she could, she really, really could.

"Well, better get back to the flat or my boyfriend will want to know what I'm doing out so late." Mandy pushed the packet of cigarettes down into the skintight pocket of her denim skirt. Then she winked. "No rest for the wicked, eh?"

Erica smiled and flushed. "If you ever need someone to talk to, or somewhere to go, I'm always here, y'know."

Another odd look flickered across Mandy's taut little face. "Thanks, babe. I'll remember that."

And then she was gone, click-clacking out of the shop and into the snowstorm. Erica sighed in satisfaction and jotted down some fresh ideas for the novel she was planning about a prostitute serial killer. Time passed, but when she looked up at the clock she saw that it still said half past midnight, which meant that it must have stopped soon after Mandy's visit. Bored again she pulled out the Wunderkind's copy of her story and decided to read through his comments, but when she looked at them she found she couldn't understand anything he'd written, except for the word "*spiegelei*" which for some reason she knew meant fried egg in German, but which made no sense at all. So much for the Wunderkind's great literary insight – admissions standards had clearly dropped at the college in recent years.

Erica rubbed a peephole in the condensation on the window and tried to peer out, but there was nothing to see except whiteness. An idea for a story seeded itself in her mind: a plucky heroine who wakes one day to discover that she's become invisible – no, not just invisible . . . Erica reached eagerly for her notebook and wrote: "Heroine wakes up to discover she doesn't actually exist". Erica paused and the surface of the counter felt comfortingly warm where her arm had been resting on it. Then she continued: "Should appeal to women. Needs historical sub-plot. Richard and Judy bookclub choice."

A few streets away, Simon sat at his writing desk by the window and lifted his eyes reluctantly from the computer screen. He could hear Mandy slamming the front door and her skittish tread on the parquet flooring of the hall. A few moments later and she was in the room, shooting him an arch look and shucking off her jacket.

"Well, did you see her?" he asked.

Mandy made a big show of emptying her pockets. Condoms, sweets and an emergency sewing kit fell out onto the coffee table. She settled on the sofa and took a sip from the glass of pinot grigio he had got ready for her.

At last she said, "She's still there, but I think she's suspicious. She kept staring at me."

"Damn." He glanced back at the screen and in particular at the last line he'd written about Justine. "Did she say anything interesting? Did you write down her dialogue?"

"Nope," said Mandy airily. "And I'm not doing it any more. It makes me feel dirty. If I were you I'd forget about her and just concentrate on the graffiti dude, the weird German kid and the mental-breakdown teacher. Just make the teacher younger and hot."

Simon sighed. Perhaps Mandy was right. He'd been getting increasingly fed up with Justine over the last few weeks; even changing her name from Erica hadn't helped. She'd be easy enough to delete from the script because she wasn't in any of the Student Union bar scenes where most of the action with his protagonist took place. He'd cut Justine and start working up Emo

Kid instead. If only he had the time to learn even rudimentary German . . . Maybe he should just cut his losses now and make him a werewolf. That would certainly solve the language problem, but it would also mean that he'd no longer be eligible for the *Ich Bin Ein Berliner* literary grant.

He glanced over at Mandy who was helping herself to pizza from the box, and skimming through an old print-out of the script.

"That's the first draft," he said. "All the names are different now."

Mandy put the pages down and pouted at him. "Why can't you put me in your film? You've made yourself the hero."

"Haven't," Simon said defensively, changing Justine's "terribly handsome" to "good-looking for his age". Damn, he'd have to get one of the other characters to think that now – but which one? "I'm just calling him Simon until I think of a better name."

"I gave you a good name yesterday. Boris. It's unusual."

He stared steadfastly at the words on his computer screen, hoping she'd get bored and go away, but she didn't.

"Well at least change the setting. Nobody wants to watch a TV drama about a bunch of students and their rent-a-quote teacher, even if they do all have superpowers."

There was a hint of mockery in her voice and Simon's shoulders slumped. Perhaps moving in with Mandy so soon had been a mistake.

"A writer writes," he said, under his breath and through gritted teeth.

"What did you say, babe?"

"Nothing. I'm calling it a night."

He had an early start in the morning – a meeting with the deputy head about the chronic staff shortages. Mandy giggled and twiddled her wine glass. A saucy look came into her eyes.

"Hey, it's my time of the month, you know. We could try and make that baby now."

She ran her fingernails down the bare white skin of her thighs – for a mortician she was pretty sexy – but he didn't feel like it tonight. He'd been writing solidly since getting home from school.

"Not tonight, love," he said, saving his changes and making a mental note to weed out all signs of Justine the following day. "You turn in and I'll be along soon." A movement at the window caught his eye and he peered out into the night. "That's funny," he said. "It's snowing."

Ten miles away, in a sleepy suburb of the city, Alice sat at her laptop with the slightly dented index finger of her right hand hovering over the Delete button. She didn't like how the story was going at the moment – the characters weren't behaving in the way she wanted and the language had begun to feel stilted. Metaphors and similes jostled together like commuters on her train of thought, and her original plot had grown baggy and weak. At least if she got rid of Simon she could concentrate more on his girlfriend – she still loved the idea of a sexy girl mortician as a lead character. But if Mandy the embalmer was going to be free to explore her sexuality and experience a passionate reawakening of her spiritual side, wouldn't it be better if she was unattached, or better still, recently bereaved? Yes, Simon should be relegated to backstory. She began to tap the Delete button, and soon Simon and Mandy's conversation about his screenplay was no more. She thought about Simon for a moment with an odd kind of tenderness. He was an amalgam of several teachers she had worked with over the years, but he wasn't really very interesting in his own right; he was grumbly and self-obsessed, and vain – like most men.

The dainty little carriage clock on the mantelpiece chimed half past midnight, reminding her that she hadn't yet taken her anti-depressants or planned what she was going to say at the staff meeting in the morning – so many teachers were leaving to take up places on creative writing courses that the school was grinding to a halt. Why couldn't they just fit it in around their jobs, like she did? She wasn't handing in her notice until she'd at least been placed in a national competition. She got up stiffly from her writing desk and went over to the window to draw the curtains.

Outside, the street was deserted and still. A lone fox with a severed human hand in its jaws crossed the circle of tungsten light spilling out of the Lit Crit and Spit speakeasy on the corner, before disappearing into somebody else's crime novel. Unexpectedly, a little snow was beginning to fall.

"Follow your inner moonlight; don't hide the madness."
– Allen Ginsberg

# The Dybbuk's Tale
## AMANDA SCHIFF

Many years ago, in a small village near the Bug River in Polish Galicia, there lived a young woman named Freidel, who was to be married to the village policeman. The marriage was an arrangement between the two families, and Freidel was not happy about it. She was full of fire and spirit, but the place and age in which she lived would not allow her to show this. So she lowered her eyes, bit her tongue until it bled and said nothing.

At harvest time the policeman went up into the blue-green forest on the high slope of a mountain above the village, to hunt a wolf that had been taking sheep from the summer pastures.

He was a brave man, but not clever, or good with a flintlock. He took aim at the wolf, which looked at him with a bemused expression, big tongue lolling out of the side of his mouth.

A sharp report issued from the barrel of the rifle, showers of sparks flew from its muzzle and a cloud of black smoke drifted on the pine-scented morning air. The ball missed the wolf by a mile, and the recoil was so powerful the policeman was flipped backwards into a steep ravine. He lay there for a day and a night before dying from his terrible injuries.

I know all this because I watched him die.

You must be thinking, "How cruel and wicked to do nothing as the man died a slow and painful death."

Why did I not help, fetch villagers to rescue him? Did I bear a grudge against the victim, that I watched him suffer, unmoved and pitiless in my vigil?

Herein lies your mistake. Do not look for rational answers.

For I am a dybbuk, the wandering soul of a dead man.

Before I departed this world, I was a carpenter by trade, named Asher. But at night in my workshop I would burn the candle at both ends to study books of ancient knowledge, away from the prying eyes of my neighbours.

The workshop's smell of new wood and rabbit-skin glue was intoxicating, yet it also anchored me to what we assume to be reality. The texts of the Cabala are expressly forbidden to the non-Jew. Nor must those Jews (like me) who are under the age of forty, who do not have children (or a beard) explore its secrets. The danger in these esoteric studies is that without your feet planted firmly in the here and now – the hurly-burly of life – you will become unmoored and float away from this world.

One morning, as I approached a tributary of the Bug River in search of fish for my mother's Friday-night table, I saw a huge carp basking in the clear shallow waters near the bank. Without thought for my safety I plunged in and pursued the fish to the middle of the river, where the current is fast-flowing. I caught it with both hands, but it thrashed so mightily that I could not maintain my grip. I dropped the fish and lost my footing as the riverbed plunged steeply away beneath me; the icy waters closed above my head. A sharp pain seared my lungs and I fought to regain the surface. Even in my panic and confusion I understood with piercing clarity that I could never return to my old life. And yet I was not ready to be taken to the Court of Death. There was still so much work to complete in my life before Dumah, the Angel of Death, came for me with the final reckoning.

I didn't want to die, and I knew from my Cabalistic research that it was possible for the soul to transmigrate into another living creature. If I was no longer able to live as Asher the Carpenter I could abandon my broken, drowned body. And thus I became Asher the Carp.

\*

Seeing the teeming underwater world through the carp's eyes was a revelation to me. Here was a great highway, busy with aquatic life. The fish himself was still alive, and none too pleased to be sharing his body with another soul, so we had to come to an accommodation. Since carp are not very smart, he recognised my superior intellect, and we got along well for a while.

Until one day, out of the blue, a huge jaw full of jagged teeth crashed down towards us, impaling the carp and scooping it up towards the river bank in a graceful arc of streaming water, fishscales glinting like diamonds in the midday sun. The carp and I gasped for air, flailing from side to side in the wolf's mouth as he struggled to prevent us from escaping back into the river.

The wily old wolf dashed the carp against a rock, and as the life drained out of the fish, I knew I had to make my move again, this time into the wolf.

He and I feasted hungrily on the fish; I, reluctantly at first because it seemed strange to be devouring my former self, then joyously as the wild, animal spirit of the wolf infected me.

When he was sated, the wolf loped away and slept off his dinner. But I did not sleep, and spent the remains of the day considering my situation. It was better not to be dead, but did I want to spend the rest of my life as a wolf? To be fair, there were benefits. The pure, physical pleasure of running through the forest at night, lit by a blue moon. The warm sun on my shaggy pelt, and a full belly.

After only a few days the novelty was already wearing thin, but I managed to show enough interest to hunt down stray sheep over the course of the summer. Yet the taste of mutton grew boring, and to be honest I was just going through the motions. The wolf was more sophisticated than the carp, but his desires were primitive and easily satisfied. He ignored my overtures of friendship with a lupine contempt for humans I hadn't appreciated before. When he could be bothered he tried to shake me out of his head by scratching his ear with a powerful hind paw. He seemed to think I was a very annoying flea.

I missed my books and learned research into the mysteries of life. The rank, gamey smell of the wolf's fur in the hot sun grew distasteful to me, and its howling at the moon all night drove me very nearly insane.

Early one morning, around harvest time, the policeman arrived with his ancient flintlock rifle. He was clumsy and inept with the weapon. I let him take aim, but knew he could never harm me from such a distance. It was a game, and I needed the amusement.

Plotting my strategy, I wondered how far I could lead him. I was as surprised as he was when the recoil threw him backwards into the ravine.

The policeman could not move any part of his body. He prayed constantly, making a bargain that if he survived he would be a good, honest hard-working father and husband for the rest of his life. He would tithe his wages to charity, and study the Talmud at night. But it was all to no avail and he died at sunrise.

When the village men arrived and killed the wolf, I gratefully transmigrated once again into the corpse of the policeman. With great relief my essence rearranged itself inside a familiar human form. This husk was only a temporary home until I could find a living host, but I was moving back up the hierarchy of creatures again.

It is very restful inside the body of a dead man, and I slept peacefully there until it was brought down the mountain back to the village.

Rigor mortis had of course set in, and in order to get the policeman into the coffin (one I had made before I died), the butcher (acting as undertaker until a new carpenter could be found for the village) had to break the bones left untouched by the fall.

The reluctant Freidel was brought by her parents to see the corpse of her no-longer-husband-to-be. The coffin lay on a trestle in the centre of the small wooden *shul*. At first I was overwhelmed by the noise of the villagers gossiping and chattering like excited magpies. Nothing so dramatic had happened for years.

The villagers thought Freidel was sobbing with misery at the thought she would remain a spinster to the end of her days. However, a dybbuk can see into the souls of others and know their deepest fears and desires, so I concentrated on Freidel's thoughts, filtering out the confusion and chaos of the room.

Thus I realised that hers were tears of joy. Freidel had been released, and it was her great good fortune that the policeman had died. While her father was in a corner of the room arguing with the dead man's uncle about the return of her dowry, she bent down and whispered in the corpse's ear: "Oh lucky day that I should see my husband laid out in his coffin before he lay in my bridal bed."

I looked into her eyes and saw the fire and intelligence burning like seasoned pine logs on a frosty night. In an instant I saw our futures intertwined. Freidel would help me complete my life's work, in spite of the restrictions on a woman scholar, and I would make her happy and fulfilled.

Freidel fell to the floor, writhing in pain and ecstasy as I entered her. I felt warm blood gushing through her veins like the river of life. The music of the spheres was the drumbeat of her heart. I was reconnected to the universe. I was a living, thinking human being, animated once again by more than mere instinct and base desires.

The villagers still believed Freidel was consumed with grief, but her mother knew her better. When the girl began to speak in a low mannish voice, her mother screamed and sent a boy to fetch the Rebbe.

"This is the work of a dybbuk. My poor sweet girl is possessed. This is all our fault for bringing an innocent, frail child to see the corpse."

I explained to Freidel the fate that had befallen her – I had impregnated her soul, but this act of *ibbur* needed her consent. I would take up residence with, not against, her will. Curiously, Freidel reacted with surprise but no fear or confusion; she ceased screaming and thrashing around once she realised she was not in mortal danger. Instead she lay still, with eyes closed, assessing the situation.

After what could have been no more than a minute (but which seemed like an hour in the crowded, airless room) she whispered her permission, but the onlookers, seeing her mouth moving and not understanding her words, took them as further proof of demonic possession.

The Rebbe confirmed Freidel's mother's diagnosis: possession by the dybbuk of the dead policeman. Freidel laughed at this, which the Rebbe took as a sign of agreement, and she fell into a trance.

Freidel made space for me inside her head, or wherever it is the soul resides, like sharing a bed with a cousin in a small attic room in the depths of a winter's night.

Her father and brothers carried the unconscious girl to their house. Her mother undressed her, washed her as if she were a corpse, and sat beside her bed on a hard wooden chair through the long night.

I had of course met Freidel before – our village isn't so large that you wouldn't have known all the inhabitants to some degree. But I have always been a solitary soul, enjoying my own company and that of my books more than the general chaos of life. My parents found me a wife when I was sixteen, but she ran off with an itinerant pedlar many years ago. She couldn't stand my moody silences, and the dusty books cluttering up the house. I would be a liar if I said I missed her.

I had the perfect life. All day I would work with my hands, and the more I worked, the more skilled I became. At midnight I would fly up into the ink-black sky, powered by thought and imagination. A few hours of sleep would be enough to refresh me for the next day's labours.

And now, a future for Freidel and me, together but distinctive equals, seemed a worthy substitution for a life cut short. This new partnership would provide me with the means to complete my great work.

When Freidel awoke from her long sleep any hopes her family had that she would be restored to her old self were dashed.

She got up late and dressed in her brother's clothes. Her voice was coarse and rough. She sat at the breakfast table, knees apart, feet firmly planted on the kitchen floor, waiting to be fed. The old Freidel would have been the first to rise, making a fire, boiling water for washing, cooking breakfast and serving the menfolk before finally eating her own modest meal.

The new Freidel ate mountains of black bread and plum jam, cured meat, pickles and *knishes*, washed down with oceans of strong black tea, slurped through a sugar lump gripped between her teeth. Her family could only act in stunned compliance to her requests for more of this and more of that. She was a force of nature, a cuckoo in the nest. Freidel's father was aghast and bewildered at this turn of events. Her mother was secretly impressed and envious of her daughter's freedom to indulge her appetites like any other man in the village.

Freidel's new life was to last a few brief weeks, until the villagers (mostly men, and the more bitter and jealous women) could stand her transgressions no longer. The sight of a pretty, young woman behaving like a vulgar, boorish man quickly palled as an amusing novelty. They demanded that the Rebbe conduct an exorcism of the dybbuk.

"She's upsetting everything. We don't know what's up and what's down any more. She's setting a bad example to the children. And the cursing and bad language . . . Enough is enough!"

During her weeks of freedom, Freidel had gone to the *yeshiva*, where the pious young men of our village studied the Jewish laws. The room fell silent when she entered. Undeterred by the stares and insults of the students, she had taken down the Mishna, the Talmud and the Zohar from the shelves.

One student, braver than the rest, challenged her. He attempted to wrestle the sacred tomes from her hands, spitting on the defiled and defiling specimen of womanhood. She stood her ground with new-found strength, flinging curses at the youth until he gave up and turned away.

She sat by herself in silence on a bench, ravenously devouring the books in the same manner as she had despatched every scrap of food in her mother's store cupboard. All around her the chatter and learned arguments resumed until her presence was forgotten.

At night, she and I would lie awake discussing the meaning of what she had read.

These were the happiest days of my existence. We would climb out of the window and fly away over the rooftops. Powered now by the imagination and thoughts of two, we floated higher than I could have achieved on my own, and from such a great distance the world looked very small and insignificant.

On the day of the exorcism, the Rebbe called upon Freidel's dybbuk to give his name.

When challenged to admit that the demon was Yossel the policeman, I called out with indignation that I should be mistaken for that simpleton: "No, I'm not Yossel the idiot, Yossel the useless wolf-slayer. Guess again!"

This caused consternation in the room.

"I command you, Yossel, to leave this poor woman. You have done enough mischief. Leave by a sneeze, or through her big toe – but leave her you must."

As in the *yeshiva*, Freidel stood her ground.

The Rebbe said: "I divorce you from this woman, Ru'ah."

But Freidel just laughed.

The Rebbe called for a black candle, salt and a brass pot of freshly drawn water into which he poured drops of oil.

He lit the candle, which began to smoke, making Freidel cough. Encouraged by this sign, he drew a circle on the floor with the salt, and pushed her inside it. He flung droplets of the oil and water at her head, all the while intoning Psalm Ten: "Why standest Thou from afar, O Lord? Why hidest Thou from Thyself in times of trouble?"

He repeated this nine times, and spat three times, saying, "Shaddai, Shaddai, Shaddai."

The villagers were silent, through fear and reverence, and the room was so hot that Freidel's mother fainted and was carried outside.

The Rebbe wrote many formulae on bits of paper, which he burned in the flame of the black candle.

Freidel and I watched all of this with amused interest.

Drawing on his final reserve of strength and cunning, the Rebbe raised his voice to a wailing shriek: "Lul, Shapham, Arigon and Anirdaphon, I sit amidst the stars, I walk among lean men and fat men. The sons of Reshpah fly upwards. Jah, Jah, Lord of Hosts, amen, amen, Selah. Be split, be accursed, broken and banned. Son of mud, son of an unclean one, son of clay, like Shamgaz, Merigaz and Istemnah."

The Rebbe had done his worst (or his best) and had nothing left to throw at the demon. The people in the room held their breath, waiting to see if the exorcism was successful.

Freidel fell to the floor, writhing in pain, sweating and screaming as she had when we were first conjoined. I was confused and frightened this time, as it was not of my doing – but nor was it the Rebbe's handiwork. She clawed at her clothing, holding her belly and cursing. One of the women recognised what was happening, and ran to get Freidel's mother. Other women in the room also understood, and ordered their husbands and sons to leave. The Rebbe sat heavily in a chair, mopping his brow, utterly spent.

After an hour or so of howling and shrieking, Freidel was delivered of a baby boy. That is, me.

Freidel's mother was torn between horror and pride. A monstrous supernatural child born out of wedlock is a source of shame . . . and yet, still, her daughter's boy.

Freidel's father refused to see the swaddled mite, but stroked his exhausted daughter's damp hair and kissed her cheek as she slept. Her brothers hung their heads in sorrow, crushing their black hats in anguished hands.

The mother of Asher, the dead carpenter (that is, my mother *before* Freidel), took the infant from Freidel's arms and tenderly pulled back the swaddling cloth. When the baby opened his eyes she gasped.

"But he has my son's eyes," she said, wiping away a single tear with her huge, rough hands. "The way he looks at me. I know this child. My grandchild. Asher."

When Freidel agreed to name the baby after the drowned carpenter, the old woman pressed on her Asher's tools and all his secret books of divine wisdom.

She knew nothing but understood everything.

The family built a cabin in a clearing in the blue-green forest, on the high slope of a mountain, where Freidel and her son could live and not bring further shame on the village with their uncanny freak show. They leave her parcels of food in the long, hungry months of winter. She sees their footprints in the snow. Although scared of the dybbuk-child, they are not hard-hearted folk.

Freidel is blissfully happy with her son, and her books. He is becoming a skilful carpenter like his father. He hews wood, builds the fire in the grate and draws water. She will become a great scholar of the Cabala, the greatest there has ever been (but only you and I will know this).

And what of me, Asher the father and Asher the son, Asher the wandering dybbuk in search of a home? For I am all of these in one body now.

My mother, my father's bride, who I name Binah for her wisdom, calls me Chockhmah for my intellect. Together we study the Cabala; we have already deciphered many of its ancient mysteries.

Together we still fly around the world at night; powered by the thoughts and imagination of two we float higher than can be achieved alone, and marvel at how tiny the earth seems from such a great distance.

# Notes on Contributors

**Sarah Alexander** has previously worked as a tomato picker, travel consultant, mental-health support worker and suitcase administrator. She is now an editor for an educational publisher in London. She has just completed the Birkbeck MA in Creative Writing and is currently writing a young-adult novel about free-diving in Scotland. She lives in Essex.

**Amy Bird** completed the six-month Faber Academy Writing A Novel course in March 2012 and, at the time of writing this story, was in the second year of her Creative Writing MA at Birkbeck. Her debut novel, *Yours Is Mine*, is being published by Carina UK (a digital imprint of Harlequin) in 2013. Aside from writing, she is a lawyer and a trustee of a theatre festival. You can follow her @London_writer.

**Barbara Bleiman** is co-director of the English and Media Centre and editor of *emagazine*, a quarterly magazine for A-level literature students. She did a degree in English Literature at Somerville College, Oxford and completed an MA in Creative Writing at Birkbeck in September 2012. She had two short stories published in issues 7 and 8 of *The Mechanics' Institute Review*, has had two children's short stories published by the English and Media Centre and is now working on her first adult novel, *Indecent Acts*, from which the story in this anthology is taken.

**Desmond Byrne** was born in Dublin but has lived in London since 1986. He is a professional tattooist, a student on Birkbeck's Creative Writing BA and is currently working on his first novel. A disciple of what he terms "the holy trinity" of Joyce, Beckett and Nabokov, he also sees in his work the possibility of a happy marriage of George V. Higgins and George Eliot.

**Louise Christian** is a solicitor with a long career acting in human rights cases. In November 1985 she set up a legal aid firm, now Christian Khan (http://www.christiankhan.co.uk/), where she currently works. She has acted for people detained in Guantanamo Bay, and for victims of disasters such as train crashes. She has received awards for her legal work, and is an ex chair of the human rights organisations Liberty and Inquest. She is a contributor to the *Guardian* Comment website and has frequently appeared on television. She is in the second year of a part-time Creative Writing MA at Birkbeck and is writing a novel about a law firm in Hackney and how people's lives are affected by the law, for better or for worse.

**Amanda Crane** trained in London as a nurse before switching to midwifery in the early eighties when she lived and worked between Balham and Bermondsey. She gave up work a few years ago to start writing up her travel diaries and is currently studying on the MA in Creative Writing at Birkbeck. She writes short stories and poems and is trying to decide which novel to start first.

**Charlie Fish** is a popular short-story writer and screenwriter. His stories have been published in several countries and inspired dozens of short film adaptations. Since 1996, he has edited www.fictionontheweb.co.uk, the longest-running short-story site on the Web. He was born in Mount Kisco, New York in 1980; and now lives in Brixton, south London with his wife and daughters. You can contact him at charlie@fictionontheweb.co.uk, and you can follow him on Twitter @fishcharlie.

**Gaylene Gould** was a student of the Birkbeck Creative Writing MA in 2008. She writes fiction and non-fiction, and works as a creative coach and broadcaster for BBC Radio 4. "The Sacrifice", a short fiction piece published in the anthology *X-24 Unclassified*, became the inspiration for her first novel. At manuscript stage, the novel, *The Sacrifice*, won the Commonword Children's Diversity Writing Prize. "Wendy", the story featured here, is an extract from it. Gaylene is currently working on her second novel, about an estranged father searching for his lost daughter, and a coaching book for writers based on her Writers' Hub series, Interior Dialogues. She is represented by the agency Peters Fraser and Dunlop.

**Colin Grant** is a historian, Associate Fellow in the Centre for Caribbean Studies and producer for BBC Radio. His books include *Negro with a Hat: The Rise and Fall of Marcus Garvey and His Dream of Mother Africa* and *Bageye at the Wheel*. He has also written and directed plays. The son of Jamaican parents, he lives in Brighton.

**Lucy Hume** grew up in rural Kent and now lives in London, working in publications and marketing for a play publisher. She completed her Creative Writing MA at Birkbeck in 2012. She is very grateful to her brother Tom, a vet, for all his help with this story.

**Kavita Jindal** is the author of the critically acclaimed poetry collection *Raincheck Renewed*, published by Chameleon Press. She also writes literary criticism and fiction. Her short story "A Flash of Pepper" won the Vintage Books/Foyles Haruki Murakami competition in January 2012. Her work has appeared in journals, anthologies and newspapers around the world including the *Independent*, *South China Morning Post*, *The Indian Express*, *Dimsum*, *The Asia Literary Review*, *Cha*, *The Moth*, *The Yellow Nib*, *The HarperCollins Book of English Poetry [by Indians]* and *Not A Muse*. Kavita's poems have been translated into German, Punjabi, Romanian and Arabic, and some have been set to music. After six years of research and writing, her first novel is now complete. www.kavitajindal.com

**Russell Celyn Jones** is the author of seven novels – *Soldiers and Innocents*, which won the David Higham Prize, *Small Times*, *An*

*Interference of Light, The Eros Hunter, Surface Tension, Ten Seconds from the Sun* and *The Ninth Wave*. His work has been translated into five languages and his short fiction has featured in a number of international anthologies. He has served as a Man Booker Prize judge and is currently Professor of Creative Writing at Birkbeck, University of London.

**Jackie Kay** was born and brought up in Scotland. Her work includes poetry collections (*The Adoption Papers* won the Forward Prize, a Saltire Award and a Scottish Arts Council Book Award), novels (her first novel, *Trumpet*, was awarded the *Guardian* Fiction Prize and was shortlisted for the International IMPAC Dublin Literary Award), collections of short stories, and the memoir *Red Dust Road*. She writes for both adults and children, and has written widely for stage and television. Jackie was awarded an MBE for services to literature in 2006, and is currently Professor of Creative Writing at Newcastle University.

**Rebekah Lin** is a full-time writer and photographer, part-time green evangelist and, sometimes, private-equity financier, from Singapore. She loves anything to do with food and can spend hours rewatching good films that make ordinary things extraordinary. She plays far more Taboo and Scrabble than is deemed normal, plays sketchy guitar and is ace at bathroom singing. Rebekah has been published in her local newspaper and fitness magazines, and her poetry has been performed at Wigmore Hall. By the time this anthology is published, she will (hopefully) have completed her MA in Creative Writing at Birkbeck.

**Adam Marek** is an award-winning short-story writer. He won the 2011 Arts Foundation Short Story Fellowship, and was shortlisted for the inaugural *Sunday Times* EFG Short Story Award. His first story collection, *Instruction Manual for Swallowing*, was longlisted for the Frank O'Connor Award. His stories have appeared in many magazines, including *Prospect* and *The Sunday Times Magazine*, *The Stinging Fly* and *The London Magazine*, and in many anthologies including *Lemistry*, *The New Uncanny* and *Bio-Punk* from Comma Press, and *The Best British Short Stories 2011* and *2013*. Visit Adam Marek online at www.adammarek.co.uk.

**Fiona Melrose** completed the Birkbeck Creative Writing MA in 2012. She has recently completed her first novel, *Guilty*, the seeds of which were sewn in writing her *MIR* submission, "The Fox". This is Fiona's second published story. She also writes book reviews for the Writers' Hub. She has spent most of her adult life living in either the UK or Johannesburg, where she studied and lectured in politics. At the time of writing "The Fox", Fiona was living in rural Suffolk with two charming dogs. You can follow Fiona on Twitter @papercutprint and her blog is papercutpublishing.tumblr.com.

**Julius Pasteiner** lives in east London. He writes freelance for *ArtReview*, *spiked* and *The First Post*. His short fiction has appeared in *Nowishere* and Issue 8 of *The Mechanics' Institute Review*. Currently he is working on a collection of short stories and a novel about a spate of mysterious teenage suicides.

**Joel Pearcey** was born in 1980 and lived the first seven years of his life on the Welsh-English border. The rest of his childhood and adolescence was spent in New Zealand, Australia and China. He moved to London in 2004 and now lives in Brighton with his partner and their three children.

**Maddy Reid** lives in London, but wants to live somewhere her eight-year-old son won't be able to hail black cabs. She is currently completing her MA in Creative Writing at Birkbeck and is working on a collection of short stories. She wrote interminable plays as a child, one of which was the inspiration for a BBC Radio 3 play. It looked at the question of why Van Gogh cut off his ear. She still hasn't been able to answer this.

**Lenya Samanis** lives in London and is currently working on a novel, *27 Magpies*.

**Amanda Schiff** is a film producer, lecturer in screenwriting, writer and artist. She was in the first cohort of graduates from the Birkbeck Creative Writing MA in 2004 and was one of the six founding editors of *The Mechanics' Institute Review* Issue 1. Her short story "Anamorphic Breakup" was published in the anthology and she was shortlisted for the Crime Writers' Association Debut Dagger Award in 2001. Her cabinets of curiosities and short stories have been exhibited in solo exhibitions at the Eleven Spitalfields gallery (2009) and at the Grant Museum of Zoology and Comparative Anatomy (2010). Although she is writing a screenplay and conventional novel, Amanda is interested in digital and transmedia writing and is working on a fiction enhanced book app.

**Jacquelyn Shreeves-Lee** was born in Tottenham, north London and can't remember a time when she hasn't written. Even before she had learned to read she pretended that she could "read" her scribbles. Jacquelyn is on the Creative Writing MA at Birkbeck and has recently had a short story published on the college's Writers' Hub website. She was shortlisted for the Saga Book Prize (1996), the London Writers Competition in association with Waterstones (2001) and the Fish Short Story Prize (2002) and was published by Virago in June 1996 as part of an anthology of new women writers. More recently Jacquelyn was a winner of the Tales of Edmonton event, her short story was dramatised and performed at the Millfield Theatre in 2008. Jacquelyn works as a clinical psychologist in her role as an expert witness but her passion rests with literature and language. She's currently working on a collection of short stories.

**Gemma Thomas** has a BA in English Literature from the University of Durham, and graduated from the Birkbeck Creative Writing MA in 2011. She has lived in London for several years, and has also spent time in Jerusalem and Madrid. She has read her work at the Open Arts Café, blogs at gemmathomas.wordpress.com and is working on a novel about the disappearance of a teenage girl.

**Dave Wakely** was raised in south London and Surrey before gaining a BA in English from Loughborough University. Since then, he has worked variously as a musician, a university administrator, a poetry librarian, a web developer and a learning-materials author and editor in locations as disparate as Bucharest, Sofia and Milton Keynes. A part-time Birkbeck Creative Writing MA student, he also currently works as a blog writer/editor and journalist, focusing mostly on organisational development and the contemporary experience of the workplace. A collector (and player) of stringed instruments and an enthusiastic home cook whose kitchen is his sanctuary, he lives in Buckinghamshire with his civil partner and too many guitars.

**Maggie Womersley** completed Birkbeck's MA in Creative Writing in 2007. Since then she has finished her first novel, and swapped city living and a career in TV for motherhood and tweeting about her unnatural passion for handicrafts. She writes a regular blog called The Pram in the Hallway for www.writershub.co.uk.

**Evie Wyld** runs Review, a small independent bookshop in Peckham, south London. Her first novel, *After the Fire, a Still Small Voice*, won the John Llewellyn Rhys Prize and a Betty Trask Award. In 2011 she was listed as one of the *Culture Show*'s Best New British Novelists. She was also short listed for the Orange Prize for New Writers and the International IMPAC Dublin Literary Award. She is included in Granta's list of Best of Young British Novelists 2013. Her second novel, *All the Birds Singing*, was published in June 2013 by Jonathan Cape and will come out in 2014 from Pantheon in the US.